The clarinet is an epic instrument
HECTOR BERLIOZ

Paul Harris
The Clarinet

The ultimate companion to clarinet playing

Acknowledgements

Huge thanks are necessary to so many who have helped in so many ways: firstly, to two particular players, pupils and friends, Georgina Lee and Ben Westlake, who have spent many hours with me discussing and debating the text. To Peter Cigleris, Jean Cockburn, Bette Gray-Fow, Melanie Ragge and Harriet Wells for much support and help over the content. To Anthony Bailey and Felicity Vine, clarinet guru Michael Bryant, Gaspare Buonomano, Xiya Cheng, Richard Ingham, Holly Isherwood, Julia Middleton, Jonathan Whiting and Emily Worthington; the legendary clarinet players Philippe Cuper, Stanley Drucker and Karl Leister for their inspiration and comments; the esteemed singers Yvonne Minton CBE, who commented on the section on breathing, and Alison Chamberlain, who helped especially on other aspects of the oral cavity; Ed Pillinger, one of the world's leading mouthpiece makers; clarinet makers and technicians Daniel Bangham and David Fingerhut; respiration specialists Dr Caroline Tjoa and Dr Timothy Hinks, Nuffield Department of Medicine, University of Oxford; physiotherapist Dr Sarah Upjohn and osteopath Hector Wells; John Atkinson, physicist and musician; and Joe Wolfe, head of the physics department at the University of New South Wales.

A deeply felt thanks to my wonderful team and friends at Faber Music – to Richard King and Lesley Rutherford, and especially to Emily Bevington who has spent many hours refining this text.

Finally, to my wonderful clarinet teacher, John Davies, who, through his long and inspirational life not only taught me (and many others) how to play the clarinet, but also the importance of a deeply enquiring mind and that life is all about sharing.

All music by Paul Harris unless otherwise stated.
Photograph credits: page 28, Stefan Rotter; page 63, TheRoff97; pages 98 and 216, Desmond Kean; pages 110 and 150, Fotomy (all Getty Images). All other photographs by Georgina Lee.

Fantasy Sonata, John Ireland
© 1945 Hawkes & Son (London) Ltd. Reproduced by permission of Boosey & Hawkes Music Publishers Ltd. All Rights Reserved.

Clarinet Concerto, Aaron Copland
© 1949, 1952 The Aaron Copland Fund For Music, Inc. Copyright Renewed. Boosey & Hawkes Inc. Sole Licensee. Reproduced by permission of Boosey & Hawkes Music Publishers Ltd. All Rights Reserved.

5 Bagatelles, Gerald Finzi
© 1945 Hawkes & Son (London) Ltd.
Reproduced by permission of Boosey & Hawkes Music Publishers Ltd. All Rights Reserved.

Sonata, II, Herbert Howells
© 1954 Hawkes & Son (London) Ltd.
Reproduced by permission of Boosey & Hawkes Music Publishers Ltd. All Rights Reserved.

Clarinet Concerto No.2, Malcolm Arnold
© 1984 Faber Music Ltd. All Rights Reserved.

Divertimento For Two Clarinets, Malcolm Arnold
© 1988 Queen's Temple Publications. All Rights Reserved.

Sonata da Camera, Paul Harris
© 1998 Queen's Temple Publications. All Rights Reserved.

Sonata in B♭ for clarinet and piano, Paul Hindemith
© 1940 Schott Music GmbH & Co. KG. Mainz. Copyright Renewed 1968. Reproduced by permission. All Rights Reserved.

Capriccio for Clarinet in A, Heinrich Sutermeister
© 1947 Schott Music Ltd, London. Reproduced by permission. All Rights Reserved.

Adagio for Clarinet and Piano, Paul Harris
© 1993 G. Ricordi & Co. (London) Ltd. All Rights Reserved. Used by Permission. Reproduced by Permission of Hal Leonard Europe Ltd.

This book features thread-sealed binding that allows the spine to be flexed, enabling the book to open easily and lay flat.

© 2022 by Faber Music Ltd
This edition first published in 2022
Bloomsbury House 74–77 Great Russell Street London WC1B 3DA
Music processed by Donald Thomson
Book design by Adam Hay Studio
Illustrations by Elizabeth Ogden
Cover image: painting by Georgina Lee
Printed in England by Caligraving Ltd
All rights reserved

ISBN10: 0-571-54218-2
EAN13: 978-0-571-54218-5

To buy Faber Music publications or to find out about the full range of titles available please contact your local music retailer or Faber Music sales enquiries:

Faber Music Ltd, Burnt Mill, Elizabeth Way, Harlow CM20 2HX
Tel: +44 (0) 1279 82 89 82   Fax: +44 (0) 1279 82 89 83
fabermusic.com

Contents

7   Before we begin ...
8   A moment for reflection:
     the point of departure

13 Be prepared!
29 Sounding good
53 Developing tone
99 Intonation and playing in tune
111 Articulation
151 Finger-work and dexterity
191 Performance
203 The clarinet

217 Further information
229 Appendices

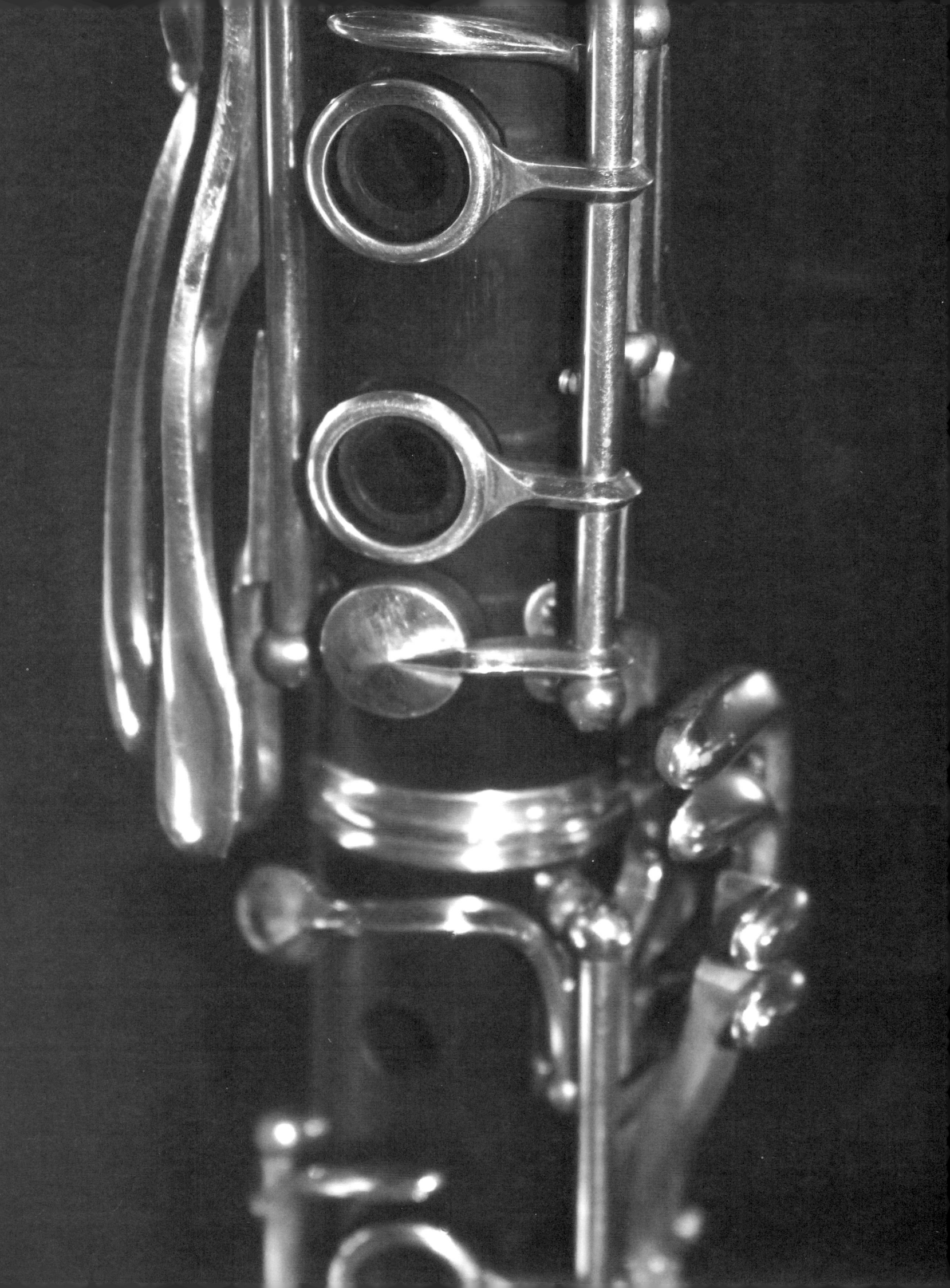

Before we begin …

Playing the clarinet is endlessly fascinating.

Some may wish to take the Monty Python approach: *Well, you blow in one end and move your fingers up and down the outside.*[1] Having this book suggests you probably want to delve rather more deeply.

No two players are the same: motor skills, the shape and formation of lips and teeth, tongue, facial muscles, oral cavity, resonating spaces and so much more will vary significantly from one person to another and contribute to every clarinet player's individual and unique voice. Then there is the instrument itself, and the different types of mouthpiece and reed. Playing the clarinet, or any instrument, is not an exact science (or art) and similar approaches will have differing effects for each individual.

The purpose of this book is to help you develop your individual clarinet personality, to open doors for thought and to open the way to unlimited progress.

I have taught some pupils who seem to make a beautiful sound virtually from the first lesson, quite naturally with little instruction. For others, more guidance and experimentation is the way forward.

As such, I encourage you to use this book in the way you find most comfortable and useful, taking into account that all aspects of playing technique are of course interdependent. Whilst books are necessarily linear in construct, learning is not, so you may wish to dart about the book continually cross-referencing ideas and exercises; or you may like to begin at page one and work through systematically. Stop if you feel you have had sufficient input on a particular aspect. And whilst I hope there always *will be* sufficient explanation on all aspects, remember that there is no end to learning and a book can only be a finite number of pages.

From an author's perspective, expressing technical and musical thoughts in words that can be universally understood is often challenging. Much of what we say and think is borne of experience, intuition and imagery, and each of us may have slightly different interpretations of those images. I have occasionally heard two people express the same thing in a seemingly entirely contradictory fashion. Nonetheless, I have done the best I can and additionally have offered scientific and theoretical explanations where this may help understanding. The scientific sections are clearly marked and can be skipped, but I encourage you to persevere. The more broadly informed we are, the more profound our understanding becomes.

For me, playing the clarinet really *is* endlessly fascinating: trying to get the better of its technical conundrums and mastering its wonderfully rich repertoire is a precious journey. Sharing this with you is the *raison d'être* behind this book. But, being a book, this can't take the place of a live teacher. Fine teachers, through their experience, their aural and visual perception and their desire to help, are indispensable.

I had the great pleasure of speaking to one of my clarinet heroes recently. I rang to wish the great Karl Leister a happy birthday. We spoke for a few minutes about the essence of clarinet playing. Is it possible to sum up your thoughts in a sentence, I asked Karl. 'It's all about the line; singing the melodic line,' he answered. That's what we do: we sing and create beauty through our instrument, and in doing so, in each of our own ways, we contribute something special to the world in which we live.

---

1. This was actually in reference to being asked how to play the flute, but I'm certain the clarinet would have produced a similar answer.

A moment for reflection: the point of departure

Every day gives us the opportunity to reflect and reappraise. Whatever the subject, reappraisal is a fundamental starting point for change, learning and development. Given you have a copy of this book, and irrespective of your level as a player, you obviously would like to re-examine or look more deeply into aspects of your clarinet playing. From this moment, your future practice sessions can be viewed as an opportunity to reappraise, but in doing so, be compassionate with yourself. Employ good judgement and always try to look for the positive.

TECHNICAL ASPECTS

When it comes to the technical aspects of playing it is important to begin with the body as relaxed as possible with no inappropriate tensions (this is dealt with in detail in *Be prepared!* from page 13) and with an open mind. You can then make some choices about how to proceed. When studying an aspect of technique, you may choose to work through the text and exercises as though starting from scratch, or you may like to use what you find here to develop, refine, revise or modify what you already do. The former will take some doing – like wiping the slate clean and beginning again. There's much to be said for doing this from time to time, challenging though it may be, especially if there are certain areas of technique you wish to rethink.

MUSICAL ASPECTS

When working and reworking musical aspects such as phrasing or interpretation, again it can be valuable and interesting to reappraise at times – to rethink from scratch. Try singing a phrase and then playing it with a beautiful sound and good control, but eliminate previously imposed ingredients – dynamics, tonal inflection, *rubato*, and any rhythmic deviation from the marked text. Then begin again, rethinking each ingredient. Reappraise. You may well find this highly refreshing and mentally invigorating.

MOVEMENT

Do you instinctively move when you perform; when playing a note, a scale or a piece of any description, whether in private or in public? Movement can represent a powerful facet to your musical expression. Again, occasionally, it may be interesting to wipe the slate clean and play with no movement at all. Be calm and relaxed. If stopping the movement seems to *create* tension, identify the tension and tell yourself gently to let go. In this way you will become much more aware of the muscles you *do* need to use. Hence, you can begin to reappraise the significance of movements that can sometimes divert and distract both you and your audience from what you actually *want* to communicate musically. By recognising the potential effect of movement whilst playing you might find your musical expression much enhanced.

Think of this constant reappraisal as something fluid, changeable and flexible. Sometimes you think about it; sometimes not – let your instincts take over. *But whenever we set out to do anything, the greater the self-awareness, the greater the potential for positive development.*

THE CLARINET

The two halves of a clarinet

The sophisticated piece of equipment we call the *clarinet* is in fact only one half of the instrument. The other half is you. Playing a musical instrument isn't so much what you do *to* the instrument but what you do *with* the instrument – how *you* are in relation to it.

The *you* half is what the greater part of this book is about. We will look at the instrument and all its component parts – how to look after them and get the best from them. But more important is the nurture and development of your side of the instrument. As you work through this book always try to remain positive, inquisitive and thoughtful. Hopefully you won't get frustrated or discouraged and will always enjoy your work. If you do occasionally stop enjoying it, take a break, take a walk, get perspective, do something else.

The best learning is a 'one step at a time' approach. The explanations and exercises will reinforce that concept, but of course you can be creative, and if you feel a technique needs to be broken down into even smaller steps, make these up for yourself. Ultimately there is no limit to the number of micro-steps we can take on our journey.

When the clarinet and the player come together with thoughtful care, the result is sound that is truly beautiful. There are many exercises in this book; treat them all as music and always strive to make your most beautiful sound. Beauty comes from the soul. Whether you're playing a scale, one of those many exercises, a simple tune, a concerto, a sonata, a jazz number, they are all expressions of our musical soul.

LIFE AND ALL THE LEARNING IN IT IS A JOURNEY
As we continue that journey – and for those reading this book, playing the clarinet is clearly an important part of it – try to see each new day, and each new practice session, as simultaneously a continuation and a new start. I very much hope *you* find it endlessly fascinating.

A MOMENT FOR REFLECTION

Terminology

The registers

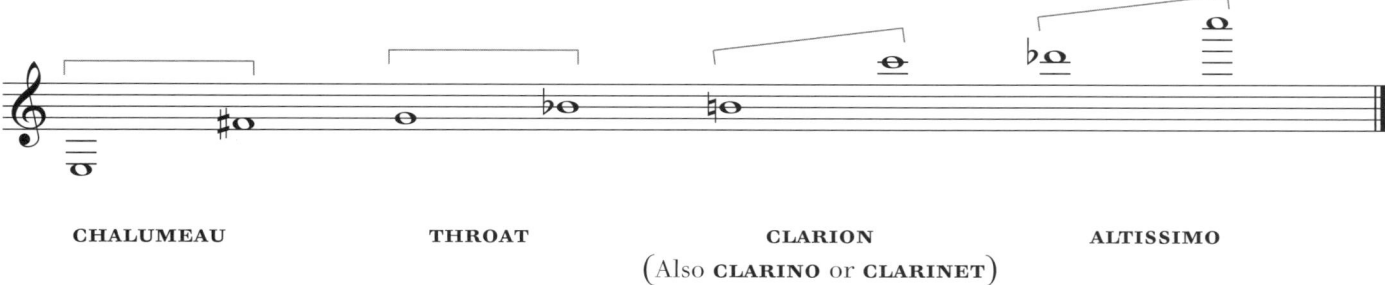

CHALUMEAU   THROAT   CLARION   ALTISSIMO
(Also **CLARINO** or **CLARINET**)

The notes

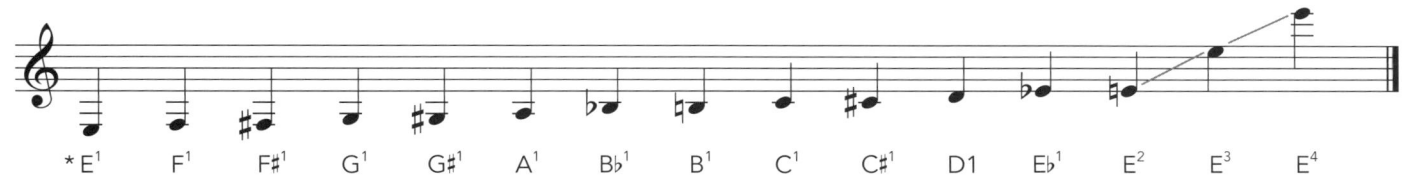

* E^1 F^1 $F\#^1$ G^1 $G\#^1$ A^1 $B\flat^1$ B^1 C^1 $C\#^1$ $D1$ $E\flat^1$ E^2 E^3 E^4

* Some clarinet makers are now producing instruments with the range extending a semitone down to E♭.

Finger numbers

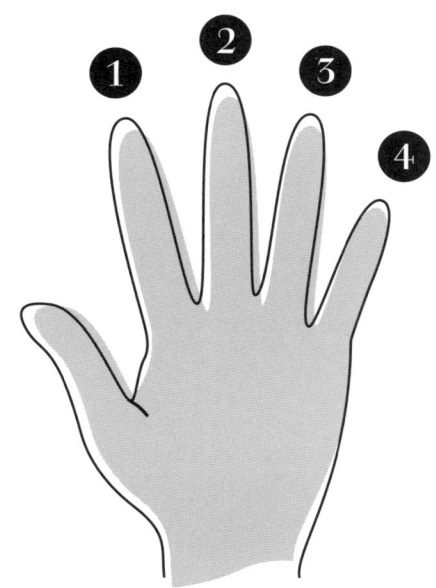

Fingering chart key

Th = Thumb hole
R = Register key

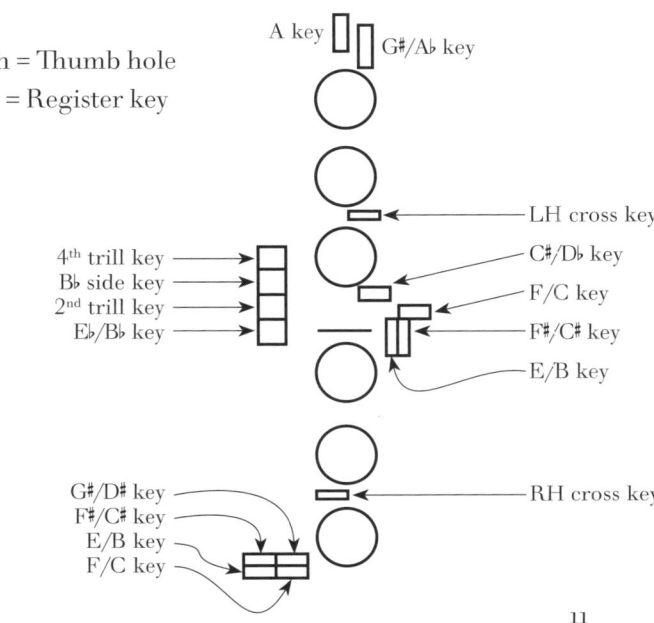

11

Be prepared!

Preparing to be prepared
Warming up without the clarinet
Limbering up without the clarinet
Brain states and deeper states of consciousness
Posture for playing
Warming up with the clarinet
Stretching (or cooling down)

Preparing to be prepared

The obvious place to start is in setting ourselves up correctly before we begin playing – whether that's to practise, rehearse or perform. Good preparation and good posture with an absence of tension are fundamental to good playing. In developing and refining technique when teaching, I often find myself spending equal time reducing or eliminating tensions alongside the cultivation of new ideas and techniques. Holding the instrument well and developing a comprehensive warm-up regime are both very helpful in realising, ultimately, our desire for effortless playing.

It seems obvious to state that optimum performance is most likely to occur when your body can move freely and comfortably, and respond as and when you want it to, free of pain, tension and fatigue. But stating it *is* important.

There are clear parallels to other fields of performance, such as dance or sport, where an optimum performance depends on how the body is prepared and used. Like dancers or athletes, there are benefits for instrumental musicians in adopting simple but effective strategies that will prepare and care for their body, and thereby enhance their performance. These can be divided into two distinct parts:

- How best to prepare and care for your body each time you play
- How best to maintain your body for playing over the longer term

Preparation for the (often significant) physical demands of playing an instrument begins before we pick up our clarinet and takes both a physical and mental form. It involves two different but complementary elements: *warming up* and *limbering up*. We shall also look at the importance of cooling down (mostly involving stretching) after practice.

All of these exercises are designed to create an *Optimum State* for achieving the most effective and productive playing experience.

Warming up without the clarinet

All athletes and dancers warm up at the start of every practice, rehearsal or training session. Similarly, we should begin each of our playing sessions by warming up.

The function of a warm-up is exactly what it says: to warm up. It increases blood flow to the muscles that you will be using; blood brings oxygen to those muscles, which is needed by the muscle cells to release energy. Warming up need not take long, but it does require you to get moving.

Examples include:
- Taking a brisk walk to the practice or rehearsal space
- Jogging on the spot
- Jumping on the spot
- Shifting from sitting to standing a few times[2]

> ### Here's an exercise for simultaneously warming up both body and mind:
> Hold your arms up in the air with fingers pointing to the ceiling. Then raise each knee in turn and touch it with the opposite hand. Breathe in as you move down to touch the knee and then out, as the arm returns to the starting position. Repeat the exercise reversing the breathing (i.e. breathe out as you move down etc.). Repeat either or both exercises for 20 to 30 seconds.

Once you feel warmer you can then begin to *limber up*.

---

[2]. If you're hypomobile, do this with care.

THE CLARINET

EXERCISES
Limbering up without the clarinet

Limbering up involves gently moving the soft tissues and joints that are involved in playing.

The function of limbering up is to:

- Make you aware of your own body;
- Give you the chance to notice areas of tension in your body;
- Reduce pre-existing tension in your muscles;
- Enable soft tissues (muscles and tendons) to begin moving smoothly prior to playing;
- Make you aware of your balance;
- Make you aware of the space around you.

Here is a collection of exercises that are useful for limbering up to prepare the body for playing. You don't have to do all of them or do them in the order given (in fact it's beneficial to vary the order), but collectively they focus on reducing and hopefully eliminating common tensions. Whichever exercises you choose, make limbering up part of your routine before each practice session or performance.

Don't forget to do a general warm-up (walking, jogging, jumping, etc.) for the entire body before you begin the limbering-up exercises, and remember, if you practise for long periods make sure you are moving regularly.

Limbering-up exercises are best done standing with feet shoulder width apart. Stand tall and comfortably.

Finding your point of balance

Here's an initial whole-body exercise to help find your central point of balance. Without shoes, stand tall: sense the connection with the floor from your toes through to your heels – in fact, the entire under-surface of your feet. Then rock forward onto your toes, keeping your heels on the floor, just enough to feel the muscles at the back of your lower legs stopping you from falling further forwards. Hold that position for a moment. Then rock back onto your heels, keeping your toes firmly on the floor, and feel the muscles preventing you from falling backwards. Hold this position for a moment. Now rock back and forth making each rocking movement smaller until you find your central point of balance. Hold that position for a moment.

Limbering up the body

TOES
You may be surprised to learn that tension can begin in the feet and may cause related tension in the hands and elsewhere. This makes it important to begin your limbering up with some toe exercises.[3] Stretch your toes up and out, creating a gap between each toe, and breathe in. Then curl your toes downwards and inwards whilst breathing out. Hold each position for a few seconds. Repeat several times.

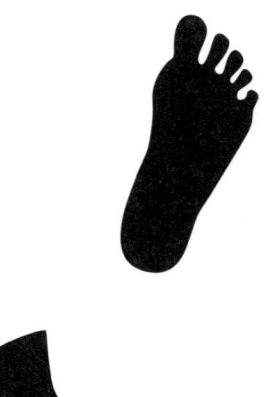
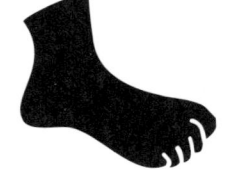

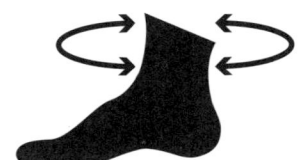

ANKLES
Gently move each ankle around in a circle in both directions.

KNEES
Stand with your knees unlocked to aid blood circulation and to prevent tension in your other leg muscles. Gently bounce with your feet flat on the floor to loosen the knee joints and engage the 'calf-pump' – a very important mechanism for maintaining healthy blood circulation.

---

3. There is a well-known story of a professional tuba player who developed debilitating tension in his fingers. Eventually it was discovered that he had excessive tension in his feet and toes and once these were freed his fingers returned to their full, tension-free use.

SPINE

Flexion:[4] stand and reach up towards the ceiling with both hands and then fold gently forwards. To return, engage your stomach muscles and uncurl gently to a balanced upright position.

Side flexion: stand and reach up towards the ceiling with both hands. Gently bend to one side and then the other. Return to a balanced standing position.

Rotation: stand and touch opposite hands to opposite shoulders. Keep your knees and hips facing forward while rotating your shoulders left and right. Return to a balanced standing position.

FINGERS

Finger exercises are important to encourage relaxation and blood flow.

With both hands, spread your fingers out as far as you can without straining them, then squeeze them into a fist. Repeat this several times.

Bend your fingers as though you are gripping handlebars, then stretch them out. Repeat several times.

With palms facing upwards, spread your fingers as far as they will comfortably go and then release them to their natural resting point.

WRISTS

Gently shake out your hands and wrists, as though they are wet.

Hold your hands in front of you and rotate your wrists a number of times, as though you are turning a tap.

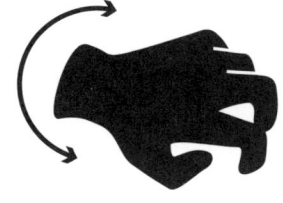

ELBOWS

Slowly extend the arms from the elbow, so they are completely straight, then reverse the motion, bringing your hands back towards your shoulder.

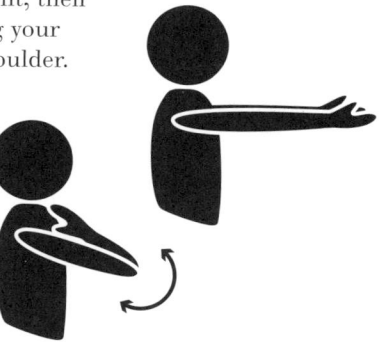

4. 'Flexion' is the scientific term to describe the action of bending.

THE CLARINET

EXERCISES

SHOULDERS
Make large windmill circles with each arm (in both directions).

With your arms relaxed at your sides, gently shrug your shoulders up toward your ears, hold for a moment and then release.

Place your hands on your shoulders and roll your shoulders in a circular movement several times slowly. Then, reverse the direction.

'Write' your name with each shoulder using joined-up writing.

NECK
Tilt your head down trying to touch your chest with your chin.

Tilt your head towards each shoulder, leading with your ear.

Look straight ahead and turn your head from side to side. Think of the front of your neck as being 'loose'.

HEAD POSITION
Many people hold their head too far forward (often known as 'Forward Head Posture' or FHP). This can have many harmful effects on the body, including neck and back pain, poor breathing, headaches and poor sleeping. Do consult an appropriate medical practitioner if you have this problem. Here's a simple exercise to feel whether your head is held correctly:

Stand against a wall, ensuring your tailbone (or buttocks) and shoulder blades are in contact with the wall.

Now, check your head position. Is the back of your head touching the wall? In a natural standing position, clearly your head isn't so straight, but it's a useful gauge of where to start.

NODDING
We tilt our head from a point virtually in the middle of the skull between the ears. Our heads are usually tilted slightly downwards when playing the clarinet. Ensure this tilt comes from that central point and not from the neck as this will create tension.

Nod your head and sense how the nodding is generated from a point in the middle of your skull and not from the back of your neck.

JAW
Wobble your jaw very gently from side to side, sensing its connection with your skull about halfway up your ears. Many players have tension in their jaw, which can affect breathing, embouchure and articulation. Gently massage the point where your jaw and skull connect if you feel any tension (the temporomandibular joint).

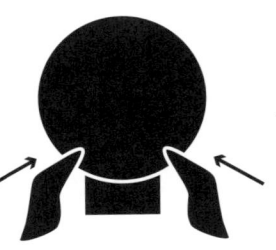

SOFT PALATE
Keeping the soft palate lifted (as good singers do) will aid the resonance of clarinet tone. Breathe in through your mouth and feel the cool air hit the top of the mouth, then quietly sing a 'ng' sound with a steady airflow. Then move to 'ah' as if you're amazed and delighted! This will raise the soft palate providing a feeling of space inside the oral cavity. Remember this sensation.

TONGUE
Run your tongue over the front of your teeth, making sure to reach to the very back of your mouth on both the top and bottom row. Begin on one side at the top and end on the same side at the bottom, then reverse the motion. This energises the tongue muscle.

BREATHING

1. Take a deep breath slowly, close your mouth and gradually engage the supporting muscles. Blow gently towards your closed lips, just enough to feel the air pressure behind them (keeping the throat open and relaxed). Feel the connection of the energised air in your lungs, trachea and mouth, behind the lips. Then release the air energetically.[5]
2. Take another deep breath and this time, close your lips keeping them close to the teeth. Then form a small natural aperture. Blow out energetically and with considerable velocity: this (with the clarinet) will result in a loud dynamic.[6] There is no particular 'force' or tension required in the blowing here. The air is released naturally and energetically.
3. Use the same lip pressure again and, taking care not to control *this* exercise with tighter lips, blow out again more slowly and with more restraint of the air. This will require *more* support and will control the softer dynamic levels.
4. Repeat exercises 2 and 3, this time positioning your tongue to produce a long 'hiss'. Take care to keep your jaw relaxed. Move your lips about with each long breath. This is an excellent exercise to train your brain to understand that the breath and the lips are entirely independent.
5. Repeat exercises 2 and 3 again, feeling that no other muscle sets are engaged, for example with no tension in the neck, wrists, shoulders, lower back, or knees. Try the exercises while jiggling around – almost dancing on the spot. We must learn to make the breathing mechanism independent from all other muscles. If you ask a non-clarinet player to take and hold a deep breath, they will often tense virtually every muscle in their body (as if they are about to jump into deep water). Clarinettists need a different approach.
6. Now repeat the second and third breathing exercises again, but every few seconds interrupt the flow of air by placing your tongue (with a quick and precise movement) just behind your top teeth. Ensure your abdominal muscles are still engaged during these interruptions. Sense that the air is still energised. This exercise strengthens the support mechanism and is particularly good for developing control at the ends of phrases or for notes when you will inevitably have little air left, and in maintaining a consistent sound during articulation.
7. Maintain the support and blow a long breath through virtually closed lips (without tension). Travel between varying degrees of velocity, as if making a *crescendo* and then a *diminuendo*, always ensuring connection to the abdominal supporting muscles. This must be controlled from the breathing mechanism and not the lips.
8. Repeat the exercise, but this time instead of pressing your lips together, hiss. Notice how the *crescendo* and *diminuendo* have no connection with the lips.
9. Maintaining a steady air pressure, blow a long breath and vary your tongue position, specifically the back of the tongue, from low ('aw') to high ('hhheee') and notice the speed of air: in the higher position it will be faster. Ensure the lips are not disturbed. This exercise is excellent for warming up your 'voicing' technique (see page 40), which can help facilitate so many aspects of clarinet playing.

Brain states and deeper states of consciousness

Here is one final exercise to practise before picking up the instrument. Making music is a multi-layered activity that combines the mental, emotional and physical, and brain states play a part in achieving the *Optimum State* needed before playing (see page 26).

Research has been undertaken on the differing ways in which the brain functions. These brain states are commonly labelled 'alpha', 'beta', 'delta' and 'theta'. Normal waking consciousness is usually considered to be in the 'beta' state, but we can *heighten* this state of consciousness to reach a little more alertness, critical reasoning and logical thinking. Ideally, as musicians, we need some 'alpha', too. An alpha brain state enhances your imagination, visualisation, memory, learning skills and concentration.

Meditation is a very good way into brain states. Doing some gentle breathing exercises will deepen the beta state and may access alpha too.

- Sit quietly. Close your eyes. Pay attention to any tensions in your body and gently release them; notice any thoughts that enter your mind and gently let them go.
- Breathe in slowly and deeply. Pause at the top of your breath until your body asks you to release it.
- Breathe out slowly, then pause and wait for your body to invite you to breathe in again.
- Repeat this process a few times until you feel yourself relaxing. In so doing, you may be accessing these heighted brain states, though you probably won't be aware of it!

---

5. For a full discussion on the breathing process see pages 32–39.
6. In fact, dynamic level is all to do with the energy that sets the reed vibrating. More energy causes the reed to vibrate with a greater amplitude which causes a louder sound. The air is what fuels that energy.

Posture for playing

Having warmed up and limbered up without the clarinet, it is now time to consider posture.[7] There is much talk and discussion about good and bad posture, yet it is rarely clearly defined, nor is the impact of different postures on our sound, our playing, our endurance and our comfort.

Some postures or positions are easier on the body and will enhance our playing, and some are less natural and may impact our playing negatively.

We all know that maintaining a good posture is vital, but it is also important to know why. In doing anything physical we must aim to apply the least amount of stress and strain on the supporting muscles, ligaments and tendons (collectively known as soft tissues). Also, correct bone alignment will assist these tissues to work efficiently and prevent injury and damage. Holding a good posture will feel as though the weight is evenly distributed without any part of the body taking on undue strain. In addition, it will allow the body to make best use of its energy, which will reduce fatigue.

Think: minimum effort for maximum effect.

Supporting the instrument

Correct posture provides the basis for technique and performance. The overall aim is to support the instrument with the least muscular tension. Consider the following carefully and re-evaluate your posture on a regular basis.

You should stand, or sit, in a comfortably upright position. This will allow you to make maximum use of your lung capacity and will help to avoid tension. If you sit, aim for position C as shown in the diagram opposite.

In this position you are sitting with your body weight going through your sitting bones (the two bones you can feel if you transfer your weight from buttock to buttock). This will be familiar to those acquainted with The Alexander Technique.[8]

Sitting for a sustained period of time in position A can cause the overuse of your back and shoulder girdle muscles, as they are busy (and unnecessarily) holding you up. This commonly results in fatigue and pain in the lower back, middle back and shoulder girdle.[9]

Position A also involves sitting up and off your sitting bones. This prevents you from taking the deepest breath you can, as some of the back muscles that are working hard in this position also attach to your lower ribs; when they are working to extend the back, the ribcage expansion is restricted.

Position B brings the base of your spine (the coccyx) into contact with the seat; in this position the lungs cannot expand fully, and your abdominal muscles will be less able to provide the necessary support for long notes.

When playing, make sure both feet are flat on the floor, with your heels approximately under your knees. Tucking your feet under the chair provides less stability, and may make you begin to tip forward, changing your balance.

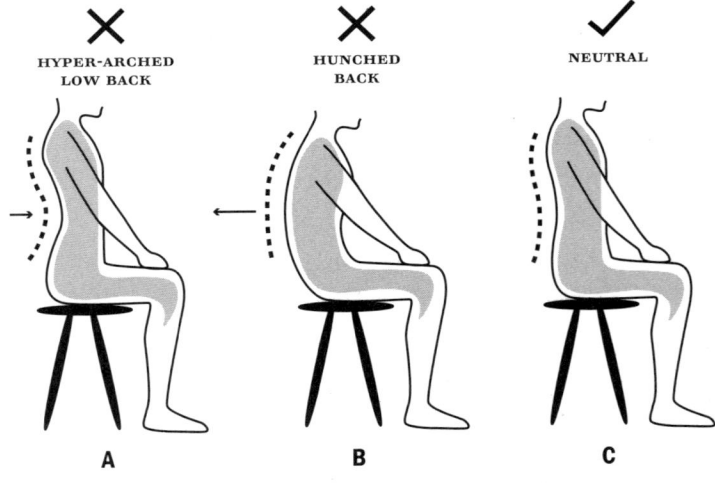

7. Posture is the first of my four P's – the four essential principles that underpin and drive all instrumental and singing development: Posture, Pulse, Phonology (sound) and Personality (of the music). For a full explanation see *Improve Your Teaching! Teaching Beginners*, Faber Music Ltd.
8. Named after the actor (Frederick) Matthias Alexander, The Alexander Technique develops understanding of movement and postural awareness. It aims to address long-standing physical habits that might cause tension, also taking into account intellectual and emotional aspects.
9. The shoulder girdle is the mechanism that allows for all upper arm and shoulder movement – it includes the clavicle and scapula and their associated muscles.

Holding the clarinet: standing   Holding the clarinet: sitting   The back of the clarinet

Place your right-hand thumb under the thumb rest (between the tip and the first joint). For many, the position of the thumb rest may need adjusting – this should be done with the guidance of your teacher or an experienced professional technician. There are sophisticated thumb rests available that reduce the strain on the thumb. If you feel strain while playing – a feeling that the thumb is overstretched, bearing uncomfortable weight, or in an unnatural position in relation to your fingers – discuss the benefits of such a device with your teacher or a reputable instrument dealer or technician.

Some players like to use a neck strap[10] that will remove virtually all weight and support from the right hand. Again, discuss this with your teacher or a professional instrument dealer. Some professional players use a neck strap, so there is no stigma attached to doing this.

The left thumb is placed on the thumb hole at an angle of about 50 degrees to the line of the instrument.

The clarinet is normally held at an angle between 20 and 40 degrees to your body, though some players play significantly outside of these parameters. There is ultimately no right or wrong way and you should experiment. There is also a connection between the angle of the clarinet in relation to your body and how much lip is in contact with the reed. This means that your teeth and lips also affect the angle.

Once holding the clarinet, allow your elbows to drop from your shoulders in a natural position, i.e. not held too closely to the sides, which will cause tension in the upper arms, or raised too high, which will cause tension in the shoulders and upper back.

Once you have considered your posture, try to avoid excessive non-essential physical movement while playing. Some players associate a particular movement with a particular phrase shape – for example, lifting or lowering the instrument when a phrase goes up or down. This may become habitual, disrupting the instrument's position in relation to the embouchure, and may be distracting to an audience. Often unwittingly, players put more expression into these physical movements than into the music. Of course, some tasteful and musical movement is a natural response to the music – just do this with awareness and not to excess! It's also important to avoid holding one position rigidly while playing.

If you are concerned about matters of posture or are interested in learning more, do consult an Alexander Technique practitioner (or other suitable practitioner in this field).

10. If you do use a neck strap be aware of any strain it might put on the neck.

THE CLARINET

EXERCISES
Warming up with the clarinet

The next set of exercises will require your clarinet. Each of the technical areas touched upon here (development of tone, articulation and finger movement) has its own chapter that explores these topics in much greater detail.

Getting started

1. First of all, here's a simple exercise to get the support muscles energised. Place the reed about 5mm above the tip of the mouthpiece and play anything you like – some notes, a phrase from a piece you're studying, a scale, a short improvisation. You'll have to work hard to create the sound. This will set up a confident approach to blowing as it will not be possible to distort the sound by over-blowing. This exercise will both engage the supporting muscles and increase your awareness of them.[11]

LONG NOTES
2. Now, placing the reed in its correct position, play G^2 as quietly as possible (see *The first tests*, page 206). Ideally the tone should be clear and warm, which means the reed is neither too hard nor too soft. Play a simple phrase, such as the opening bar of Debussy's *Première Rhapsodie*. The three notes should sound warm in tone, and the *legato* easy to manage, especially across the break. You may wish to make some small adjustments to the reed at this time, or simply move on.

Debussy, *Première Rhapsodie*, bar 2

3. Play E^2 blowing energetically and with a considerable velocity of air to produce a resonant ***f***. Listen carefully to the evenness and consistency of the sound. Now play it again restraining the air to produce a warm and resonant ***p*** note.

4. Play E^1, E^3, and E^4 as above, and then repeat using other pitches across the registers.

5. Play the key note and explore dynamic levels from the pieces you are currently studying.

LEGATO
6. Choose any two notes a second or a third apart and play with a smooth *legato*. In these small intervals take care to keep the embouchure still and the airflow constant – the only movement is in the fingers.

7. Play the following sets of *legato* paired notes. Work on each pair carefully in this order:

---

[11] Use this exercise any time you feel the supporting muscles may need a little waking up.

BE PREPARED!

8. Now play the following exercise. Consider the position of the tongue (see page 40) as you move from E^3 to E^4.

9. Work on these bars similarly in preparation for exercise 10 below:

10. Now play this *legato* phrase:

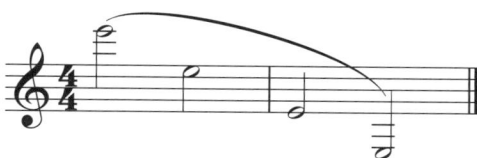

11. Repeat using other pitches across the registers and other intervals. Also explore particular *legato* phrases from pieces you are currently studying.

ARTICULATION

12. Play F^2 as a long note with your most beautiful sound followed by a single *staccato* note:

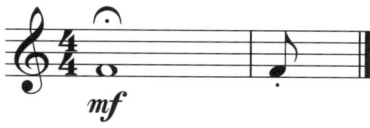

13. Now play just a single *staccato* F^2 at ***mf***. Next, play a *staccato* descending F major scale at ♩= c.60 down to F^1, one note per beat. Make sure the tongue is independent from the finger movement.
14. Play an ascending F major scale *staccato* at the same tempo from F^2 to F^3. Listen carefully, particularly to the quality of the throat notes.
15. Now extend the scale from F^3 to F^4. Aim to make all notes the same length, the same dynamic and with clean beginnings and endings.
16. Repeat at a faster tempo, exploring other dynamic levels and using other pitches. Explore varying the length of the notes and the gaps between them.

THE CLARINET

EXERCISES

Here's a particularly useful warm-up articulation exercise that can be adapted to other scales (those of pieces you are learning, for example) and other octaves. Ensure you maintain even airflow and lip pressure, taking care not to engage the throat.

EXERCISES

INCREASING ARTICULATION SPEED

1. Choose a comfortable metronome speed and a note and articulate (tongue) a bar of semiquavers (sixteenth notes), probably four ♩'s worth, but do whatever is comfortable. A louder dynamic is preferable.
2. Playing the same note, increase the number of beats – maybe by one beat every few practice sessions.
3. Also increase the tempo in very small, imperceptible increments (for example, by one bpm each time).
4. Repeat the exercise above using notes in each of the registers. *Remember that the tongue is a muscle that will need constant exercising.*

FINGER-WORK

1. Cover all tone holes, simultaneously depressing the F^1 key with the fourth finger of your left hand and the E^1 key with the fourth finger of your right hand. Now lift and replace each finger (and thumb) in turn *slowly* between about three and five times. Work out how much energy you need in the finger action: aim for as little as possible. Don't move any of the other fingers and keep them relaxed. Play this exercise as if playing a long note – you'll hear some strange sounds but it's very good for the fingers!
2. Play a slow and even trill using a strong finger of your choice. Keep both notes of the trill equal in length in relation to each other, and don't over-emphasise one note. Keep going for a full breath. Then explore other slow trills using each finger in turn. Try a number of different trills for the fourth finger. Explore one or two of the more unusual trills (maybe using a fingering book).
3. Play one or two scales and arpeggios, preferably in the key of the pieces you are currently studying. Play at a slow metronome mark to begin and gradually, over a period of weeks and months, increase the tempo.

MEMORY WORK

Choose a phrase or a passage from a piece you are currently learning and play it from memory. Listen to the tone, and explore varying phrase shapes, speeds and dynamic levels.

> **Optimum State**
>
> If you have worked through these exercises, you are now in the *Optimum State* and ready to carry on. If during your practice you do experience tensions, come back and revisit the appropriate exercises.

It is unlikely that you would have time to work through all these exercises each time you practise or perform. Get used to picking and choosing those you feel are most appropriate at the time, but try to do a variety on each occasion. How long you spend warming up will depend upon how long you intend to play, but always spend a proportion of that time warming up – it will pay you significant rewards.

Stretching (or cooling down)

In sport and dance, stretching is commonly part of the end of a training session. Stretching at the end of playing (whether a practice, rehearsal or performance) can also be helpful to instrumental musicians.

The function of slow and sustained stretching after playing is:

- To help muscles that have been working hard in a shortened position to relax and lengthen;
- To avoid muscle soreness the next day by preventing lactic acid build up and removing lactic acid that has built up in the muscles;[12]
- To maintain overall soft tissue flexibility.

Any stretching should be done to the point of feeling resistance and then held at this point for a short time. Don't hold your breath while stretching. Each stretch should last the time it takes for a few normally paced breaths in and out; most sports therapists recommend between 10 and 15 seconds. You can direct your 'mind's-eye' to the tightness and ask it to 'soften', 'melt', 'lengthen' or 'loosen'. Do not stretch to the point of pain and never force a stretch.

> **EXERCISES**
>
> **EMBOUCHURE**
> - Relax your lips and blow air through them to make a horse-like whinnying sound.
> - Push your lips together and then make circles.
> - After a long practice or playing session, massage and gently stretch the embouchure muscles with your index fingers.
>
> **WRISTS**
> - With one palm facing upwards, gently push your fingers towards the floor with your other hand. Repeat with opposite hands.
>
> **SHOULDERS**
> - Bring an arm across your body, raise your other arm so that the crook of your elbow supports the extended arm and bring it towards you. Repeat with your other arm.
> - Stand and extend your arms sideways. Push your shoulder blades together, whilst breathing in. Then, keeping them straight, bring your arms in front of you, whilst breathing out.
>
> **SPINE**
> - Raise your arms slightly and twist from the waist about 60 degrees in both directions.

> In summary, habits that promote musculoskeletal well-being will profoundly help instrumental musicians stay healthy and enjoy years of successful playing.
> - **Prepare** by warming and limbering up
> - **Establish** postures that help your body work well
> - **Avoid** fixed positions
> - **Cool down** (stretch) afterwards

---

12. Lactic acid is produced (naturally) when we over-extend muscle use and can cause a burning sensation in active muscles. This is a signal to stop using those muscles temporarily until they relax again. The actual cause of the soreness is a little more complex – there are medical books and journals on the subject if you want to investigate this further.

Sounding good

The science of sound

Reed, fingers, air and the tube

Breathing

Breathing exercises

Planning your breathing

The oral cavity

Embouchure

Special sonic effects

All about squeaks

Sounding good

Fundamental to playing a musical instrument is the sound we make. Clarinet sound (or 'tone') has changed over the years – listen to early recordings and you'll hear the difference (see page 227).[13] Listen also to other recordings and go to hear great players when you can for inspiration in developing a sense of what you'd like your own sound to be. Somewhere, in your imagination or your 'mind's ear', you need to have a sound to which you aspire.

There are three essential components involved in the production of our sound: breathing, oral cavity and embouchure. All three interconnect and are *absolutely* interdependent in making the sound. We now find ourselves in a kind of 'chicken-and-egg' situation: which component comes first? Let's start with breathing – perhaps the most essential, as that is where the sound is generated. We will then move up through the throat into the oral cavity and finally to the embouchure, which is where the player is joined to the instrument. So this section is very much about *your* side of the clarinet.

But before we do that, let's look at what this thing we call *sound* actually is. Some understanding of what we are trying to control, and how sound works within the clarinet, will help considerably in understanding the development of that control.

The science of sound

Sound is a type of energy that travels through the air in the form of waves that vibrate the air molecules. In our case, the clarinet sound (or tone) is created by the vibrations of the reed which, in turn, vibrate the column of air inside the clarinet.

Longer wavelengths produce sounds of a lower pitch than shorter wavelengths. The sound made by a clarinet, or any musical instrument for that matter, consists of several different simultaneous soundwaves, the longest being the pitch of the note we hear. The other, shorter waves help to create the characteristic timbre of the instrument by adding to the sound of the fundamental, heard as higher notes known as harmonics or overtones. When listening to lower pitches it is possible to hear these overtones, which is something we'll explore later.

The clarinet is a cylindrical pipe – one end is open, but the other is closed due to the presence of the vibrating reed and the player – this produces a different harmonic pattern from an open pipe (such as the flute) or closed conical pipes (such as the oboe and bassoon). For scientific reasons we don't need to go into here, a closed pipe produces very strong odd-numbered harmonics and very weak even-numbered harmonics. This is both why the clarinet's second register is a 12th higher than the fundamental register and the reason for its characteristic tone (see page 44 for more on harmonics).

---

13. Victoria Samek's recording label Clarinet Classics includes many fascinating historic recordings. Of course the sound is partially the result of less sophisticated recording techniques, nevertheless these recordings are of considerable interest.

Soundwaves and harmonics

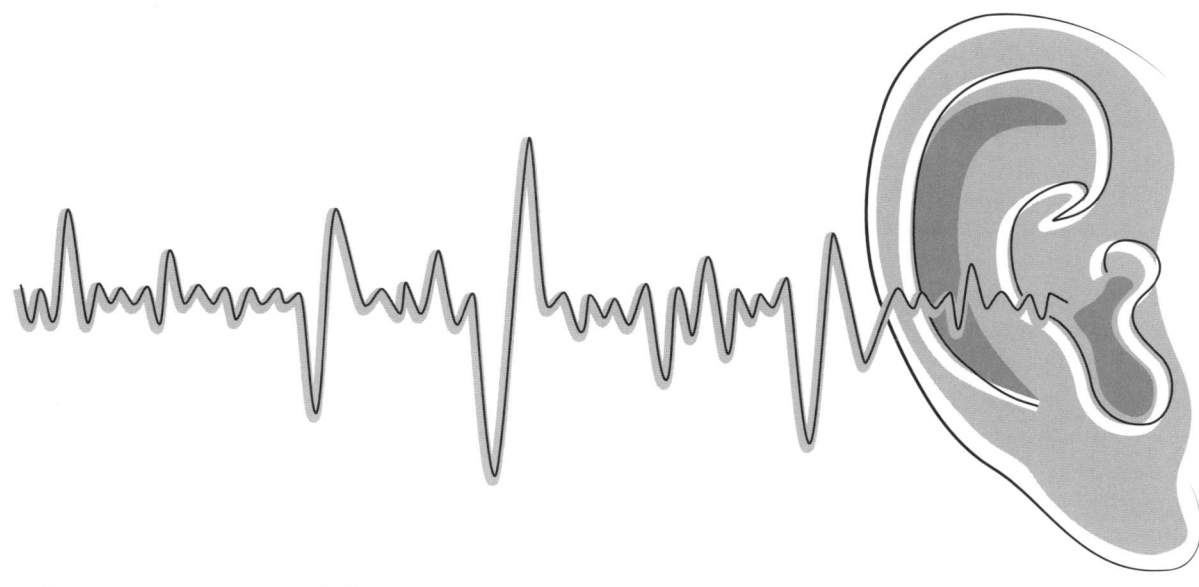

The fundamental wave	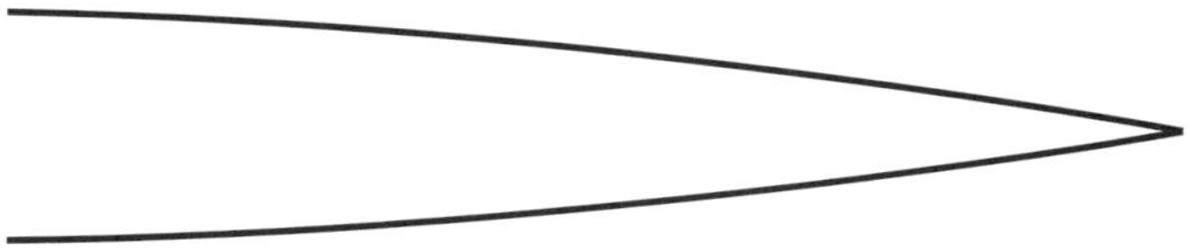
2nd harmonic An octave above and characteristic of an open pipe (e.g. flute and recorder) and of closed conical pipes (e.g. oboe, bassoon and saxophone) causing the overblowing of an octave.	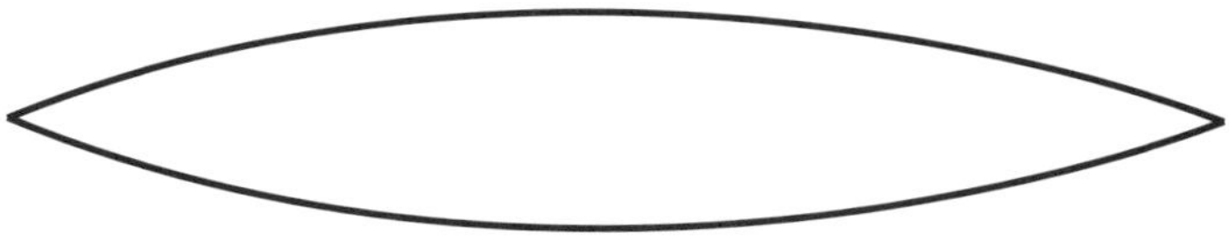
3rd harmonic A characteristic of a closed pipe (clarinet) producing notes a 12th above the fundamental, i.e. the second register.	
4th harmonic A characteristic of an open pipe, producing notes two octaves above the fundamental.	
5th harmonic A characteristic of a closed pipe (clarinet) producing notes two octaves plus a major third above the fundamental, i.e. the third register.	

Photograph © Denis Gliksman for Buffet Crampon.

Reed, fingers, air and the tube

When activated by blowing, and with an appropriate embouchure, the clarinet reed vibrates, moving up and down on the mouthpiece creating a valve. This opening and closing process causes alternating high and low pressure that vibrates the air column, which then vibrates the surrounding air to make the sound we hear. The air column inhabits the mouthpiece and the rest of the tube (the instrument[14]). The length of the air column determines the pitch of the note. So as fingers open or close tone holes they shorten or lengthen the air column (and hence the wavelength of the sound) and the pitch becomes higher or lower.

Now here's an important point: the sound is not so much the product of air *flowing through the instrument*, like wind blowing through a tube, but rather the result of the air being *energised*. Imagine it as a tube of water. If you slapped the end of the tube, a wave would be created that travels along to the other end, but the water stays where it is! The energised air is vibrating and causes the air around it to be energised too, and so we hear the wonderful sound that is the clarinet. We'll explore this further shortly.

When talking of clarinet sound, it is usually referred to as the *tone*. So from here onwards the word 'tone' will be used interchangeably with 'sound'.

Let's now have a close look at how we create the sound and how all our three components (breathing, the oral cavity and embouchure) work together to produce the tone we're aiming for.

Breathing

We begin with the engine itself – the point where the air that makes the sound is generated and energised. Breathing is the most important aspect of tone production and its success depends on the correct use of the muscles supporting the air column. Let's start by looking at the science behind breathing. You may wish to skip this section, but an understanding of the theory (as in so many instances) can really help you to apply the underlying principles in your own playing (and teaching).

The science of breathing

Breathing is about moving air. It is controlled by increasing and decreasing the air pressure in the thorax (the section of the torso between the neck and the abdomen).

As a general rule, air moves from areas of high pressure to areas of low pressure. For example, if we were to blow up a balloon, the air pressure inside the balloon would be high, making its skin firm to the touch. If we were to release the neck of the balloon, air would start to flow out because the air is at a lower (atmospheric) pressure. In releasing the balloon, we create a pressure gradient, as shown in the diagram opposite.

When we breathe in, the air pressure inside the thorax drops below the atmospheric air pressure, causing air to move into the lungs. When breathing out, the opposite applies: the air pressure inside the thorax increases to above the atmospheric air pressure, forcing air out of the lungs.

As we inhale, the diaphragm[15] contracts and flattens and the intercostal muscles lift the lower ribcage upwards and outwards, increasing the volume of the thorax enough to cause the needed change in internal air pressure. When breathing out, we simply relax and the diaphragm goes back to the domed position, assisted by the elastic recoil of the lungs and chest cavity, like a spring returning to its resting shape.

---

14. The technical term for the instrument in this context is the *resonator*.
15. A large dome-shaped muscle extending from the front to the rear of the body that is attached to the lower ribs and separates the chest from the abdomen.

SOUNDING GOOD

The thorax
The primary muscles of inspiration

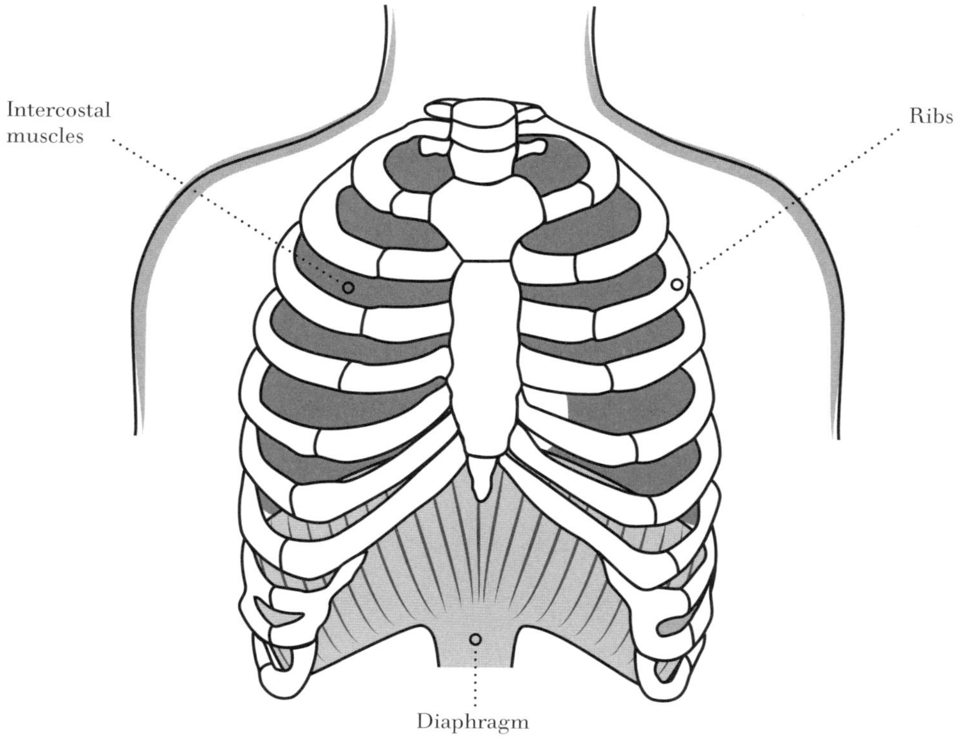

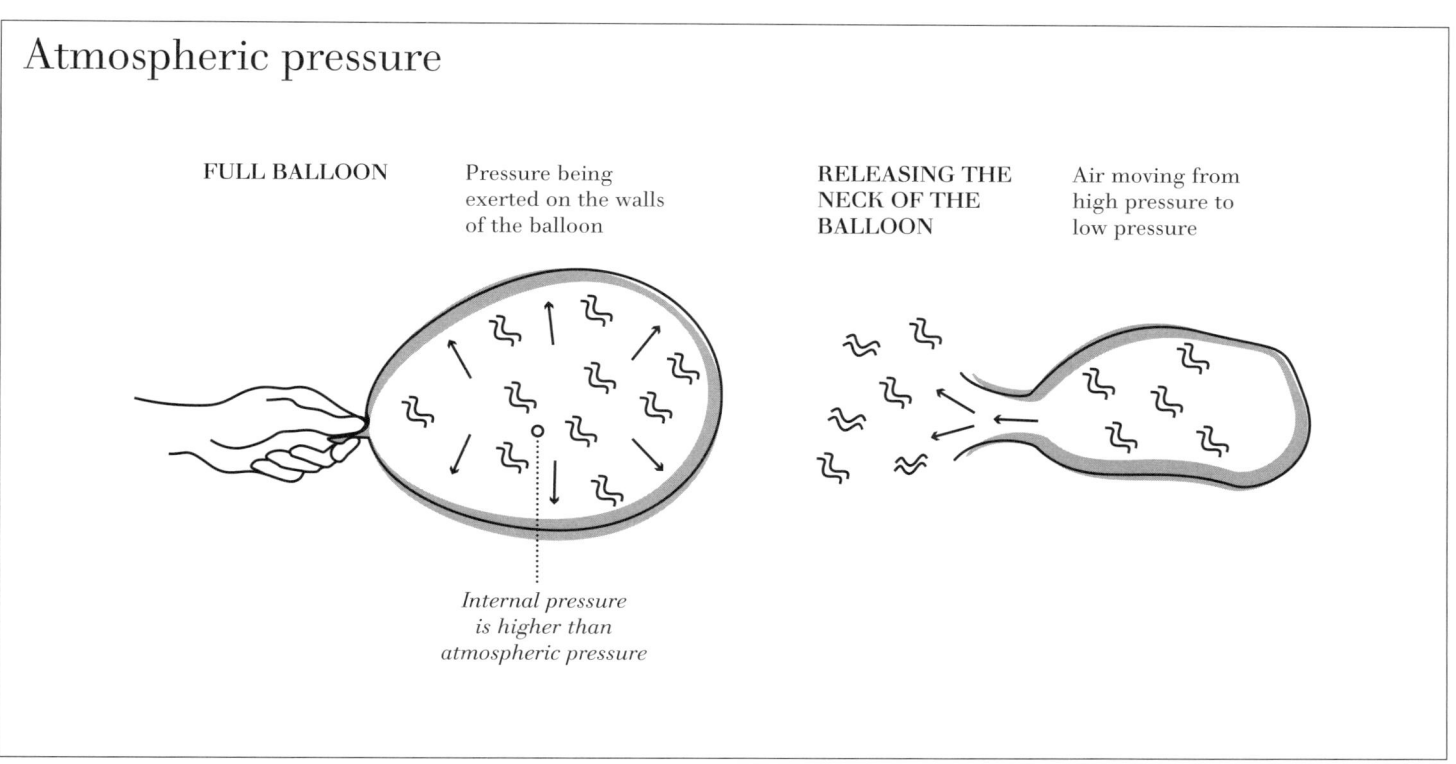

Intercostal muscles

Ribs

Diaphragm

Atmospheric pressure

FULL BALLOON — Pressure being exerted on the walls of the balloon

RELEASING THE NECK OF THE BALLOON — Air moving from high pressure to low pressure

Internal pressure is higher than atmospheric pressure

THE CLARINET

Breath control in clarinet playing

There are important differences between breathing at rest and breathing when playing the clarinet. Involuntary breathing is subconscious and automatic. *Controlled* breathing while playing is a very *conscious* action – we *take control* of the process, we *take control* of the air. The player actively chooses when and how much to breathe in and how the air is then released.

In order to understand this controlled type of breathing, we need to look closely at some of the muscles involved. These are the diaphragm, the intercostal and other chest-wall muscles that control the movement of the ribcage, and the support muscles of the abdominal wall (rectus abdominus, transverse abdominus, the external and internal obliques and, to some extent, the lower back muscles).

When playing the clarinet, the only difference when breathing in is that we take in more air than normal. In breathing out, we assist the relaxing diaphragm with what is called 'support'; without this, there will be insufficient control to maintain a supported column of air that will:

- produce a beautifully controlled tone,
- sustain longer musical phrases and
- control varying dynamic levels.

To support the diaphragm as it relaxes, you must actively engage the various muscles of the abdominal wall. These are the same muscles that we use in coughing or shouting.

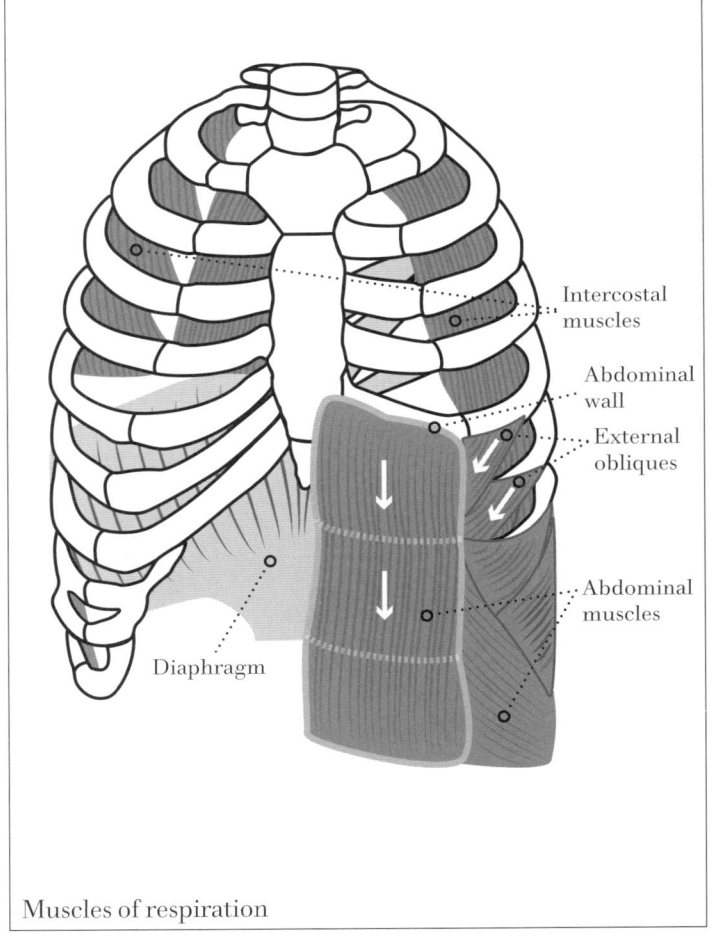

Muscles of respiration

What support really means

We often hear teachers give the instruction to 'support more' or observe that a particular player's tone 'lacks support'. But what does this actually mean?

When we support something we give it assistance. Whether it's a structure, a mechanism, a person or a cause, it's about giving stability, strength and, often, durability. In a similar way, *breath support* gives the air column strength, stability, and durability. There is nothing particularly complicated about playing loudly – beginners often do – but as we get quieter we need to increase the support, which means increasing the control. That control results from the opposition of two forces, but a very particular kind of opposition.

Imagine holding a bow (of the bow-and-arrow variety) with the arrow pointing upwards. Pull down on the relatively slack string and you'll feel a tautness. Imagine holding that position. You have created an opposition between two forces: your hand pulling the string with the arrow attached, and the string wanting to move upwards.

Now imagine the string is the diaphragm and the arrow is the air. The loading up of the air (as with the loading up of the arrow) causes your diaphragm to descend. If you simply let go of the string, the arrow will shoot away with considerable velocity. Similarly, if you let go of the air it will be expelled quickly and without much control. In this metaphor we're not going to let go of the arrow at all, but carefully control its movement back to its original position. The slower we wish to move the arrow back to its home position, the more control we need over it.

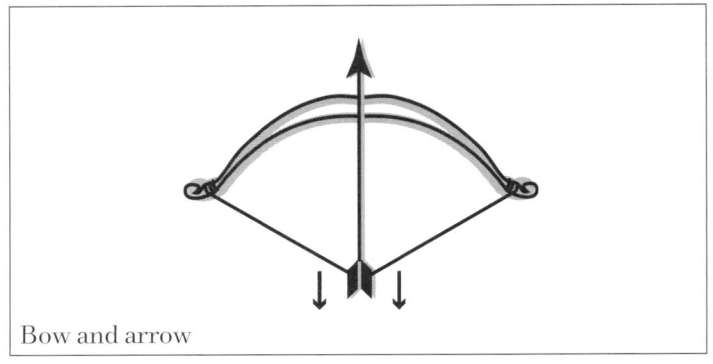

Bow and arrow

SOUNDING GOOD

Similarly, in expiration, the quieter we wish the sound to be, the more control we need, as the air movement is slower. The abdominal and other muscles (the hand holding the string in our image) now come into play to control the exhalation of the air. This is what we mean by support. Support is controlling the air and managing the volume and evenness that we require to energise the reed to make the sound we want.

- To experience this, take a deep breath.[16] Keeping your mouth open and throat completely relaxed, release the air as slowly as you can. Feel the control of the air being expelled.

Without that control the air is expelled too quickly (we've just let go of the arrow). Beginners usually run out of air very quickly for this reason.

We now need to learn to feel the connection between B (the place where the sound is created, controlled by the reed, embouchure, mouthpiece and tongue) *resisting* A (the diaphragm, assisted by the other breathing muscles).

- Take another deep breath. This time press your lips together, and again keeping the throat open and completely relaxed, blow and feel that resistance.

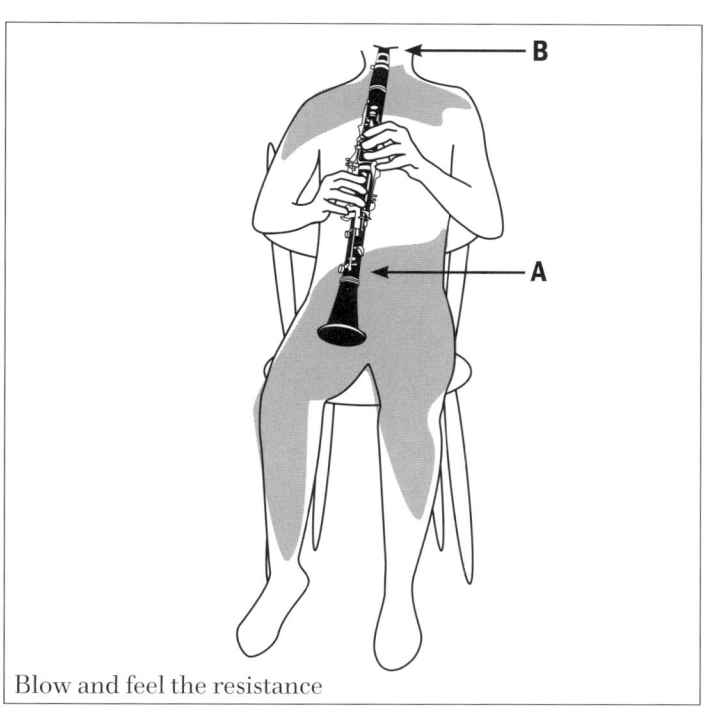

Blow and feel the resistance

Why the phrase 'breathe from your diaphragm' is only part of the story

We often hear expressions like 'diaphragmatic breathing' or 'breathe from your diaphragm'. The diaphragm is indeed the main muscle of breathing in, however, it has a less prominent role in the controlled exhalation necessary in playing the clarinet.[17]

When you breathe in deeply, you'll feel and see an expansion of the midriff area as the diaphragm lowers. In blowing out, the abdominal muscles play an important role in producing stable and strong support which prevent the diaphragm from returning to its natural position too fast. The player must make a conscious effort to control the tension in those abdominal muscles *without the back tightening*, which then controls the release of the air. Returning to the bow-and-arrow analogy, this control is like the hand drawing back the string until it is taut, and then gradually controlling its movement back to its rest position.

The feeling of this controlled tension in the abdominal area is *similar* to the firmness you would automatically create if you were about to receive a punch to the stomach. Take care not to clench or tighten these muscles (especially the back and the neck). Think of the muscles as being firm and controlled – not tense or stiff.

In playing the clarinet this process becomes quite sophisticated (we shall be considering this later). For now, remember – loud playing needs less 'support' because the fast-moving air has its own 'power'. As you become quieter the more support (or restraint) is required.

By 'diaphragmatic' breathing, we really mean a deeper type of breathing, engaging not just the diaphragm but also other accessory muscles. This type of breathing enables the lungs to fill to a much greater capacity as opposed to the gentle tidal breathing at rest or sleep, and facilitates both greater power and control.

In addition to the diaphragm and the abdominal muscles, the muscles of the ribcage also have a role to play. The ribcage is not fixed rigidly in one position, but expands upwards and outwards (a little like an umbrella opening) when breathing in. This expansion further enlarges the lower part of the chest cavity and allows more air to be drawn into the lungs, producing more space for resonance.[18] As you blow out, the combined conscious control of the abdominal muscles and the natural action of the ribcage provides the necessary support.

---

16. The instruction to take a 'deep breath' throughout this book doesn't mean you should attempt to fill your lungs to the point of discomfort, like a balloon filled virtually to the point of bursting. Breathe deeply but comfortably.
17. The diaphragm is unusual and interesting because it is made of skeletal muscle (the type of muscle we have control over, as compared, for example, to the muscles in the iris of the eye), yet it can also switch into automatic mode when we're sitting quietly or during sleep, working without any conscious effort. You can't move your diaphragm in the way you can move an arm or a leg. But you can move it when you breathe in (breathing in is the only way you can move the diaphragm) and in association with the abdominal muscles when you breath out, and that's what we're doing when playing the clarinet.
18. Body resonances are also important in sound production, as well as those produced in the instrument, oral cavity and the actual space in which we are playing.

EXERCISES
Breathing exercises

Exercises for controlled breath support

The following exercises – practised without the clarinet – will demonstrate the contraction of the abdominal muscles and the relaxation of the muscles controlling the ribcage when breathing. Take in a good breath with relaxed abdominal and intercostal muscles before each one:

1. Press your lips together and blow out in fast, short, sharp breaths. Make sure each breath is pushed out by the contracting muscles of the abdominal wall. Ensure the throat doesn't close when you stop blowing.
2. Now apply the same procedure to a continuous breath by blowing out a long stream of air, maintaining a constant speed and volume. If you place your hands about 3cm below the navel, you will feel the firmness of the abdominal wall as it controls the upward movement of the diaphragm. As you blow out you must be constantly aware of this firmness, as though you are being squeezed about the middle (again, around the navel area) by a tight, wide belt. Simultaneously, 'push' against that 'belt'. With repetition, this technique will become automatic.
3. Just to feel the action of the abdominal wall, hold the flat end of a pencil firmly to a spot a little above your navel. Push the pencil towards you and, engaging the supporting muscles, feel them pushing against it. Make sure there is no tightening of the back.

Holding your breath the clarinet way

The natural way to hold one's breath usually involves closing the throat (think of jumping into the deep end of a swimming pool). As clarinet players, we must take great care to avoid this. The air column, from the energising abdominal muscles through to the embouchure, must remain as uninhibited as possible.

Try this exercise. Take a deep breath and then hold the breath (restrain the air from moving) with:

- your throat (the glottis) (think 'uh' as in under);
- the back of your tongue (think 'k'). Be very particular to make sure you don't involve the throat here;
- the tip of the tongue, held behind your top teeth;
- your lips.

Compare and 'feel' the difference between each.

Now simply hold your breath keeping both your throat and mouth open.[19] Close your mouth, *engage the supporting muscles* and blow (keep your cheeks held against the sides of your teeth). Feel the air pressure behind your lips but don't let any air escape. Now relax your lips slightly and let the air begin to move out of your body.

---

19. Having taken a breath and held it in this way, there is no pressure gradient.

SOUNDING GOOD

Developing awareness of the breathing process

Here are some more exercises – still without the clarinet – to help develop awareness of the breathing process.

1. Whilst nasal breathing is not practised when actually playing the clarinet, it is a natural way to breathe and we all breathe correctly and healthily in this way. Exploration of this type of breathing will help you to feel inhalation in a more vivid fashion and avoid any improper use of the throat. First, take a deep breath, breathing through your nose.

2. Now breathe in slowly and deeply through the mouth (remembering what it felt like when breathing in through the nose) over a period of eight seconds. Sense you are breathing from a reservoir of air below the waist and feel the cool air hitting the top of the mouth. This will encourage you to raise the soft palate (see page 40). As you breathe in, feel your ribcage expanding to full capacity and the lungs filling up. Then close your mouth, engage the breathing muscles and briefly feel the supported column of air behind your lips. Hold this position for a few seconds. Now blow out through pressed lips, also for eight seconds, supporting the air column with the muscles of the abdominal wall and keeping the intercostals free from tension. Do this a few times, really sensing the feeling as the air is moving.

3. Now repeat the exercise but this time inhale for four seconds, hold for a couple of seconds and similarly exhale for four seconds.

4. Now inhale, still as deeply as you can, for one second, hold the breath for a moment and exhale for one second.

Note: in taking a breath to play you will be inhaling much more deeply than normally. In particular, there should be greater expansion of the ribcage in all directions (at the back as well as at the front and sides). It may take some time for this to feel natural. Avoid lifting your shoulders or tilting your head back while breathing in or out; such movements will constrict your throat and breathing system and will undermine your tone production.

20. Any tension that might inhibit, disrupt or impede the process.

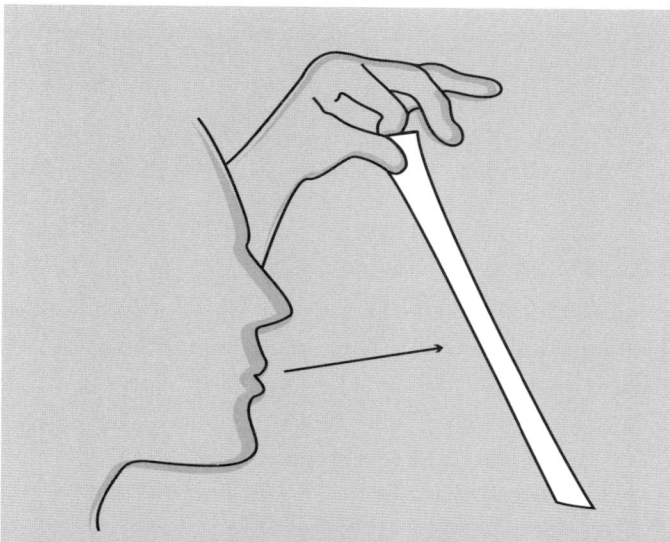

Here is a simple breath control exercise:

Hold a sheet of paper vertically from above, fairly close to your mouth. Now, aiming at a central point on the piece of paper, blow out as described above, through pressed lips so that the paper rises. If your support is working, you should be able to keep the paper at a constant angle for the entirety of the breath.

Positive control versus negative tension

Although breathing requires considerable control and practice, it must never involve or create *negative* tension.[20] Equally your control in the embouchure as you shape your lips around the mouthpiece and the opposition in the abdominal muscles should be without any tightness, stiffness or rigidity. You are aiming for a state of perfect balance. Take your time working through and reworking these exercises. If any *negative* tension creeps in, stop. Go back to your *Optimum State* (see the warms-ups in *Be prepared!*) and begin the exercise again. Your goal is to use and develop the muscles without straining them.

THE CLARINET

EXERCISES

Taking a breath with the clarinet

- Hold the clarinet comfortably and with good posture (see pages 20–21).
- Choose a note, form an embouchure (see page 41) and then breathe in deeply through the sides of the mouth. Avoid any movement or disturbance of your upper teeth on the mouthpiece, or the position of the lower teeth (jaw) and lips as you breathe in.
- Play a long note, breathe in again and play a second long note. Keep relaxed throughout this whole process.

Taking a quick breath

We need to learn to take breaths quickly, effortlessly and as fully as possible. With practice, taking a quick deep breath will become instinctive.

- Standing, without the clarinet and in a relaxed state, exhale as much air as you can.
- Now simply allow the body to refill quickly and naturally. Keep the throat relaxed.
- Do this a few times and sense the refilling process. Avoid sucking in or pulling in the air. There will inevitably be some noise in the throat but if it sounds like a gasp or an extended hiss then the throat is too tense. Some singers describe this process as feeling as if the body is opening. Taking a normal deep breath usually takes around a second or just over.
- Now with the clarinet, play a long note and then consciously refill using this technique.

Imagine the reservoir of air you're about to fill up from is below your waist level – this will help to avoid tensions in the throat and upper torso.

- The refilling process needs to feel relaxed. By relaxing we are facilitating a deeper breath when the next breath is taken.

The following exercises will help you develop the ability to take a deep breath quickly by progressively reducing the time available for inhaling. It is important to breathe only during the rests. Hold the notes for their full value, keeping a steady beat. Never let your breathing alter the length of the notes. Breathe in through the sides of your mouth, with the minimum of adjustment to the embouchure. Aim to keep the throat neutral.

Play the exercises several times. When you have mastered them at the slowest tempo, vary the tempo within the limits set by the metronome marks. Also play them at different dynamic levels and throughout the entire range of the instrument.

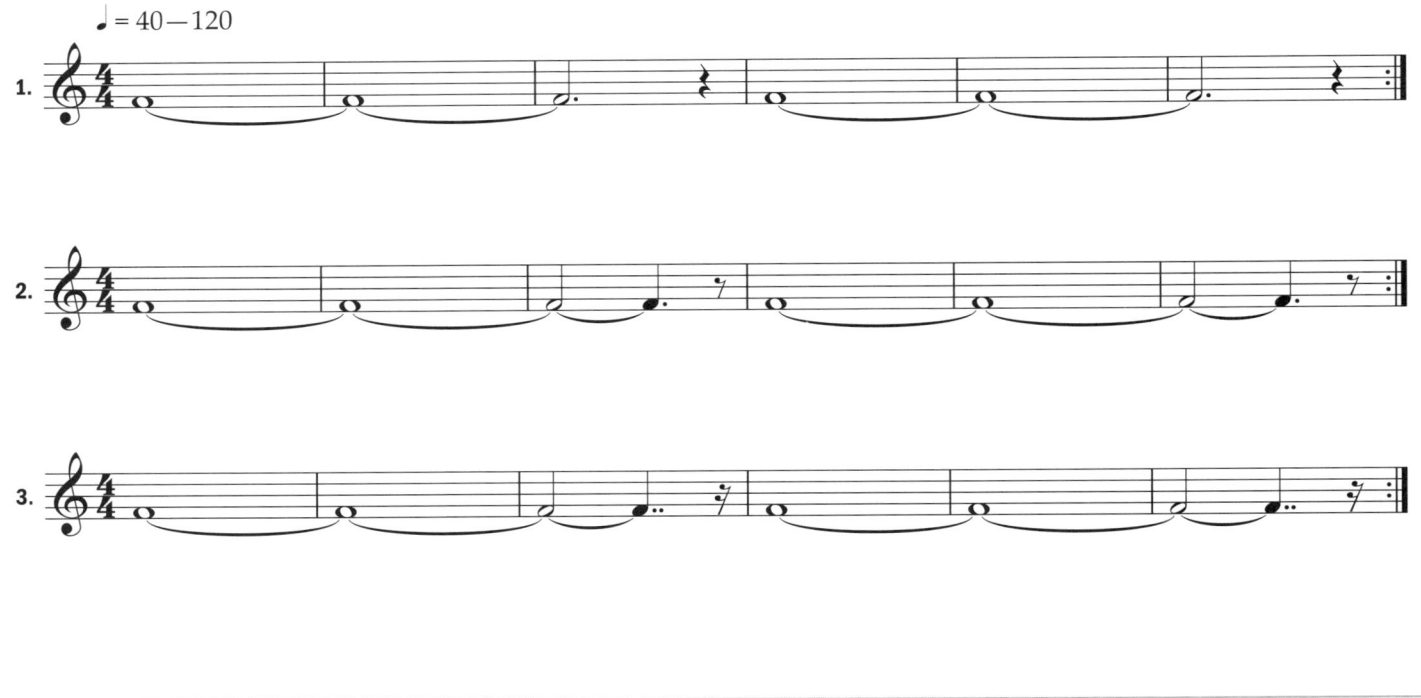

Planning your breathing

Breath control during a performance needs careful planning and is an essential part of practice and preparation. When preparing music for performance, mark on your copy the places where you are going to breathe, bearing in mind that your breathing should support the phrase structure of the music as well as your general physical comfort. Once happy with your breathing places, aim to breathe in the same places every time, both in practice and in performance. Though as you develop your performance, you may wish to change your mind over these.

It is beneficial to take a full breath at the beginning of any piece and whenever you breathe thereafter, to ensure the optimal engagement with the breathing muscles. Therefore, dependent on the length of the phrase (and your next breathing point), it might sometimes be helpful to release unused air to avoid discomfort or even feeling a little lightheaded (a technique often employed by oboe players, as they expel far less air while playing).

There are certain cases where careful planning for breathing can help with intonation. For example, softer entries can be slightly sharper if they begin immediately after taking a breath.[21] This might be employed deliberately to sharpen a note – for example, taking a quick breath before the final note of the first movement of the second Brahms Sonata. In the same way, try to avoid breathing immediately before a note that is likely to play sharp.

The oral cavity

So we now move onto the oral cavity, which is essentially the inside of the mouth and a part of the vocal tract.[22]

Quite what effect any changes in the oral cavity have on the tone, tuning and timbre has been the subject of much discussion, and even disagreement, among players for many years. Fortunately, there has been some serious scientific investigation of late, where players have subjected themselves to various kinds of scans in order to determine exactly what is going on.

If you simply take a deep breath (as deep and as full as you can) and then blow all that air out with nothing blocking or impeding its journey, i.e. with a relaxed, open throat, tongue low in the mouth and no embouchure, you would expel a complete lungful of air in a fraction of a second. There would be no control. Sustaining a good clarinet tone requires a lot of control. This is where the oral cavity has an important role to play.

As the air flows through the oral cavity, it enhances the resonance of the sound. When the air *exits* the oral cavity, the embouchure, reed and mouthpiece (acting as a unit) form a kind of bottleneck where the air is forced through a small aperture (the space between the reed and the mouthpiece tip) and therefore naturally speeds up. We need to look at what happens to the airflow before it reaches the embouchure.

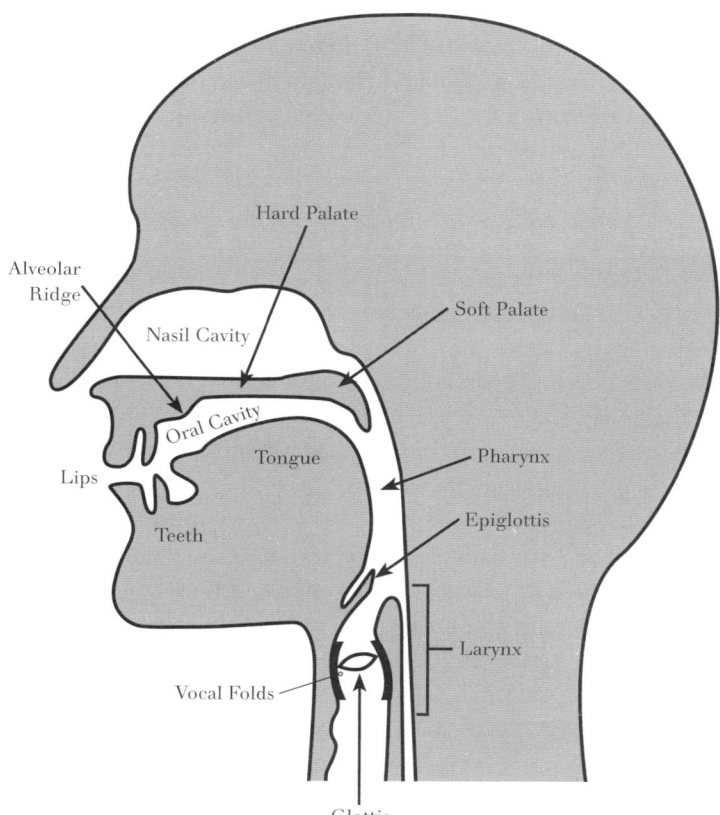

---

21. This is due to the relative levels of oxygen and carbon dioxide (CO_2) in your breath. Gas exchange happens in the lungs; the column of air in the airway above the lungs will have less CO_2, so the first note after a breath will be CO_2-light and have a higher frequency, thus sounding very slightly sharp. For more detail, see Leonardo Fuks' paper *Prediction and Measurements of Exhaled Air Effects in the Pitch of Wind Instruments*, available freely at the time of publication: https://www.speech.kth.se/music/publications/leofuks/IIIbism97co3.html.
22. The vocal tract is made up of the larynx, the pharynx, the oral cavity, and the nasal cavity. In clarinet playing it is mainly the use of the oral cavity – tongue shape and position, and soft palate – that contributes to the resonances.

THE CLARINET

Tongue position (or voicing)

The air enters into the oral cavity at the back of the throat (the pharynx). Some players speak of the importance of keeping the throat 'open'. In fact, the natural process of breathing in causes both the soft palate to rise and the larynx to lower automatically. For the clarinet player this is really all that is necessary to maintain a good throat position. If you do experience any tension or discomfort in the throat, jaw, neck or tongue, it may well be the result of trying too hard to *keep* the throat open.

EXERCISES

It is helpful to understand the benefit of a *raised soft palate*: it increases the resonance of the sound by increasing the resonating space.

- Sing a 'ng' sound (where the air will travel down the nose) and then change naturally to an 'ah', as though you're suddenly delighted to see a long-lost friend! This will raise the soft palate.[23] Yawning has a similar effect.
- Sense how this feels and then play a long note with the same sensation. You should hear a particularly resonant sound. Eventually you will assume this shape instinctively.

In clarinet playing, the main factor in developing best use of the oral cavity is the position of, and shape adopted by, the tongue – in particular the back of the tongue. This is sometimes referred to as *voicing*. The position of the tongue will significantly affect the direction and speed of the air and is thus of considerable importance. Make sure that you consciously relax your tongue as part of your warm-up routine – sense the front, middle and back of the tongue are all relaxed.

Some players only minimally alter their vocal tract formation to control *all* notes from the *chalumeau* to the top of the *clarion* register. It seems that a 'hhheee' shape, which funnels and speeds up the airflow, creates the most conducive conditions for a focussed sound.[24] Some players do alter the position of the tongue in relation to different registers, and other shapes will be considered in the next section, however, in passages that move quickly around the registers a consistent shape is ideal. Experiment and see what works best for you.

EXERCISES

Here's a quick exercise to develop awareness of the 'hhheee' tongue position:

- Without moving the jaw, alternate between silently saying 'aw' and then 'eee', to feel how the tongue changes position and in the process, changes the shape of the resonating oral cavity. The first time you do this, start with a gentle 'k' sound (as in 'key') which will place the back of the tongue in the ideal position.
- Prepare to begin the sound 'khheee' – you'll place the back of the tongue against your hard palate. Sense this position.
- Now release the 'khheee' and make a hissing sound. Sense the position of the tongue and keep going until you run out of air.

Other oral cavity shapes

'Aw' (as in 'paw' or 'saw') is another useful shape. Here the tongue is relatively low in the mouth and air speed will be slower. This can be helpful for creating darker tone colours and for giving throat notes more resonance. It can also be useful in negotiating wide downward intervals by moving seamlessly from 'hhheee' to 'aw', and similarly some wide upward slurs by utilising an 'aw' (or 'ah') to 'eee' movement – although much care needs to be taken not to impair the intonation or quality of the sound. It can help to flatten notes, but only by a small degree. It contributes to pitch bending and *glissando* (see page 46). Because the vocal tract is slightly more open with 'aw', this formation may need more breath. You might like to experiment with further oral cavity shapes to see what works best.

Try playing long notes with these shapes and listen for any variation in tone colour, but bear in mind that changes of oral cavity shape may also impact embouchure by causing small unintentional adjustments to the lip and other nearby muscles. This should be avoided; oral cavity shape should not have any effect on the embouchure or throat.

---

23. Just for clarity, *raising* the soft palate causes it to move back and up, which keeps the throat space open and wide.
24. There has been a lot of research to support this. Many players were scanned while playing. The finding was that a 'hhheee' formation (when the back of the tongue is held high in the mouth) was the most frequently adopted position for playing in all registers.

Embouchure

We now arrive at the point at which we, the player, connect with the instrument. The term 'embouchure' has evolved from an eighteenth-century French word *emboucher* meaning 'to put to one's mouth'. The word is used to describe the formation and operation of the lip muscle and other muscles around the mouthpiece.[25] It is the way that we adjust the mouth to make the most efficient fit with the mouthpiece and has a significant effect on the production, character and quality of tone and on fine tuning.

Forming and developing an embouchure

The reed should be positioned on the lower lip at about the point where the reed and mouthpiece begin to separate (the 'breakpoint'). The lower lip is drawn over the bottom teeth, although exactly how far will depend to a great extent on the shape and thickness of each player's lips. Depending on the shape of the lower lip vermillion (see below) some or all of it may slide over the teeth.

Feel where the lower lip connects with the reed. Experiment and feel what is comfortable and works best for you, ensuring the reed is free to vibrate. The chin should be stretched slightly downwards to avoid any flabbiness in the skin under the lower lip.

The lower teeth (the jaw) should give support, but always avoid undue tension (see page 37) or biting.[26]

Place the top teeth lightly on the mouthpiece. The upper lip is held firmly and directly on the top of the mouthpiece and it is important to feel both a certain amount of downward pressure and also some pressure backwards (or inwards) onto the upper teeth.

A NOTE ON 'DOUBLE-LIP' EMBOUCHURE

This is where the top lip is drawn under the top teeth in a similar manner to the lower lip over the lower teeth. Double-lip embouchure was probably used exclusively in earlier clarinet playing before the 1820s (where the mouthpiece was generally played with the reed on top[27]) and is the technique employed by double reed players. Interestingly, oboists often doubled on the clarinet when it first appeared in early orchestral music. Many well-known players of the past used double-lip embouchure and it seems, again, to be growing in popularity. Those who use it comment on the increased resonance of the sound, owing to the slight natural change in oral cavity shape and embouchure pressure.

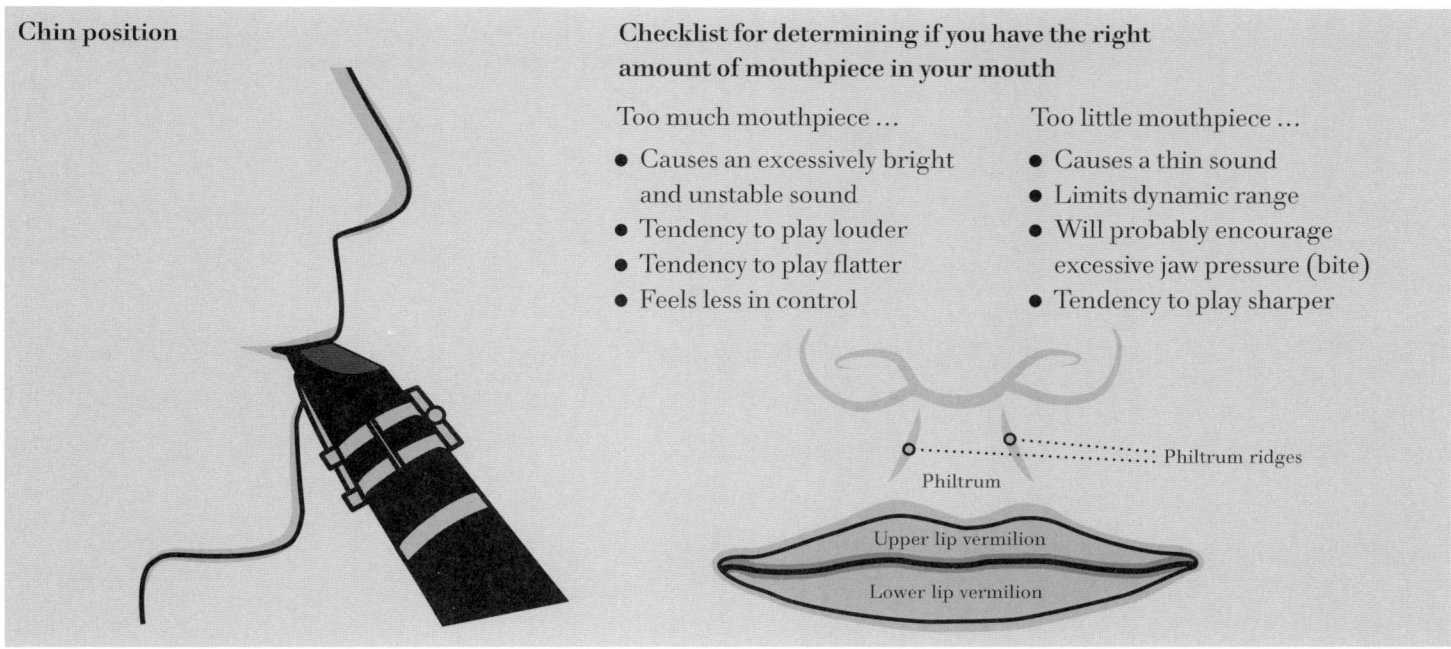

Chin position

Checklist for determining if you have the right amount of mouthpiece in your mouth

Too much mouthpiece …
- Causes an excessively bright and unstable sound
- Tendency to play louder
- Tendency to play flatter
- Feels less in control

Too little mouthpiece …
- Causes a thin sound
- Limits dynamic range
- Will probably encourage excessive jaw pressure (bite)
- Tendency to play sharper

---

25. The muscle in and surrounding the lips is called the *orbicularis oris* (from the Latin meaning little circle around the mouth). It is actually a number of connected muscles.
26. 'Biting' is a term often used by many players and teachers, and in this book. It really means using a lot of upward jaw pressure (a *biting* movement) that pushes the reed very firmly onto the mouthpiece limiting its ability to vibrate freely. It can also cause pain (and damage) to the lower lip.
27. Anton Stadler, Mozart's clarinettist, interestingly, played with the reed on the underside of the mouthpiece.

Embouchure control

Embouchure control is the result of a balance between a number of factors:

- Engaged lips: the upper lip, lower lip and the sides are both independent and interdependent. They are all part of the *orbicularis oris* muscle.
- The side lip muscles (indicated by the arrows): these act as 'side-struts' that support the upper lip as it pushes downwards, and the lower lip as it pushes upwards. They are particularly important in preventing air escaping and in controlling the cheeks.
- Cheeks: these are held firmly against the teeth and not usually allowed to 'puff out'.
- The chin (the jaw), which is slightly pulled down (see diagram on page 41).

Our objective is to create a firm embouchure without tension or tightness. An effective embouchure is ultimately about durability, flexibility and awareness.

A player with an under-developed embouchure will usually compensate by tightening the lip muscles and biting with the jaw, causing the tone, intonation and articulation to all suffer (and may also cause physical discomfort).

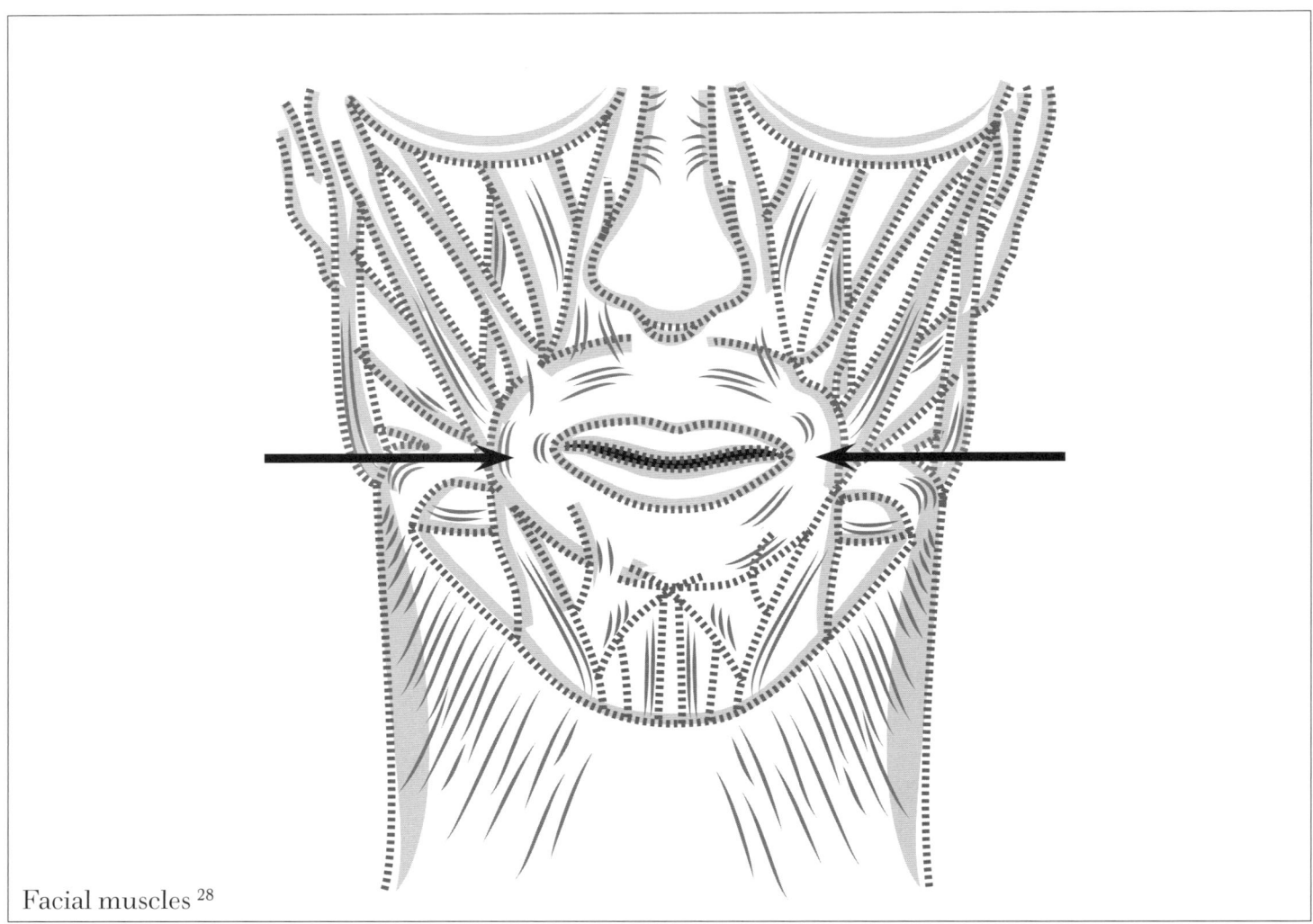

Facial muscles [28]

---

28. See *The Embouchure* by Maurice Porter (Boosey & Hawkes Ltd, 1967) for an in-depth and very detailed explanation of the embouchure.

SOUNDING GOOD

EXERCISES

Here is a sequence of exercises to develop the embouchure's durability and flexibility:

1. Without the mouthpiece, push your lips together. Push down with your upper lip muscles, up with your lower lip muscles and laterally inwards with the side muscles.

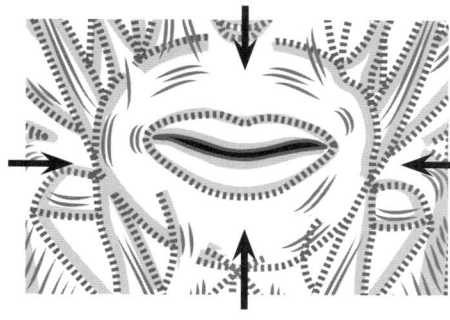

Don't exert too much pressure but sense all the muscles working together. Now, maintaining this position, gently chew without crashing your teeth together. Feel the independence of the embouchure muscles and the jaw.

2. With your lips pressed together, hold your jaw open and still, and 'chew' with your lips. First try to engage just the upper and lower lips, then just the two sides, and finally the entire circle of embouchure muscles (the whole of the *orbicularis oris*).

3. If you can find an old (unwanted and unloved) bassoon reed, here's a rather useful exercise to help develop an awareness of the lip muscles, especially the often less-developed upper lip. After disinfecting it, cut around 5mm to 1cm from the tip of the reed and then, with your jaw held apart and relaxed, and without your lips covering your teeth or your cheeks puffing out, blow a long, loud note. Both upper and lower lips will have to work equally hard. In addition, you'll feel the vibrations going through your lips which will give you more awareness of the muscles. As a development of this exercise, try placing the reed at different positions along your lips, from one side of the embouchure to the other.

4. Now repeat exercise 1 (without the chewing) but this time apply more pressure from the four sides of the embouchure simultaneously. Feel the muscles working hard.

5. To develop the top lip, use one, two or three fingers to push upwards underneath from the centre of the lip, and with your top lip, simultaneously push downwards.

6. Form a double-lip embouchure (where the upper and lower lips slightly cover the teeth, see page 41) and repeat the lip-chewing exercise (2) without moving your jaw. Feel the independence of the lips and jaw. This more accurately represents the lower lip when playing but will exercise both the upper and lower lip.

7. Take just the mouthpiece (complete with reed) and form an embouchure. Sense the shape of the mouthpiece as it's surrounded by the lips. Be *aware* of the muscles of the upper and lower lips and especially the muscles at the sides of the embouchure. Spend time sensing how all these muscles 'feel'. Sense how they interact. Sense the balance, the firmness, and the lack of tension. As you are concentrating on the embouchure muscles make sure that your tongue, jaw and throat remain relaxed.

8. Repeat exercise 7, but now with the whole instrument. Be aware of the angle of your head as you connect with the clarinet – *tilt it from that central spot* (see page 18). *Don't bend from your neck or push your neck forward.* Bring the clarinet to you.

9. Form your embouchure but with your upper teeth slightly raised off the top of the mouthpiece. Play a long note. Feel the muscles in the upper lip working hard and the lower lip supporting firmly and without tension.

10. Play E^3, then release the register key (hence fingering A^1) and try to keep the note sounding. Maintain a fast air speed and feel your lip muscles working hard. Don't allow excessive jaw pressure or your lower teeth to 'bite' into your lip. Try this using other notes in the same register. This is a good lip strengthening exercise.[29]

11. Try these exercises varying the lateral position you place the mouthpiece in your mouth.

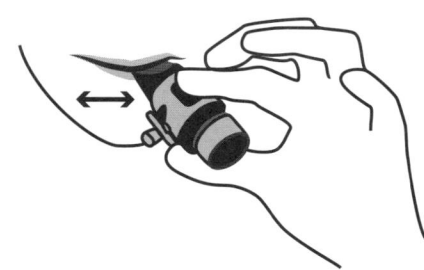

12. Ideally, after playing (especially a long practice session or performance) you should stretch the muscles of the embouchure carefully. This will release any tension and a potential build-up of lactic acid that can cause stiffness. Over time this will aid embouchure health.

---

[29]. The human brain can object to being asked to do the same thing too often. Very occasionally, as a result, the neurotransmitters (chemicals in the brain that send messages) can miscommunicate and send the wrong message to the muscles: this very rare condition is called *focal dystonia* and occurs when instructions from the brain do not cause the desired movements. This exercise can help prevent focal dystonia in the embouchure.

Special sonic effects

We can now use our tone control to create certain special effects like *glissando*, note-bending, multiphonics and more sophisticated slurring. To begin, it's useful to understand harmonics.

Harmonics

Whenever you generate a note on the clarinet, in addition to the fundamental (the note you are playing), a series of higher-frequency harmonics are created. These higher-frequency notes sound at the same time, and although they are almost inaudible, they are partly responsible for giving those notes their characteristic tone quality.

Because of its physical characteristics, the clarinet naturally favours the odd harmonics causing the second register to overblow at the 12th – not at the octave like the flute, oboe, saxophone and bassoon. Here are the harmonics on E^1:[30]

Here's an activity you can try with an acoustic piano that will demonstrate the principle of harmonics. Depress C^4 silently and play a short C^2 loudly and with an accent. C^4 will sound even though you haven't played it, as it is vibrating sympathetically with the low C (or the 'fundamental'). It is an 'overtone' or 'harmonic'. Depress a C major triad (with C^4 as the root) silently and repeat the experiment. Notice how the whole chord sounds even though you haven't played those notes. They are all harmonics of the fundamental. There is, in fact, a major chord in every note.

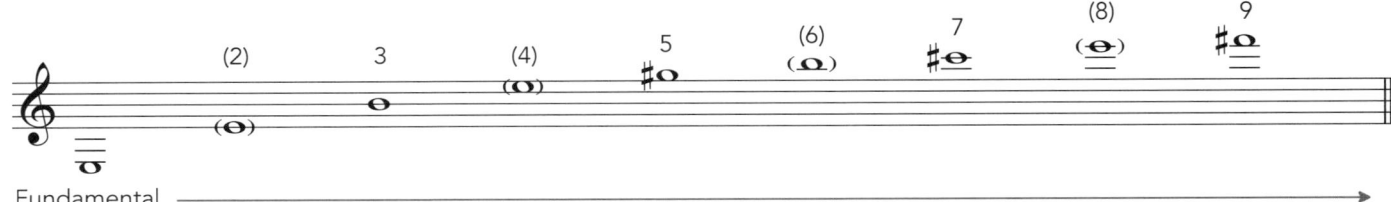

Fundamental

Knowing the harmonics of particular notes is helpful in understanding two important aspects of the clarinet's behaviour:

- Why some notes may be 'naturally' out of tune
- The explanation behind many of the *altissimo* fingerings

Being able to produce these harmonics is also very helpful in a number of other ways:

- It will further develop the embouchure by both strengthening it and helping to increase flexibility
- It will contribute to the improvement of tone quality and secure intonation
- It will help develop the use of the vocal tract which particularly aids in *altissimo* note production
- It will aid in the production of multiphonics (sounding more than one note simultaneously)

30. Basically, those of a partially cylindrical closed pipe (see pages 30–31).

EXERCISES

Have a go at these harmonics exercises (sometimes known as 'bugling'). They may take a while to master, but it's worth the effort.

1. Play E^3 then sound each of these harmonics without changing the fingering. Start each note with the breath and explore tongue positions that change the shape of the oral cavity. Think of the syllables '*aw – ah – ee*' as you ascend. Make small adjustments in your breath and lip pressures.[31] The lower lip will be very slightly pushing up and into the thicker part of the reed approximating to the breakpoint on the mouthpiece – if you do this on the vibrating part of the reed, it won't work. Take great care not to 'bite', either downward which will ultimately dent the mouthpiece, or upward, where the jaw (lower teeth) pushes upwards into the lower lip, which may cause pain. In time, you will probably be able to find two harmonics above E^3, and maybe a third harmonic with more practice:

Aw   Ah   Ee   *Ee*

Try the same exercise on each of the following notes: **F, F♯, G, G♯, A, B♭, B**

2. Try exercise 1 again, this time starting with notes in the *chalumeau* register. Notes from C^1 to E^2 are the most responsive. Higher or lower notes in this register will not give harmonics as easily. Aim to find the various harmonics (all notes in the registers above the *chalumeau* are harmonics) using a combination of oral cavity shape and breath pressure. This exercise also aids in the control of notes in the *clarion* and *altissimo* registers.

3. Beginning with E^3 again, go up the harmonics and then slur back down. Use the changing oral cavity shape *ee – ah – aw* to help accomplish each slur.

4. Play C^1 and then find the 12th (the third harmonic) on the same fingering, G^3.

5. Now play all the notes as harmonics using the *chalumeau* fingerings. Fast air will be required, the embouchure should always remain relaxed and you will need to experiment with the voicing (the oral cavity shape).

More challenging

6. Now play C^1 and then find the 15th (the fifth harmonic) on the same fingering, E^3.

7. Again, fast air will be required for this exercise. Experiment with finding the appropriate embouchure and oral cavity voicing to control the notes.

Though challenging, exercises 6 and 7 will eventually give you a lot of flexibility, control and understanding, leading to more control of intonation, crossing registers and tone colour.

---

31. These harmonics can also be found by taking in slightly more mouthpiece, but try to limit this to your first attempts. Without moving your head, lowering the angle of the clarinet can also help, but this shouldn't become a habit.

THE CLARINET

Pitch bending

Being able to bend the pitch of notes is a useful technique for playing contemporary, jazz and klezmer music and in *glissando*. It also allows you to control subtle changes of intonation. In all cases this is ideally done with the vocal tract, in particular the oral cavity, rather than the lips (often termed 'lipping' up or down, see page 102) which can have the less helpful side effect of compromising the quality of the sound.

EXERCISES

Try these exercises to get started:

1. First, sing: 'eeeee ... yaw'.[32] Sense the change in oral cavity shape, particularly the position of the tongue, as you move from 'eeeee' to 'yaw' and allow the pitch to drop naturally. Avoid any movement in the embouchure.
2. If you can, whistle a note and bend it downwards. Then repeat without making the whistle noise – listen to the pitch of the airflow and sense the change of oral cavity shape.
3. Now, just using the mouthpiece, play a long note. The pitch of that note will be a slightly flat $E♭^3$. This is a very bendable note.
4. Play it again, and once the note is well established try bending it downwards by changing the oral cavity shape seamlessly from 'ee' to 'aw' (or 'oo') as ex. 1, while increasing the air speed as you move from one to the other. In 'aw' or 'oo' the throat is more open, with the air moving more slowly, which is why you need more air. The note should bend downwards easily. With practice you should be able to bend the note by the interval of a third or more.
5. Now, with the mouthpiece attached to the clarinet, play $E♭^3$ and repeat the bending manoeuvre in ex. 4. Practise on other notes. *Chalumeau* register notes will only bend a fraction of a tone, *clarion* register notes may bend up to a third (higher notes maybe more) but *altissimo* register notes will bend easily, as much as an octave.

Glissando

The *glissando* opening of Gershwin's *Rhapsody in Blue* is possibly the most iconic moment in the entire orchestral clarinet repertoire.[33] In one sense it's a complex manoeuvre requiring a subtle combination of the use of oral cavity, tongue position, throat opening via the vocal tract, air pressure, and fingers, but we are in danger of paralysis by analysis if we think too much about it! So, being practical, it's done by gradually uncovering each successive tone hole by sliding the finger sideways across each one, slightly altering the bore's effective length, whilst simultaneously using changes of shape in the oral cavity (vocal tract) to assist in moving the pitch.

Some science

Clarinet pitch is determined by the frequency of the vibrating reed. The frequency of vibration is produced by the resonances created by the player via the oral cavity, which then combine with the resonances occurring in the instrument itself to create pitch. As we have seen, lower notes won't respond much to changes in the oral cavity, but higher notes in the *clarion* and *altissimo* registers are much more responsive to oral cavity changes, central to the success of making an effective *glissando*.

EXERCISES

1. Establish an even B^3 then gradually slide the first left-hand finger off the tone hole. Don't let the pitch move; keep the B sounding. To do this you need some flexibility in the lower lip but much more important is to feel an 'ee-aw' movement with your tongue, simultaneous with the finger movement. You should now be fingering C^3 but still sounding B^3, as though you have caught the resonance of B^3 and can hold it there irrespective of the fingering. Now gradually raise the pitch up to the fingered C with an 'aw-ee' movement in your oral cavity, possibly with a very slight adjustment of lip pressure and lots of air. Practise this until you can do it easily.
2. Finger C^3 but try to sound B^3 with the appropriate oral cavity shape and lower lip pressure. With practice this will become achievable.
3. Now repeat ex. 1, but beginning on A^3 and *glissando* up to C^3.
4. In time you'll find you can affect a *glissando* from D^2 up to C^3. Start a C major scale with a trill on G^1, ascend to D^2 and *gliss* from there – you're playing the opening of *Rhapsody in Blue*!

Multiphonics

Some contemporary music requires the performance of multiphonics, which is the sounding of more than one note simultaneously. These will usually be chords of two notes, though it is possible to play chords of three or even four discernible notes. Bruno Bartolozzi, who wrote the first important book on multiphonics, describes it as 'the generation, at one and the same time, of a number of frequency vibrations in the single air column of an instrument.'[34]

Given that there are a number of excellent websites and books available containing exhaustive fingerings and other information on playing multiphonics, this technique will only be discussed here in general terms.

As in all sonic effects, the main controlling elements are the manner in which the embouchure (in particular, lip pressure), the use and position of the tongue and the air pressure combine.

Whether or not you ever intend to study or perform pieces that include multiphonics, it's quite interesting to spend a little time exploring and practising the technique to deepen your awareness of tonal production.

EXERCISES

1. Here's a fingering that generates a multiphonic without too much difficulty:

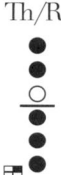

Try playing with a slow airflow (low tongue position), a little more mouthpiece in the mouth than usual, and a slight 'bite' with the embouchure. If the notes don't sound easily, avoid the temptation to support more.

2. Here's a more specific multiphonic. The fingering is C#3 played with the thumb hole covered and without the register key:

Play the fingering concentrating on producing C#3, then try to produce the low D#. Find the balance in control and both notes should sound. With luck the middle G will emerge too.

Giuseppe Garbarino's *Metodo per Clarinetto* and Phillip Rehfeldt's *New Directions for Clarinet*[35] are essential reading if this is an area you wish to develop. *Metodo per Clarinetto* includes a large number of fingerings with which to experiment as well a significant section on microtones.

---

32. Alternatively replace the 'aw' with 'oo' or 'yoo', which also creates a good shape.
33. In fact, Gershwin actually wrote the opening as a simple scale. In the first rehearsal (in early February, 1924) Ross Gorman (clarinettist in the Paul Whiteman orchestra) tried it partially with a *glissando*. Gershwin was delighted and the rest is history!
34. *New Sounds for Woodwind* (OUP, 1967).
35. *Metodo per Clarinetto*, Giuseppe Garbarino, Edizioni Suvini Zerboni (Milano, 1978); Phillip Rehfeldt, *New Directions for Clarinet* (Scarecrow Press, 2005).

Quarter tones

Semitones can be split to make two quarter tones. Such microtones might make an appearance in two main musical contexts. First, as a slight flattening or sharpening of notes for effect. It would be both stylistic and effective, for example, to bend notes in this way in some folk styles like klezmer. In such instances the slight alteration of the pitch would probably be best executed by very small adjustments to lip pressure or oral cavity shape (voicing). Precise intonation would not be necessary in such situations.

The second context is in some modern music, where the quarter tones are both precisely notated and do demand absolute precision in intonation. Though lip and air pressure will be important factors here, players who wish to develop an ability to play quarter tones need to study special fingering charts (see the books referenced on page 47 or search online).

In addition, some traditional national music, for example Syrian and Turkish, contains quarter tones. These are differently nuanced however (and more correctly described as microtones). Consult a specialist if you wish to investigate these further.

There are quarter-tone tuners available should you wish to delve deeper and train your ears.

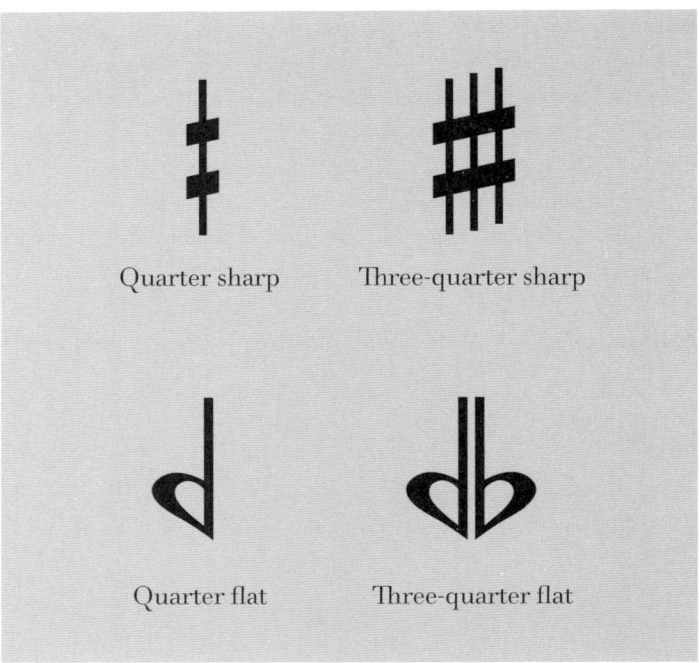

Quarter sharp — Three-quarter sharp

Quarter flat — Three-quarter flat

Circular breathing

Two very good and highly respected clarinet-playing friends of mine have very different views on one particular aspect of breathing. One teaches students to take as many breaths as they feel necessary, maintaining that the best sound and control is near the start of the breath, and to shape longer phrases in such a way that they don't suffer for the taking of these breaths. The other insists students learn to take and control the longest possible breaths they can, for minimum interruption to the line. You may also have a preference, though the results of both approaches are, musically, equally acceptable.

If your view does lean more towards the second approach, you may wish to develop the technique of circular breathing, which can allow the player to sustain a continuous sound for long periods without seemingly stopping to take a breath. In brief, this requires the ability to breathe in by the nose whilst simultaneously pushing air out by using the cheeks as a kind of bellow-mechanism. It's not a complex process but will take some time to perfect and feel comfortable. The process may be broken down into five stages as shown in the flow chart.

This all has to happen seamlessly. Transferring from normal breath to 'cheek air' and then back needs practice, but once this aspect of the process is mastered, the ability to circular breathe should present little difficulty.

Towards the end of a breath allow the cheeks to puff out and fill with air.

The air stored in the cheeks is then pushed out using the cheek muscles and …

… simultaneously breath is taken in quickly through the nose – the soft palate lowers allowing this to happen.

Once the cheek air is used up there is a return to normal breathing – the soft palate rises back to its natural playing position and …

… the cheeks return to their natural playing position.

EXERCISES

WITHOUT THE CLARINET

1. Fill your cheeks with air and then, holding that air in your cheeks, breathe in and out through your nose.
2. Take a deep breath and then fill your cheeks with 'lung' air and slowly blow the 'cheek' air out using the cheek muscles. Continue refilling with lung air until the lung air is used. Repeat the exercise until you can do it comfortably.
3. Now take a shallow breath, fill your cheeks with air and blow out keeping the cheeks puffed out. Near the end of the breath, keeping your cheeks filled with air, close your mouth and breathe in quickly through your nose.
4. Repeat the previous step but at the moment you begin breathing in (quickly) through your nose, transfer the blowing energy to the cheeks and squeeze out the cheek air.

WITH A GLASS OF WATER AND A STRAW

1. Slightly pinch the straw near the top to create some resistance, and simply blow bubbles into the glass of water.
2. Now fill your cheeks with air and blow some bubbles with cheek air.
3. Blow again (with normal air), and this time catch some air in your mouth by allowing your cheeks to puff out, and then push that air out with your cheeks simultaneously breathing in through your nose (similar to step 4 above).
4. Now try to swap continuously between lung and cheek air, doing your best to keep the bubbles bubbling at an even pressure. This will take some time to perfect. Once you feel in control of this process, it's time to apply the technique to the clarinet.

WITH THE CLARINET

1. First of all, play a long note alternating between your normal embouchure and an embouchure with cheeks puffed out. Try to keep the note steady and even. Aim to do this without any effect on the embouchure and take care not to bite, which will cause the reed to stop vibrating and so stop the sound.
2. Now swap between lung and cheek air (similar to the previous step). The tone won't be absolutely even yet, but you will be circular breathing!

Don't expect immediate results – it may take several months to perfect the technique – but the transfer from lung air to cheek air will eventually become seamless. The quality of cheek-air sound inevitably will not be as good but should only be very short-lived within the process. Choose your moments to use this technique carefully. Circular breathing works best with mid-range notes – those just above and below the throat register – and when playing trills. Avoid using circular breathing when crossing the break or in articulated passages.

It is interesting that certain players have noticed that audiences sometimes feel uncomfortable when a player is circular breathing. You may wish to take this into consideration. Musically speaking, phrases need to breathe and music needs to breathe. Most composers take into account the fact that players need to breathe. Indeed, much of the clarinet repertoire is vocally inspired, so taking a breath is very much part of the music. In summary, circular breathing is probably a technique most useful in certain contemporary music.

FUN FACT

The Swedish virtuoso Martin Fröst can play, sing and circular breathe simultaneously!

THE CLARINET

All about squeaks

This chapter has been about creating the most beautiful and controlled sound possible, but just occasionally that ambition may be interrupted by what clarinet players from time immemorial have called a *squeak*.

A squeak (usually a particularly high note or harmonic) is an unwelcome intruder into the sound we produce. By having some understanding of the possible causes of squeaks, we are in a stronger position to avoid them. Squeaks usually occur at the beginning or the end of notes.

Here are the most likely reasons we might squeak:
- A momentary lack of control in the embouchure
- Too much mouthpiece in your mouth
- Inappropriate air flow or pressure
- A mismatch between the resonance in the oral cavity and the resonance in the instrument as a result of the particular fingering
- A 'leak' in the instrument caused by the player through some slight lack of coordination in finger movement or from imprecise covering of tone holes
- An instrument that has some ill-fitting or worn pads or some mechanism that has become slack
- Water in the tone holes
- A poor, broken or split reed or an over-used one that has become calcified from saliva deposits

Assuming the instrument and reed are satisfactory, if the appropriate support is maintained and the embouchure is firm without being tight, squeaking should be rare. If you do squeak, particularly in a performance (it does happen!) move on; put it out of your mind. It's not important.

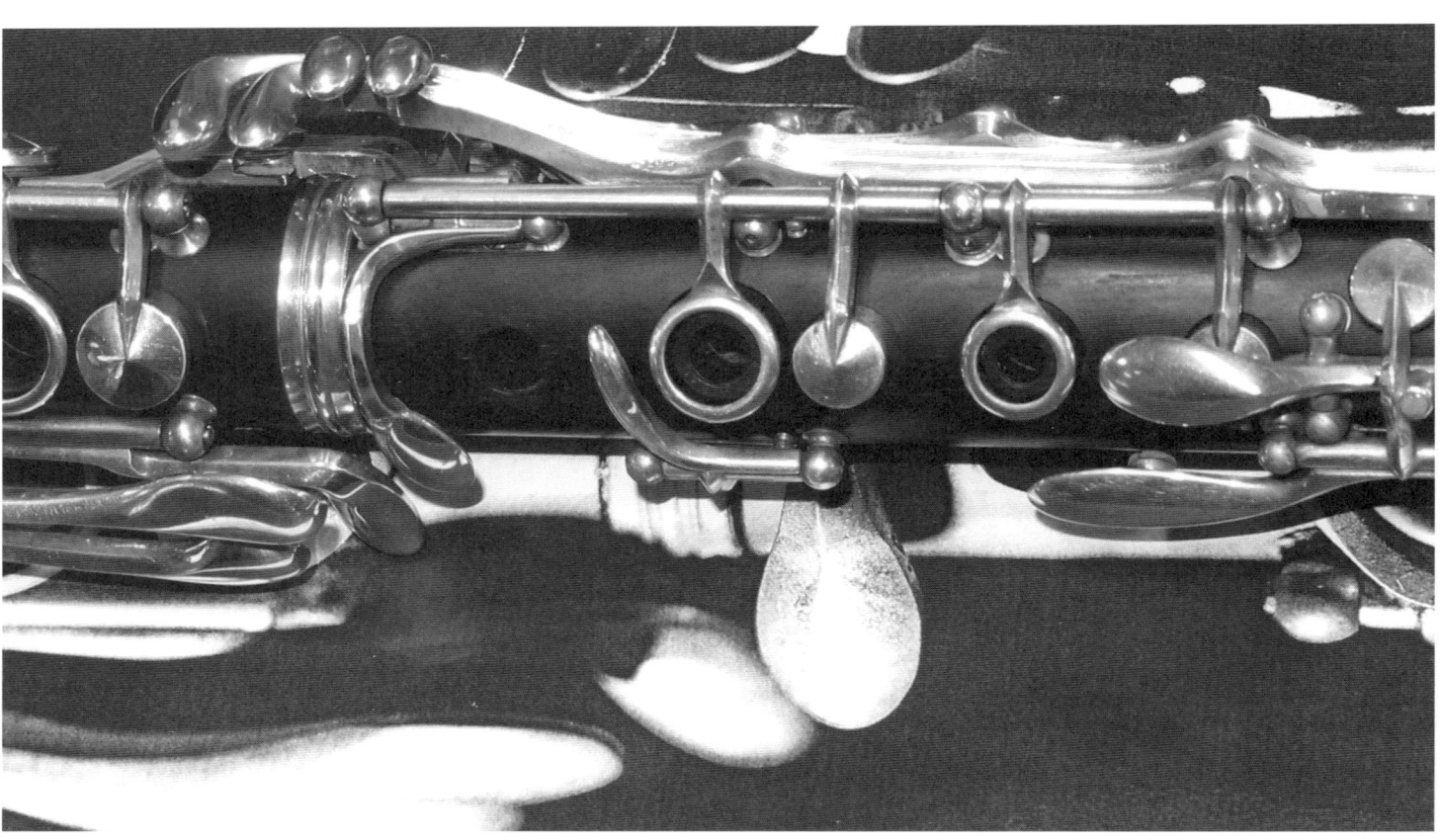

Making the sound – the journey of a breath

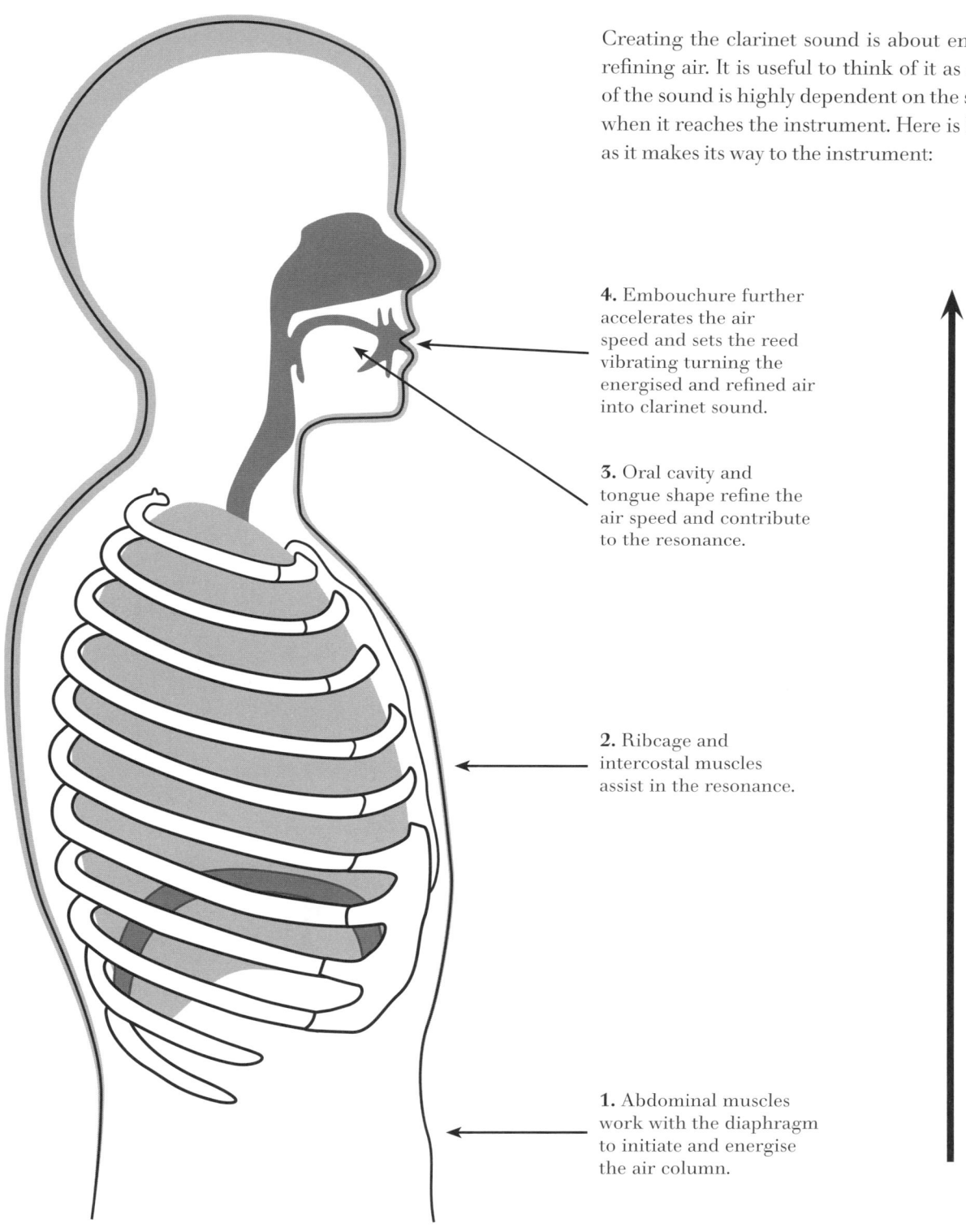

Creating the clarinet sound is about energising, moving and refining air. It is useful to think of it as a journey. The quality of the sound is highly dependent on the state of the air column when it reaches the instrument. Here is how that air is refined as it makes its way to the instrument:

4. Embouchure further accelerates the air speed and sets the reed vibrating turning the energised and refined air into clarinet sound.

3. Oral cavity and tongue shape refine the air speed and contribute to the resonance.

2. Ribcage and intercostal muscles assist in the resonance.

1. Abdominal muscles work with the diaphragm to initiate and energise the air column.

Developing tone

Tone

Dynamics

Bulging

Projection

Pitch – the registers in detail

Joining the registers

Application of tone control to playing a melodic line

Useful words

Tone

The manner in which we use and move air in clarinet playing is central to the control of tone. The main purpose of moving the air is to energise the reed which makes the sound. So before we get going, let's clarify the three aspects of the control of air to be considered: air volume, speed and pressure.

Air volume: the amount of air that is moving at any particular time. That volume is controlled essentially by the amount of restraint applied by the breathing muscles as we blow out.

Air speed: the speed of the air when it reaches the reed. The amount of support will obviously have a substantial effect on air speed, but more significant is the position of the tongue. Below are two exercises to demonstrate fast and slow air speed.

EXERCISES

- Fast air speed: form a 'hhheeee' shape with your tongue, take a full breath and blow freely. The high tongue position will constrict the path of the air, thus speeding it up. This is similar to constricting the water flow through a hosepipe with your finger and thumb.
- Slower air speed: repeat the exercise but this time place your tongue much lower in your mouth (behind your lower teeth) creating a 'huhhh' and blow freely. The air that reaches the front of the mouth is more diffuse and slower. The difference in the sound of the two air speeds is audible.

Air pressure: air is always under pressure, so let us explore that.

EXERCISES

- Press your lips together firmly, keep your mouth closed and your throat neutral and relaxed. Engage your breathing muscles and blow. No air should escape but you will feel the air pressure – the result of compressing the air towards the mouth.

Understanding these elements will ultimately give you a greater control, which will further develop a flexible and comfortable approach to tone production and a greater range of tonal colour and dynamic levels through the various registers of the instrument.

36. See *Sounding good* for exercises to support these aspects of your playing.

Long notes

Playing and practising long notes will help you to develop a controlled and beautiful tone. Many of the world's leading players spend considerable practice time on long notes. Students of the clarinet often know the substantial benefits of practising long notes but don't always put this knowledge to use!

There are many ways to practise long notes, and these will be introduced later in this section. To begin, let's look at the concept of *evenness* in long notes which involves *tone*, *pitch* and *dynamic level*.

The evenness you are aiming for must come about through the controlled movement of air and must not cause any physical or psychological rigidity. Your mind will be creating and sustaining energy and your body will be continually adapting in order to maintain dynamic evenness in producing a controlled long note, particularly as you run out of air. The lower your air supply becomes, the more control is required as the opposition between the embouchure and the breathing muscles becomes weaker. Sustaining a long even note is not a static process. The exercises in this section will help to improve this control.

When practising for *consistency of tone*, listen for three kinds of unevenness:

- An occasional 'kick' in the sound
- A mostly even sound but with occasional 'waves', or small bulges
- A more persistent and uneven wavering

In each of these cases the most likely cause will be uneven breath control. Less likely, but still possible, may be tension or movement in the embouchure or oral cavity, or movement in the throat.[36]

Pitch: Make sure there is always sufficient speed of air as you move through the note; a significant lack of energy in the air may cause the pitch to drop. Take particular care not to tighten the embouchure as you run out of air as this may result in sharpness. Pitch fluctuation can be the result of changes in oral cavity shape.

Dynamic level: An uneven (or unintended) dynamic level is most likely to be the result of uneven air pressure and support but can also be caused by small variations in lip pressure. Remember to keep the throat relaxed – tension here will affect air speed, particularly towards the end of the note.

DEVELOPING TONE

Travel

My wonderful clarinet professor at the Royal Academy of Music, John Davies, often talked of the concept of 'travel' when it came to maintaining tone quality throughout a note. It is a very useful and enabling thought. As you play a long note, or indeed a note of any length, sense the *movement* of the sound as it travels forward; feel as though your mind or imagination is travelling along with the sound. You'll find that this perception adds a real sense of direction and movement to the tone and aids in the technical production of the note. Very occasionally, for example the beginning of Messiaen's *Abîme des oiseaux*, you might desire a rather static and bleak sound with minimal internal movement in order to create the effect, but such moments are very rare.

Getting to the centre of a note

It is useful to consider the idea that every note has a *centre*, a kind of pure and absolute focus of both intonation and tone quality. The German school of playing, exemplified in the sound of players like Karl Leister, typifies a really 'centred' sound.

Every part of the instrument and aspect of tone production is involved in finding that centre of each note: the mouthpiece and reed setup, the instrument itself, the position and use of the tongue, jaw, lips, other facial muscles and pharynx, the control of intonation, breathing and the support mechanism. Each of these will play its part. It is also important to have a tonal conception strongly in your mind – you need an internalised aural model with which to compare the sound you actually make.

Now put this list out of your mind before you try the following exercise.

EXERCISES

Finding the centre of the note:

- Once warmed up, close your eyes and play a long note. Listen to it deeply and with all your concentration.
- If your chosen note is in the *chalumeau* register you may hear three component parts: a stable fundamental, a slightly less stable tone 'around' the fundamental, and some higher harmonics. If it's in the *clarion* register and higher you'll probably just hear the harmonic you're playing (all notes above the *chalumeau* register are harmonics).
- Experiment and manipulate with tiny adjustments of airflow, keeping the soft palate raised, voicing (oral cavity shape) and lip pressure, in order to try to match the core (almost French-horn-like sound) with the slightly less pure 'surrounding' sound. Concentrate on the sound, not on what you are doing. Don't think too much about it, just play and listen, and you *will* find the centre of the note. It *is* there.

THE CLARINET

EXERCISES
Dynamics

Controlling dynamics

The clarinet possesses a very broad range of dynamic variation – some suggest it has the widest range of all the orchestral instruments – but dynamics are not just a case of decibels.[37] Listen to a recording of a loud piece of music on very low volume. Would you still be aware that it was a 'loud' piece? The answer is almost certainly yes. Hence, dynamics are not always reflected by decibels, but are equally the result of character, intention, expectation and projection.

So, when thinking about dynamics, we need to detach the relative dynamic levels (*p*, *mf*, *f*, etc.) from any specific decibel value.

A *pp* would be very different in decibel level depending on whether it was played in a solo clarinet piece, in a piece accompanied by a piano or in the woodwind section of a large orchestra. In choosing your dynamic level, your first thoughts must be about context, and then the character of the passage in question. Then you can apply the appropriate level of projection and decibels.

From a scientific point of view, dynamics are about energy. For loud playing, you will need to impart more energy to the reed, causing it to vibrate with a greater amplitude, and so producing a louder volume.[38]

The threshold of sound

Here's an exercise to explore starting a note from silence:

- Prepare to play your chosen note – begin with something in the upper *chalumeau* register. Take a breath, form a good and relaxed embouchure and hold your breath for a moment or two, taking care not to close the throat.
- Now, maintaining the relaxed embouchure, begin moving the air gently. Listen to the sound of the air movement; there will be no clarinet tone at this point. It has a certain seashore quality about it.
- Now, *very* gradually increase the air movement, taking care not to increase embouchure pressure. At some point soon the note will sound.
- Try to sense the very moment the note begins and hold it there. Listen closely to maintain a good quality of sound.
- Repeat this with notes in each of the registers. You have found the threshold of sound.

37. A decibel is a unit that denotes a particular loudness. It is named after Alexander Graham Bell, the inventor of the telephone.
38. For those who are more scientifically inclined: this essentially means the maximum height of the sound wave has increased.

Developing the dynamic range

In this next exercise, try to make the transition between *f* and *p* as quick as possible. This will help you to feel the muscles you use to make changes in dynamics. Be careful not to lose the sound after *f*. Try it throughout the range of the different metronome markings suggested, but no slower than 90 bpm.

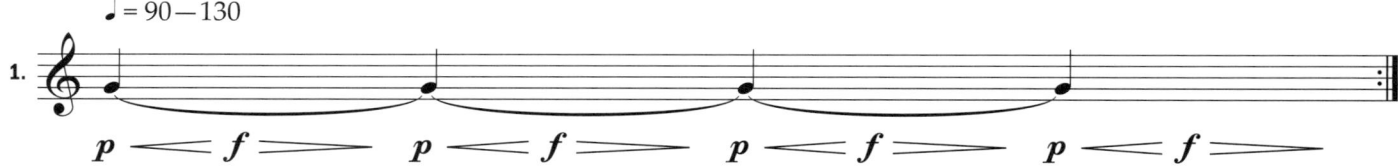

In the next exercises make a clear distinction between each dynamic level, remembering that the softer you get the more support is required. The embouchure should remain stable and firm without any tightness.

DEVELOPING TONE

Think also about these levels in relation to solo playing and ensemble or orchestral playing. Think how you might adjust these levels dependent on the context of your playing – are you playing the solo line, the top of the texture, within the texture or an accompanying role? Always listen to maintain your best tone quality and projection at all the levels. Repeat using a range of other notes across the registers.

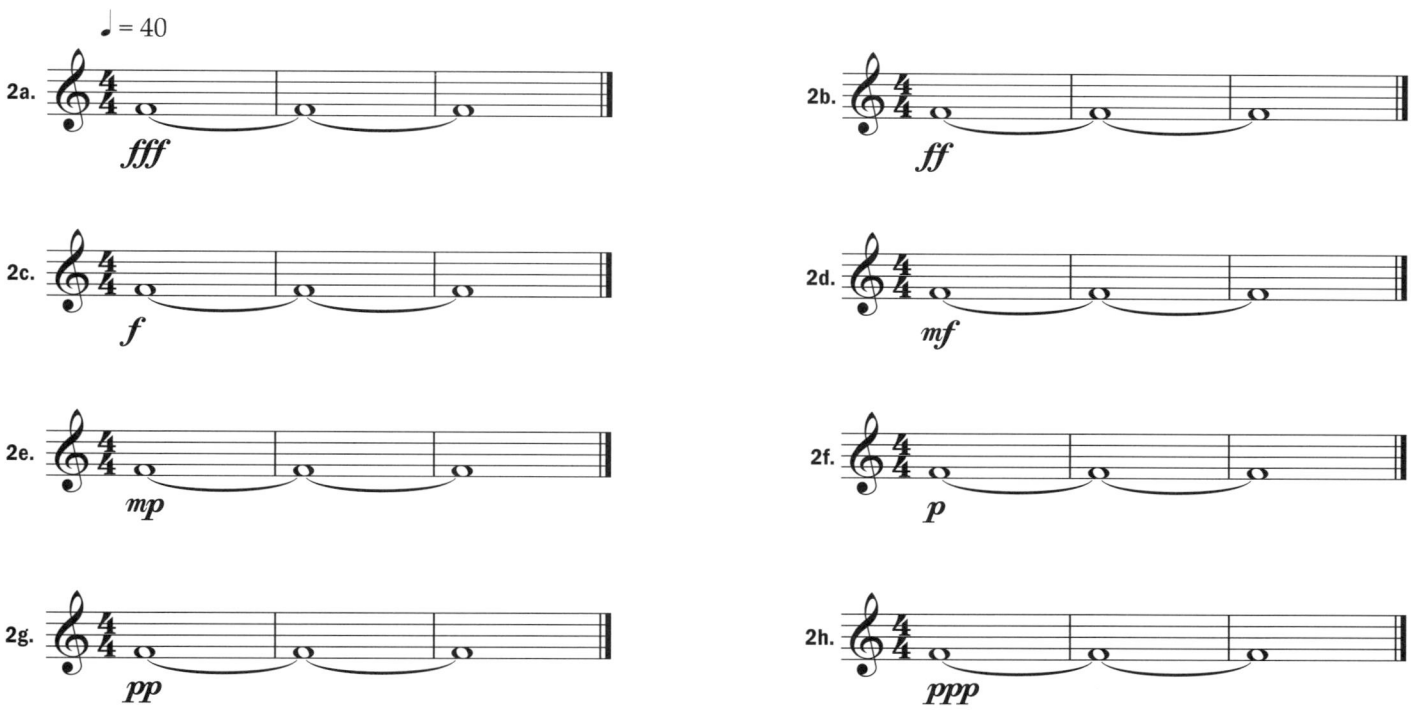

In the next exercises, ensure there is no change of dynamic level at the end of each note. Take as many breaths as you need.

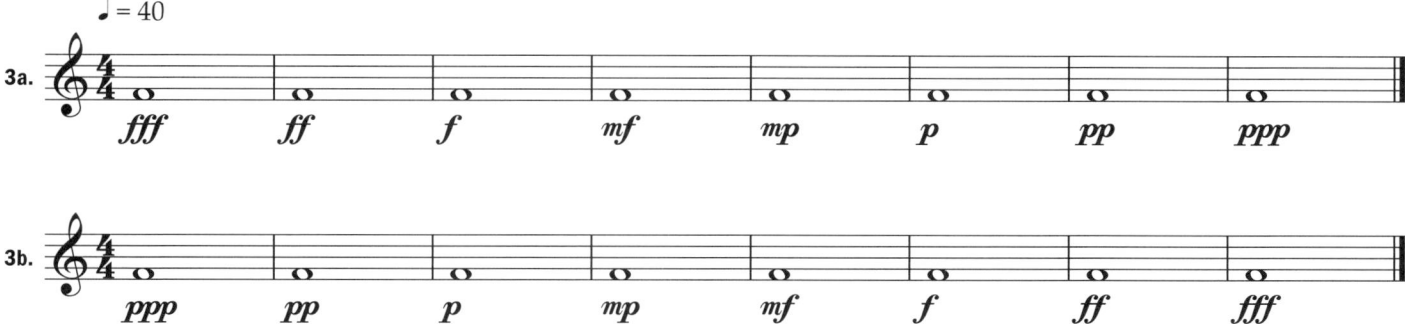

Play exercise 3a again, but this time put the eight dynamic levels in a different order, e.g. *p*, *fff*, *mf*, *pp*, *f*, *ppp*, *mp*, *f*. Aim to make each dynamic as contrasted as possible. Play them to your teacher or a colleague and see if they are able to identify each level aurally.

EXERCISES

Crescendo and *diminuendo*

'No other wind instrument is able, like the clarinet to voice a note quietly, make it to swell, decrease, and fade away. Hence its priceless ability to produce a distant sound, the echo of an echo, a sound like twilight.'[39]

Pianists are often told to 'pedal with their ears'. In the same way, the most important controlling mechanism for clarinet players in producing effective *crescendo* and *diminuendo* is also the ears. Listen intently. Play the *crescendo* or *diminuendo* by listening to the sound with extreme concentration. As you are playing the *crescendo* or *diminuendo* simultaneously *imagine* it in your inner ear and allow the breath control (together with a certain degree of oral cavity flexibility) simply to do the job for you. Your aim should be to increase or decrease the volume at a constant rate, i.e. accurately related to rhythmic duration.

- Repeat the *threshold of sound* exercise on page 56 but this time, once you have the note established, carry on building a *crescendo*.
- In the next exercise, start the note as quietly as possible and build the volume gradually and evenly over the entire length of the note. You should not reach the maximum volume until the very end of the note. Count each beat internally, hearing a gradual increase in volume *through each beat*.

In order to stop pitch and tone varying as the volume increases, you may need to consider your oral cavity shape (specifically the tongue shape and position) and the effect of any changes of breath pressure on your embouchure. Remember that as you become louder you'll need less support.

1.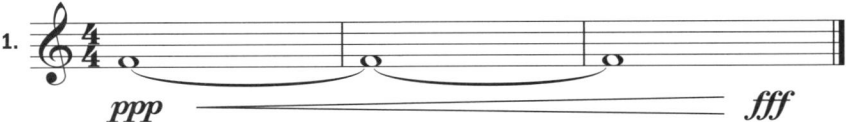

You'll need to work very carefully at support in the next exercise to effect the *diminuendo* and to maintain pitch and tone quality as the dynamic level decreases. Feel the gradual and increasing restraint in the control of the airflow as you *diminuendo* (caused by the reed vibrating with less energy). Softer playing requires more support. This will enable you to achieve a resonant sound and stable intonation at the softest dynamics. Players often lose this support in quiet playing, thus compromising the quality, intensity and energy of the sound.

2.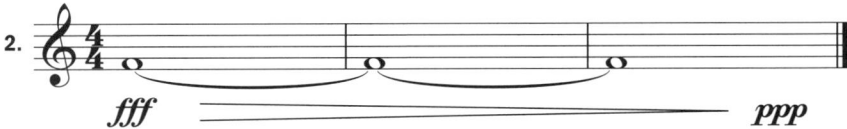

The clarinet is capable of making a *diminuendo al niente* (to nothing). Think of the sound as it travels through the *diminuendo*. It requires *a lot of support* and effort to ensure the sound disappears with perfect consistency. You need to control the airflow really carefully. In a way, you hear the *diminuendo* in your ears, whilst simultaneously employing a *crescendo* (increase) in your support – this should create a consistency of intonation and tone quality. *Diminuendo* and *crescendo* – opposite concepts that when combined will ultimately give you the desired control.

3.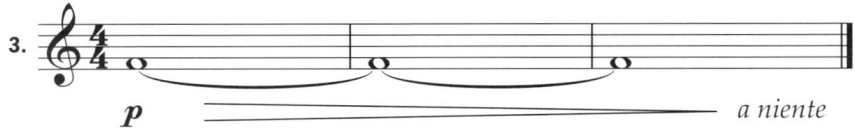

39. Wrote Berlioz in his *Grand Traité d'Instrumentation et d'Orchestration Modernes*, first published in 1843/4.

DEVELOPING TONE

The following two exercises will further highlight the support mechanism:

4.

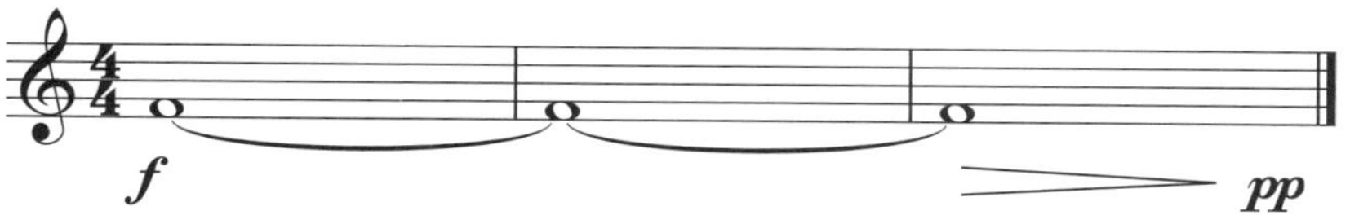

5.

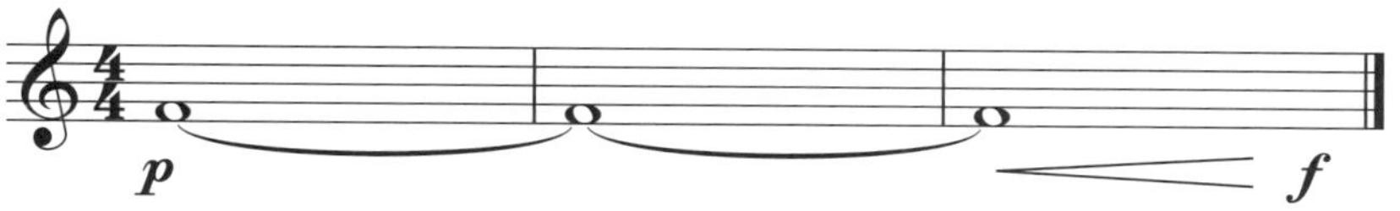

Listen carefully when playing the next exercises to make sure that your tone does not vary and that the changes in volume are smooth and even.

6.

7.

8.

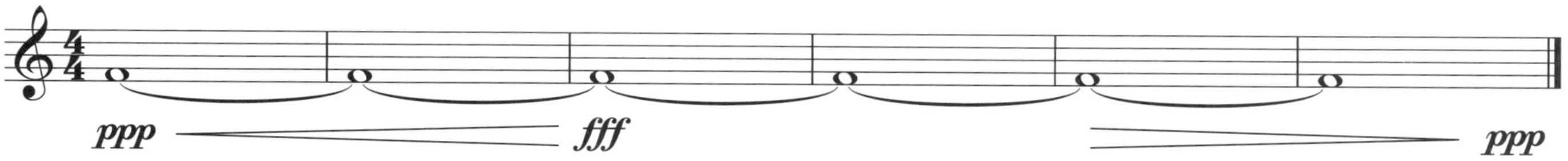

9.

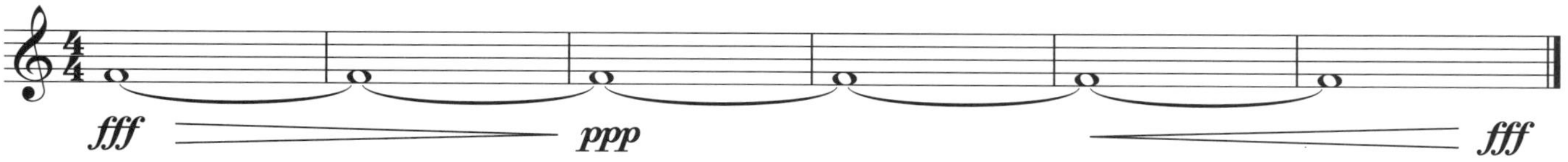

10.

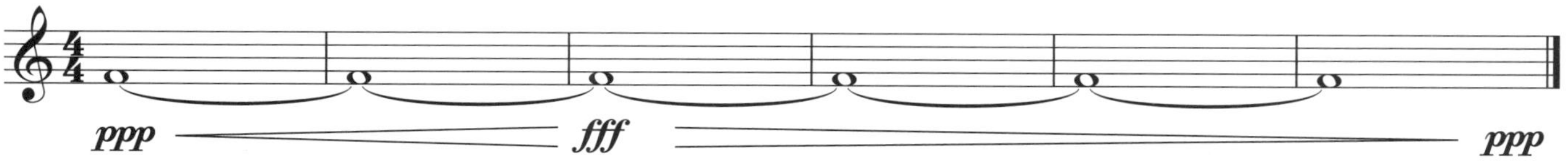

11.

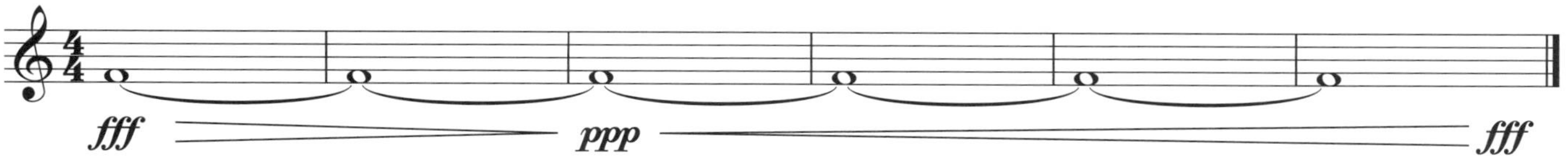

12.

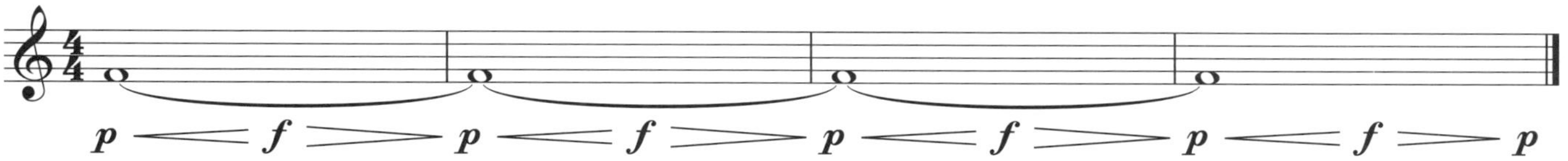

EXERCISES

The uneven long note

Here are two exercises to encourage flexibility, creativity, and freedom:

- Having worked hard to perfect absolute evenness of control in a long note, now try playing one that continually moves from one dynamic level to another, gradually or dramatically, maybe staying in one place for a moment or two, or maybe constantly on the move.
- Choose other notes and enjoy improvising these sound journeys. Keep the throat and embouchure neutral and relaxed, with no biting or movement of the jaw. Just enjoy the freedom and the result. Ultimately, when performing, we need this freedom to allow a constantly active, flourishing and living musical expression.

How loudly can you play?

In developing a wide dynamic range, occasionally practise playing very loudly indeed.[40] Don't worry if the sound lacks refinement at first. Eventually, knowing a refined tone quality *is* possible at such levels will give you more possibilities and confidence if you find yourself having to project through a large orchestra in a large hall.

Repeat exercises 6 to 12 on page 59 and work on extending the potential dynamic range – don't simply play a very loud note out of any musical or dynamic context. To begin, go further with each *crescendo*. Take care over the tone quality at the start of the *crescendo*, but at first don't worry over the quality at the loudest extremes. In this way you'll begin to develop the ability to manage the control of the reed that will now be vibrating with greater amplitude owing to the extra energy. A stronger embouchure, without biting, is needed to resist and control this energy.

Crescendo and *diminuendo* in a *legato* phrase

Make sure that a *crescendo* or *diminuendo* does not lose its energy and direction when changing notes. Always aim for a gradual increase or decrease of sound *through* the notes. Sometimes you may hear a bulge (see page 62) at the start of a new note – listen carefully to avoid this. Make sure not to adjust your breathing or lip pressure when changing notes.

In the following exercises, aim for a continual and gradual change in volume. Sustain the *crescendo* to the beginning of bar 3 in each case.

Make up similar exercises of your own in different keys using all the registers or use passages from pieces you are studying.

In the Classical repertoire, often these shapes are implied rather than written out. Even if dynamics are absent, almost all phrases will benefit from subtle changes in dynamic level.

---

40. This is a physical exercise for developing the control of more power. See also the section on projection (page 64).

DEVELOPING TONE

Tapering notes ('phrasing off')

As part of shaping notes and phrases, it's important to develop the ability to make very short, subtle and sometimes almost imperceptible *diminuendos*. Think of this as a very rapid decrease or decay of reed energy, especially as this is what is actually happening! The degree of reed vibration is simply decreasing. A reduction of air volume will be necessary but don't think too much about this.

- Before playing the next exercise play a long note **pp**. Listen for a warm and even sound that is easy to control. If the reed and mouthpiece are well set-up, this should not be a problem.
- Now play the next set of exercises carefully, both vividly imagining the beautifully controlled *diminuendos* at the ends of notes in your musical ear and sensing a reduction of air speed and volume – and listen to the results.

Take care to sustain the dynamic level through the first two beats in each bar, only beginning the *diminuendo* when marked.

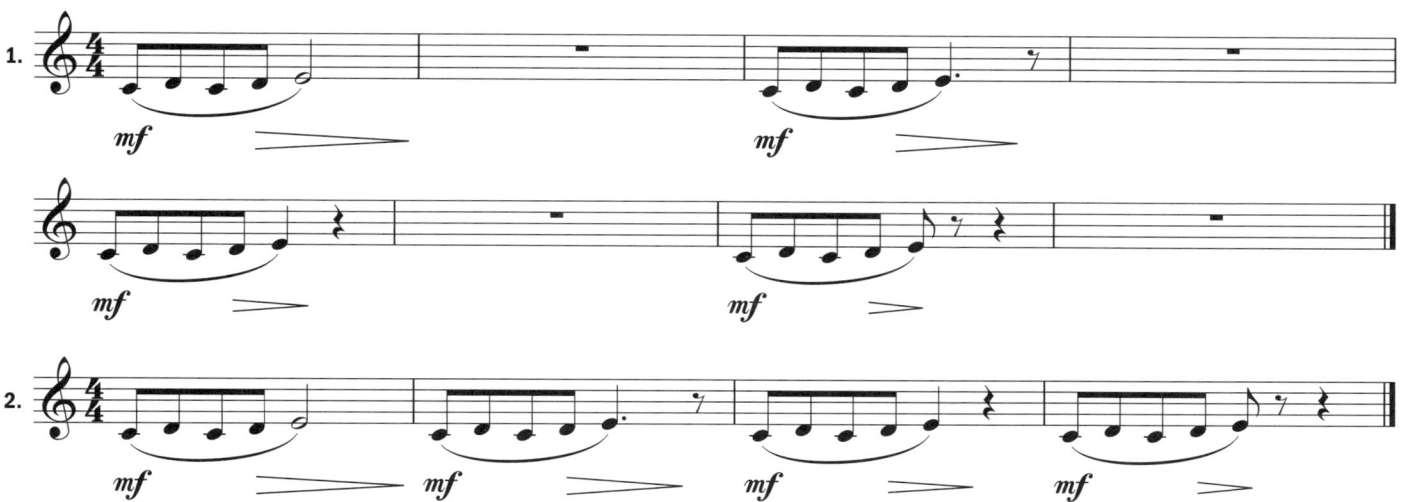

Repeat the exercises in all registers, then try these examples from works by Brahms and Beethoven:

Brahms, Sonata No. 2, Op. 120, III, bars 7–8

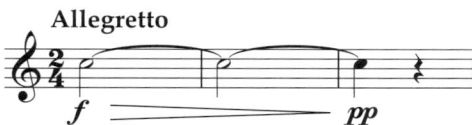

Beethoven, Symphony No. 7, II

Bulging

It's useful to be aware of unintentional 'bulging', that is, playing a note with a noticeable and ungainly *crescendo* and *diminuendo* where the sound doesn't match or support the metre and the appropriate musical shaping. If the airflow or reed energy is not sufficient at the absolute start of a note or diminishes at the point where notes change, players will immediately adjust the sound by suddenly increasing the airflow. This produces a bulge that will either spoil the control of that opening or the quality of the *legato*.

The first two notes of the Mozart Concerto are an interesting case in point. They are usually best interpreted with a sense of movement, direction and travel, but if the air is not energised and controlled from the start, both notes might end up with a less than satisfying bulge.

EXAMPLES FROM THE CLARINET REPERTOIRE
Practise the following openings. In each case, take care to control the level of sound from the moment of articulation to the beginning of the second note. The note must travel and have glow, vigour and direction, but not bulge!

Andante

Weber, Concertino for Clarinet, Op. 26, bars 38–39

Allegro amabile

Brahms, Clarinet Sonata No. 2, Op. 120, I

Adagio

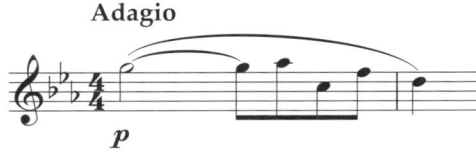

Baermann, Adagio, Clarinet Quintet No. 3, Op. 23, II, bars 6–7

Similarly, a lack of breath control can cause bulging during phrases that can become habitual and might give too much prominence to a note, so disturbing the flow. Here are some notes (marked with an arrow) in well-known phrases. Practise them and aim for the notes to sparkle with vitality without bulging. Maybe sing them as part of your practise, or make up some words to help find a shape.

Andante con moto

Weber, Variations Op. 33, Theme

Allegro animato

Saint-Saëns, Clarinet Sonata Op. 167, II

Appassionato, ma non troppo allegro

Brahms, Clarinet Sonata No. 2, Op. 120, II

There are, however, instances for what might be termed 'intentional' bulging. In some Romantic works, single notes are marked with a very short *crescendo* and *diminuendo* giving the impression of a bulge, such as the following (and many other similar moments) from the first movement of Schumann's Fantasy Pieces:

Zart und mit Ausdruck (♩ = 96)

Schumann, *Fantasiestücke* Op. 73, I

Projection

Projecting your sound is a matter for consideration when practising. Don't necessarily expect it to simply happen in a performance, be it a recital, an examination, an audition or when taking part in orchestral or chamber music. Below is a list of thoughts to reflect upon during practice to develop a sense of tone production that will allow your sound to be heard clearly in all situations.

- Always imagine that you are playing to an audience.
- Play with confidence and without tension.
- When practising, imagine the room is larger than it is.
- Feel you are projecting your sound behind you as well as in front of you.
- Always play with your best resonant sound.
- Feel the resonance inside your head.
- Remember to maintain a sense of travel.
- Don't let go of your sound – always stay connected to it.
- Broaden your dynamic range (see page 60: *How loudly can you play?*).

When performing, it is also important to take into account the size of the space in which you are playing:

- In a small space such as an exam or audition room, judge your appropriate dynamic range sensitively – levels at the louder extremes can distort and make audience members feel uncomfortable. To some extent, people absorb sound, so the more people in the room the louder you can play without risk of causing discomfort.
- In a large space, sense yourself being close to those furthest from you. Feel you are playing to them.

Classically trained singers are able to project their voices and make vibrant sounds across their range by creating a 'ring' to their vocal quality that can project over an orchestra. This is broadly about controlling and increasing the intensity of the sound through its harmonic content.[41] A clarinet tone that is rich in the higher harmonics will project in the same way. Notes in the *altissimo* register will naturally project. If the notes of the *chalumeau* and throat registers are intense, resonant and well-focussed in quality (which means harmonic rich) they will also project.

The legendary clarinettist Stanley Drucker, who was principal of the New York Philharmonic for 49 years, told me that projection is all about enhancing the sound of the players around you whilst they are enhancing your sound in return. It's also, he says, about your ears and instinct and ensuring that your *pp* tone is fundamentally the same as your *ff* tone.

Go to concerts and sit both close to and far away from players you would like to analyse. Much understanding can be gathered in this way.

Introducing the 'grace-note gambit' (GNG)

The 'grace-note gambit' (GNG) is a very useful practice strategy. It simply involves lightly rearticulating a note immediately before moving onto the next note and can be applied to any *legato* phrase of any length. Just like the essence of a magician's work, it is borne of misdirection or distraction. The benefit of the GNG is that it will help you avoid any tension in the throat or extra pressure in the embouchure, or changing (usually slowing down) the air speed immediately before you change notes which may otherwise spoil a beautiful *legato*.

Play each note for its full value and place the grace note as close as possible to the note it precedes. Concentrate on keeping the sound continuous.

So with the GNG, the following phrase:

... would be played like this:

---

41. For those who would like to investigate this more, it's all about the use of *formants*.

DEVELOPING TONE

EXERCISES
Pitch – the registers in detail

As well as developing a controlled, beautiful, *cantabile* tone, you should also be aware of the different tonal characteristics of each register of the instrument. Use a variety of dynamics for the exercises in the following sections.

The *chalumeau* register[42]

The characteristic tone of the *chalumeau* register is rich, dark, warm, mellow and sonorous. You will often need to project more in this register because of the slightly hollow quality that can make it somewhat lacking in carrying power.

Play the following exercise, listening carefully for a beautifully controlled *legato*, joining each note seamlessly to the next, maintaining the rich tone. Listen intently to the moment the note changes.

Each note should be equally loud and have the same tone quality. Try to avoid 'bumping' when moving from one note to the next by maintaining the air pressure throughout each note and moving the finger gently in both directions. Play the exercise again, taking great care to avoid any unevenness. Make sure that the first note is tongued without accentuation.

Select several of the following exercises and play a few bars from each at every practice session.

42. The term *chalumeau* derives from the Latin for 'reed' (although in modern French it means, amusingly, blowtorch!).

THE CLARINET

EXERCISES

Vary exercise 4 as per the pattern of 2a, aiming for the smoothest *legato* possible.

Now vary exercise 7 on the pattern of 2a.

DEVELOPING TONE

67

THE CLARINET

EXAMPLES FROM THE CLARINET REPERTOIRE

The following are examples of passages written in the *chalumeau* register. Play them with the characteristically rich, dark tone colour. Take care to keep the tone quality even throughout and consider the musical personality of each.

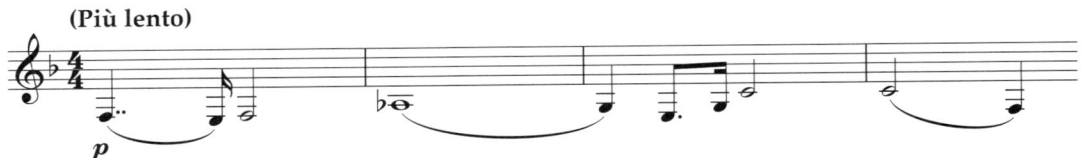

Weber, Concertino for Clarinet Op. 26, bars 138–141

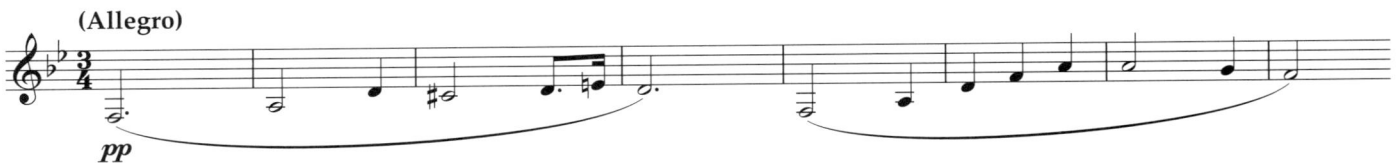

Weber, Clarinet Concerto No. 1, Op. 73, I, bars 170–178

Spohr, Clarinet Concerto No. 1, Op. 26, II, bars 18–20

Brahms, Clarinet Sonata No. 1, Op. 120, III, bars 107–110

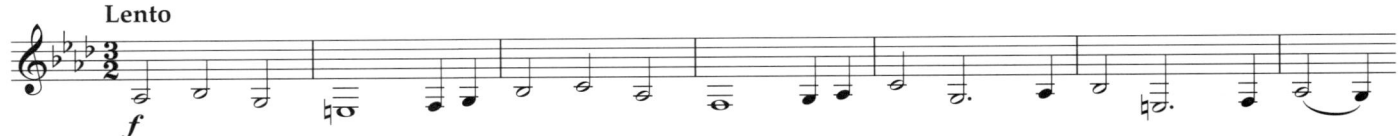

Saint-Saëns, Clarinet Sonata Op. 167, III, bars 2–8

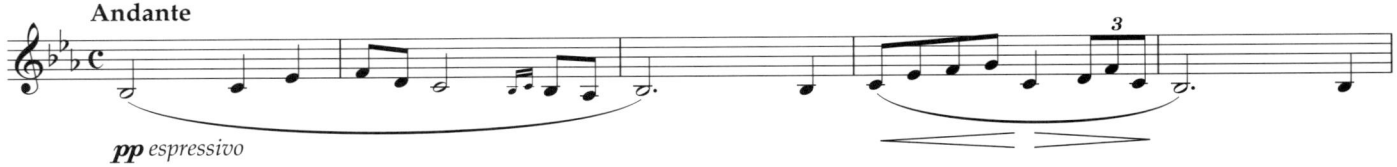

Messager, *Solo de Concours*, bars 55–59

DEVELOPING TONE

EXERCISES

When playing the extended studies in this chapter consider the following:

- The tonal character of the register
- Dynamic levels
- Maintaining the quality and projection of tone
- Careful articulation – avoid tonguing the first note of a phrase with undue accentuation
- Places in the music where you are going to take a breath – suggested breathing places are marked
- Breathing in quickly and quietly

STUDY IN THE CHALUMEAU REGISTER

THE CLARINET

EXERCISES

The throat register

Because of the acoustic characteristics of the clarinet, notes in this register are generally inferior in both quality and quantity. As a result, tone production requires special attention.

- Blow some warm air onto your hand – what kind of vowel shape helps you achieve this warm air? Consider the position of your soft palate and tongue.
- Play the notes below, and experiment with the vowels 'aw' and 'oh' while keeping the soft palate raised (remember the breathing-in position). Throat notes, particularly in slower expressive passages, will benefit from this warm air approach.

You will also find that alternative (resonant) fingerings can bring about improvements in the quality of your sound. These cause a lengthening of the vibrating air column and thus increase resonance. Bear in mind that they may also affect intonation. Some players like to avoid covering their tone holes with left-hand fingers as this might alter the tone too much, so experiment both with the fingerings indicated (see the *Fingering chart key* on page 11) and with ones you devise yourself to find those most suitable for your own particular playing and instrument.

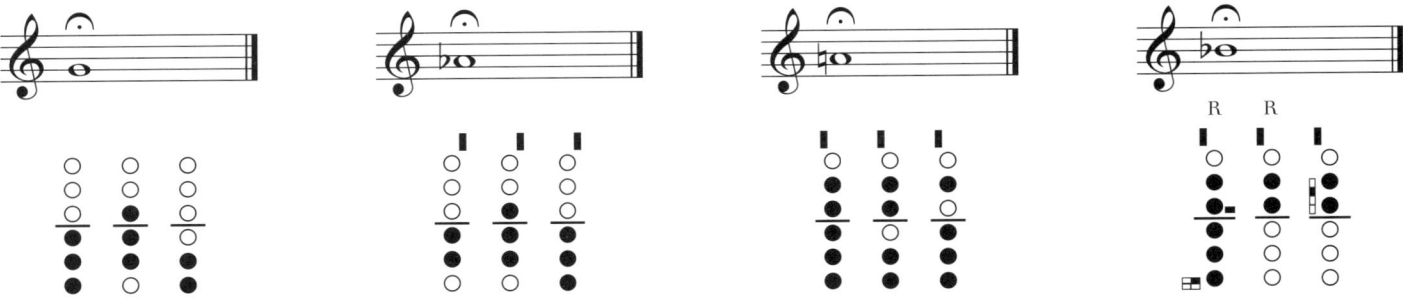

Aim for a full, well-rounded tone when playing the next set of exercises. Take care to maintain and match the tone quality throughout.

Vary exercise 1 using the following patterns:

DEVELOPING TONE

Moving out of the throat register

The following exercises are designed to develop an intuitive awareness of the use of the oral cavity and breath pressure in maintaining the best and most even tone quality as you move out of the throat register. As the intervals get wider, experiment with subtle adjustments of the oral cavity and air pressure. Listen really intently to the sound. Use alternative fingerings where appropriate and check your intonation carefully, using a tuning machine or an appropriate app.

Prepare for exercise 2 by practising the 'grace-note gambit' (see page 64). Remember to play each minim for its full value and the grace note as close to the note it precedes as possible. Keep the sound continuous.

In playing the following exercise without the grace note, aim for your best *legato* – *think* the grace note is still there, but don't play it. It will help stop you from making any unnecessary adjustments immediately before changing notes.

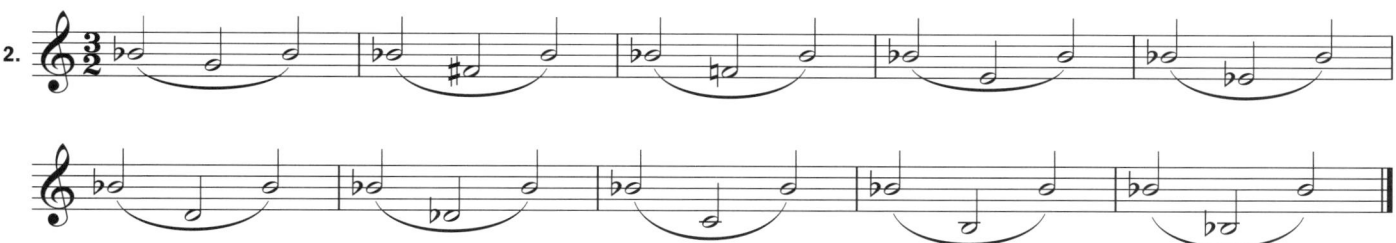

Vary these exercises following the pattern of 2a on page 65. The GNG is particularly helpful in preparing for the next two exercises.

THE CLARINET

EXAMPLES FROM THE CLARINET REPERTOIRE

Orchestral writing (especially for the second clarinet) and much chamber music often contains passages in the throat register. It is therefore very important to develop a fine tone of equal richness to its adjacent registers, and of course, accurate intonation.

Brahms, Clarinet Quintet Op. 115, II, bars 9–13

Brahms, Clarinet Sonata No. 2, Op. 120, I, bars 133–135

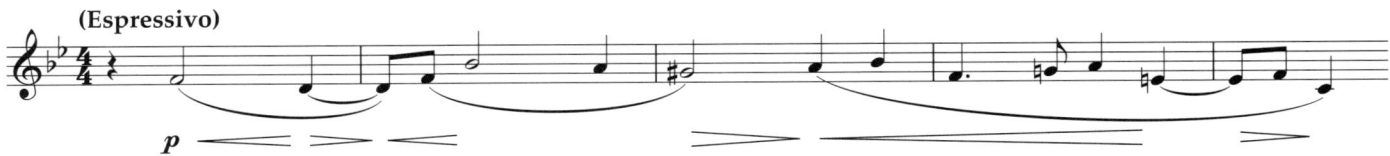

Reger, Clarinet Sonata No. 1, Op. 49, I, bars 114–118

Mendelssohn, *Elijah*, No. 29, Chorus, Clarinet II, bars 41–48

Debussy, *Petite Pièce*

Mozart, Serenade in B♭ K. 361, 'Gran Partita', Clarinet II, bars 223–227

Elgar, 'Enigma' Variations, III, Clarinet I

DEVELOPING TONE

EXERCISES

STUDIES IN THE THROAT REGISTER

Take note of the instructions given on page 69 when playing these studies. When throat notes appear in passing in quicker passages, you probably won't be able to give them quite as much individuality in oral cavity control, so simply match them as best as possible.

THE CLARINET

EXERCISES

The *clarion* register

The *clarion* (*clarinet* or *clarino*) register has a brilliant, ringing and clear quality. Many of the great chamber music melodies and orchestral solos for the instrument are written in this register, so it is very important to develop a pure tone and the ability to project it. Try to maintain a matched tone quality and a feel for the travel and direction throughout the notes in each of the following exercises. Aim to move seamlessly from one note to the next.

Vary this exercise using the following pattern:

Aim to match the quality of the bell notes with those of the lower *clarion* register.

When playing the following notes it is possible that an 'undertone' may occur, that is, an unwanted splitting of the sound that results in a note of a lower pitch (usually the equivalent fingered note in the *chalumeau* register) sounding at the same time as the upper note.[43] A firm embouchure (but no biting) and sufficient breath with optimal voicing will generally solve this problem. If you do experience undertones (or even if you don't), practise these notes with the register key[44] closed. Once you can produce them clearly in this way, they should pose no problem with the register key open. Undertones may also occur if you have too much of the mouthpiece in your mouth.

As a preliminary exercise, play the fundamental and then the harmonic using the appropriate voicing (oral cavity) technique:

5.

Now try this exercise. Play the first two bars with the register key closed aiming for the cleanest sound possible, i.e. trying to eliminate the undertone. Experiment with air speed (fast), embouchure (firm with no biting) and oral cavity shape ('ee'). Open the register key for the final note – playing it cleanly should feel easy!

6.

Prepare each of the following notes in the same way and then practise them until they have a pure, ringing quality.

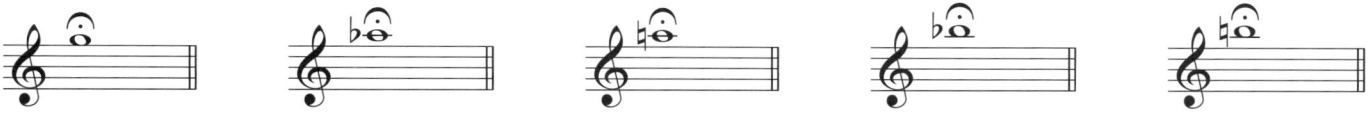

The problem of undertones may also occur with other notes in this register, and in the *altissimo* register (page 80). They should be dealt with in the same way.

Fast air and, only if necessary, slightly pushing the clarinet up towards your upper teeth will help you to control C^3. Take care not to bite or squeeze the embouchure:

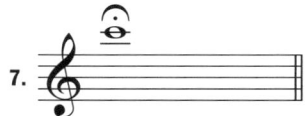

7.

Listen for that pure ringing tone in the next set of exercises. Aim for a perfect *legato* and try not to 'bump' from one note to the next. Prepare using the GNG.

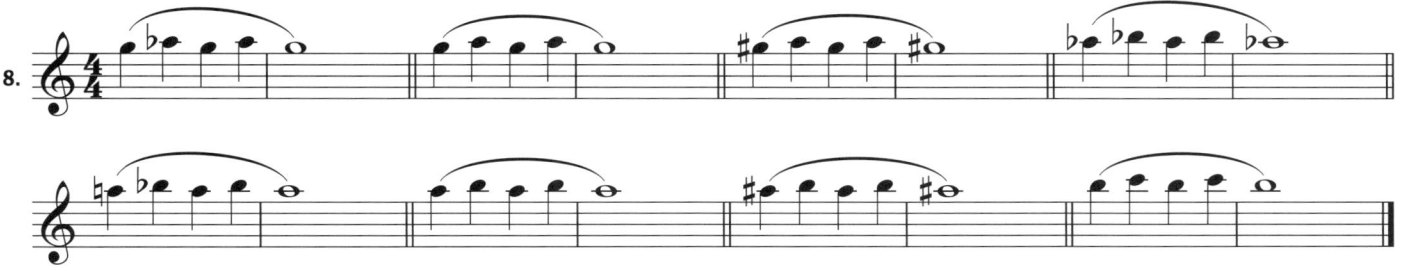

8.

---

43. 'Undertones' are also a 'series' that represent the opposite, or an inversion, of 'overtones'.
44. The register key is also known as the speaker key and the two terms are used interchangeably in the clarinet literature.

THE CLARINET

EXERCISES

The next two exercises will build your ability to make well-controlled *legato* slurs in this register. Work at each segment individually and then begin to put them together. As you build up the melodic line, slur *all* the notes. Breathe as necessary. Listen to match the sound of each note in each interval as closely as possible. Maintain a stable embouchure (no biting or squeezing) and be aware of your breath support at all times.

9.

10.

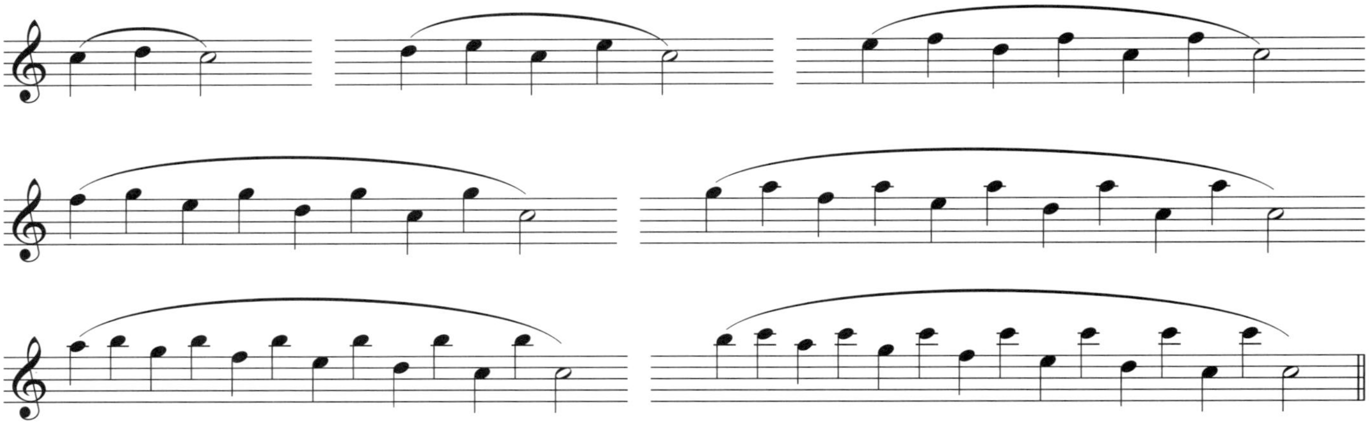

Play the next exercise first using the GNG. Aim for a stable embouchure and firm breath support. This will help you avoid squeezing the embouchure or slowing down the air. Sustain each crotchet for its full value.

11.

DEVELOPING TONE

Similarly, prepare each of the following three exercises using the GNG first.

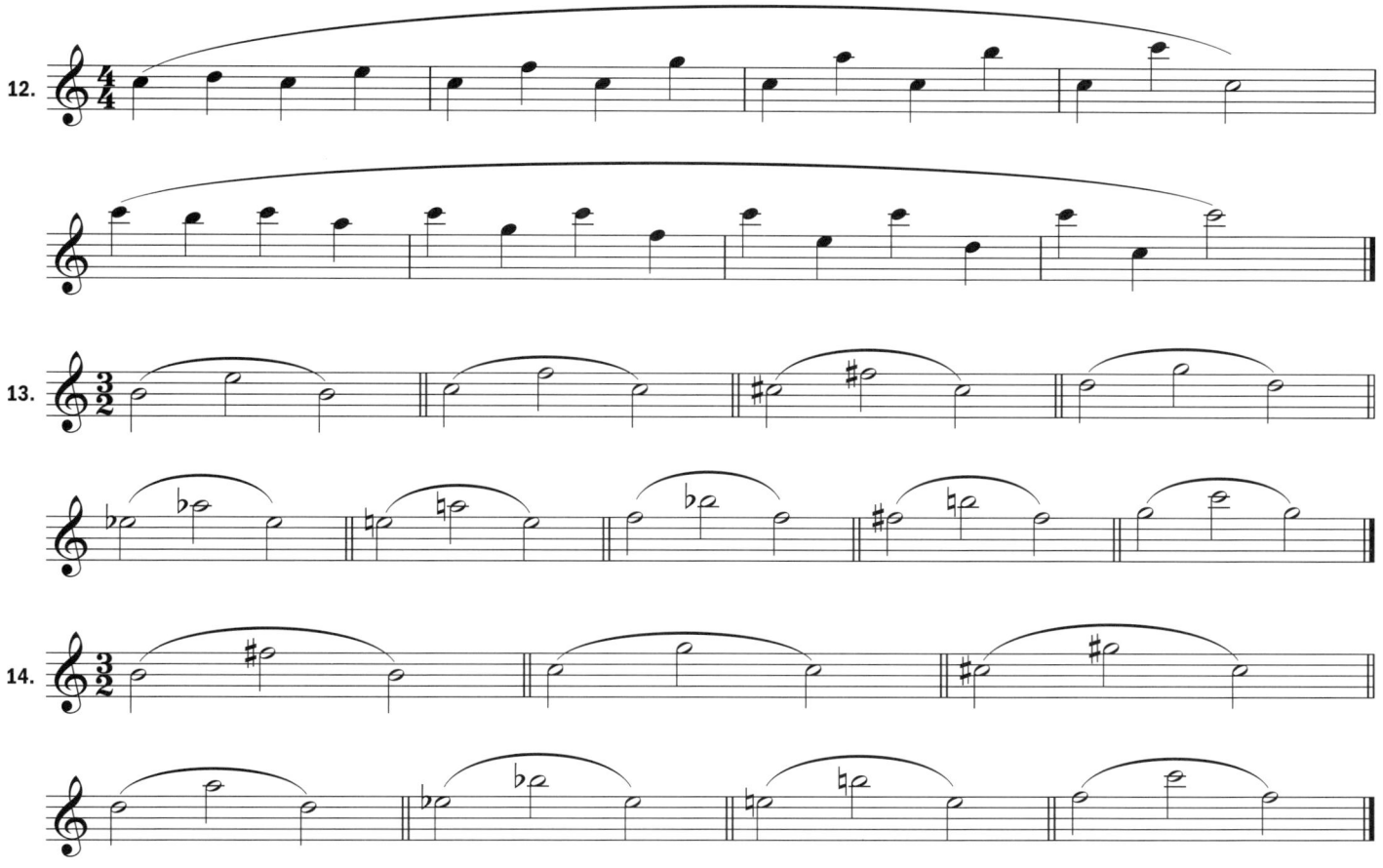

Vary exercises 13 and 14 on the pattern of exercise 1a on page 70.

Make sure that the first note in each of the following exercises begins clearly. A controlled embouchure and good supported breath control are essential. You may wish to explore varying dynamics in these exercises. The GNG is very helpful here.

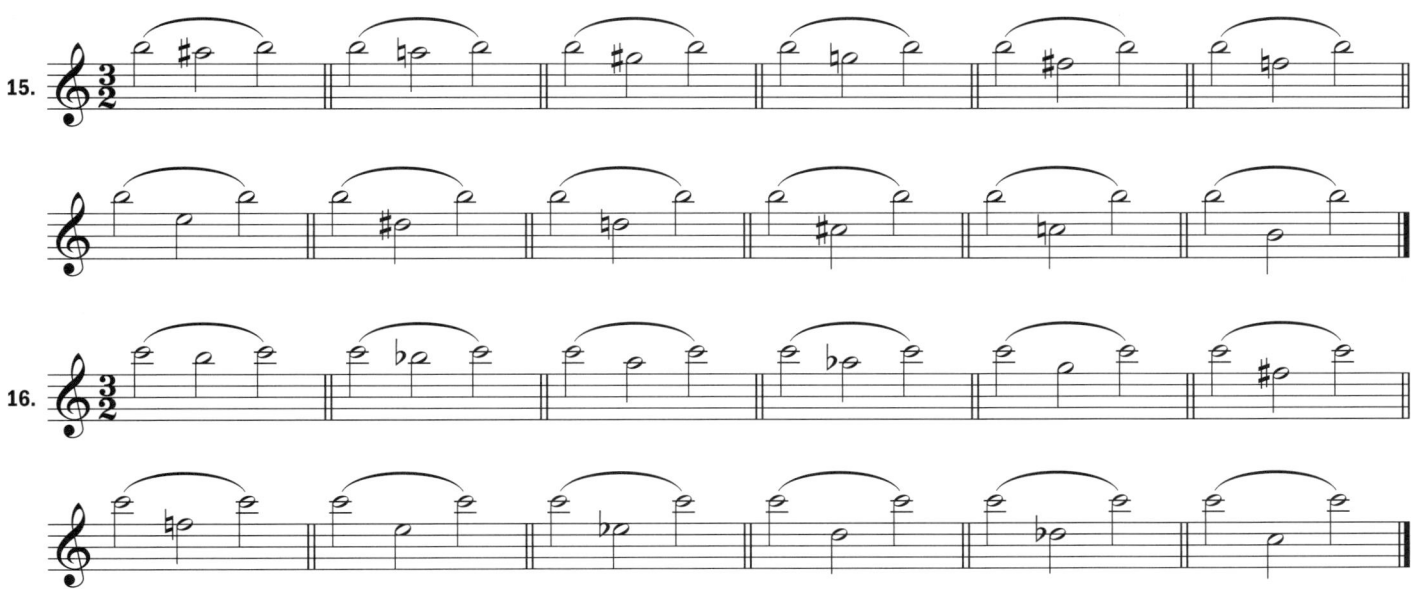

Vary exercises 15 and 16 on the pattern of exercise 1a (page 70).

THE CLARINET

EXERCISES

In the next exercise, the dynamic shape will feel curious as your instinct will be to *crescendo* to the top note and then *diminuendo* back down. This shape encourages a very even *legato*.

EXAMPLES FROM THE CLARINET REPERTOIRE

Here are some examples of beautiful melodic lines set in the *clarion* register. Aim for your most pure and ringing tone quality.

Mozart, Clarinet Concerto K. 622, II

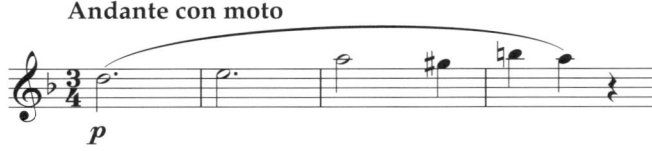

Weber, Grand Duo Concertant Op. 48, II

Brahms, Sonata No. 1, Op. 120, II

Reger, Sonata No. 1, Op. 49, II

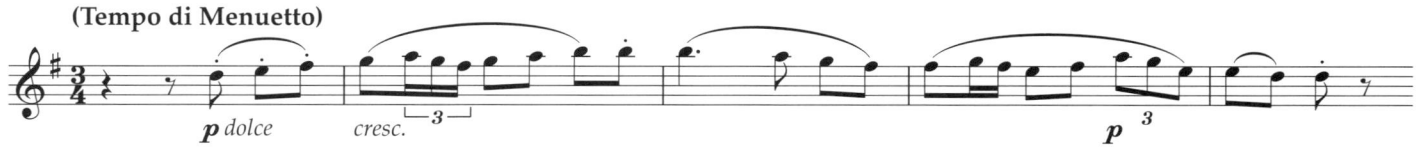

Beethoven, Symphony No. 8, Op. 93, III, Clarinet I, bars 48–52

Donizetti, Clarinet Concertino, I, bars 2–5

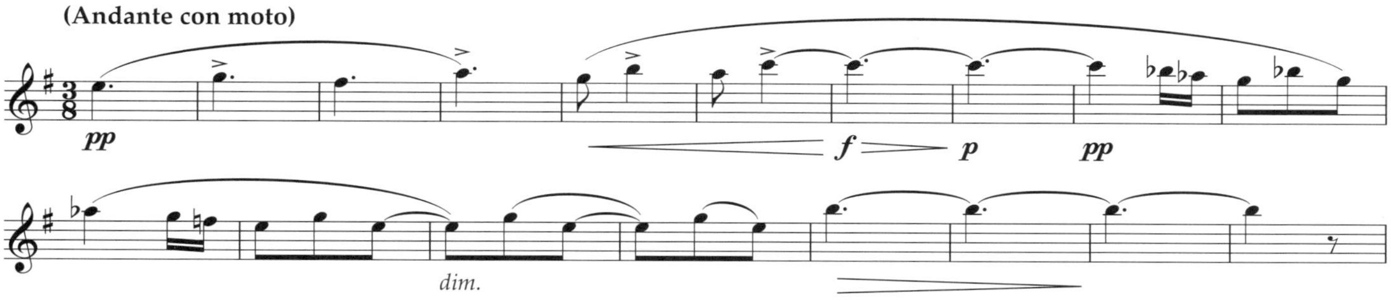

DEVELOPING TONE

Schubert, Symphony No. 8 D. 759, Clarinet I, II, bars 66–83

EXERCISES

Refer to the instructions given on page 69 before playing the following studies.

STUDIES IN THE CLARION REGISTER

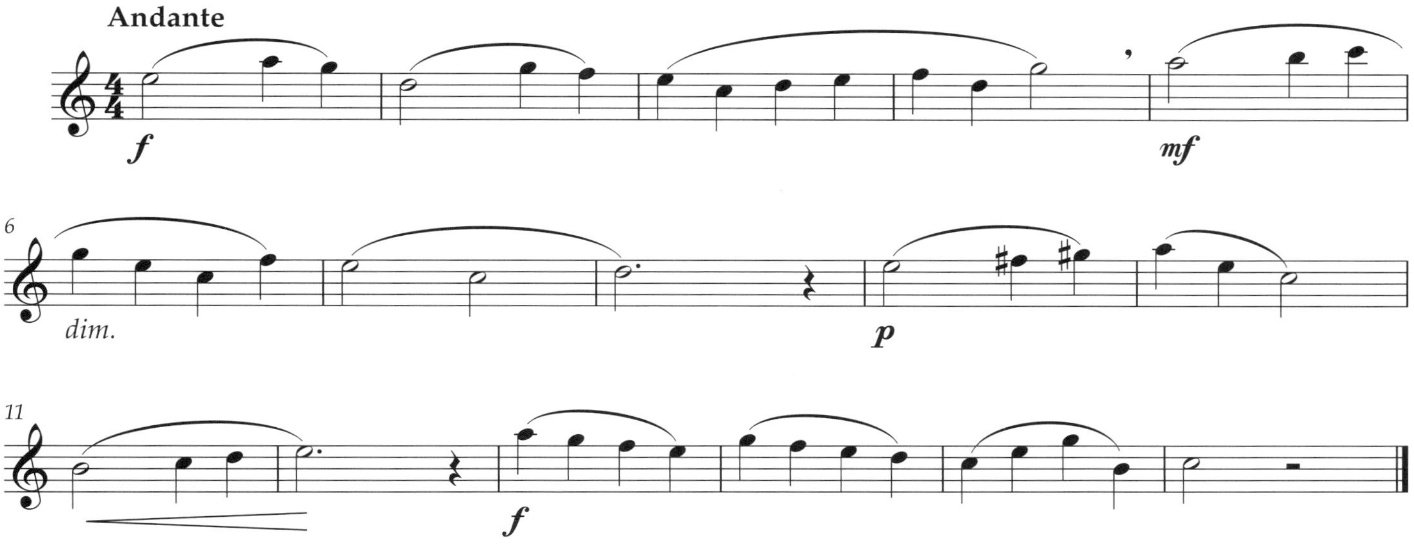

THE CLARINET

EXERCISES

The *altissimo* register

Notes in the *altissimo* register have a bright, incisive quality. They always project well and never need forcing. Great care should be taken to develop the fine balance of embouchure and breath control. Avoid any tightness of the embouchure or jaw pressure (biting), as both will produce a thin sound. Fast air and suitable voicing (tongue position) is essential. Our intention must be to produce a beautiful warm sound in this register unless there is a particular necessity owing to the demands of the character for a less than pleasant sound.[45] Experiment with various fingerings (such as those provided below). Different makes of instrument have varying acoustical qualities, and some fingerings may suit your instrument better than others.

Do invest in specially designed ear plugs if you wish to spend a lot of time on the exercises in this section. Excessive exposure to high frequency sounds can damage your hearing.

The next two exercises will really help you to feel how best to set up your side of the clarinet when playing these notes. It is very important to use instant fast air aided by a high tongue position. Be careful not to exert any more embouchure pressure than you would use for lower notes. Try to play each in one continuous breath and keep some air moving down the instrument throughout, making sure the embouchure does not tighten. Listen for an instant, pure and consistent sound. Practise starting notes without, and then with, the tongue.

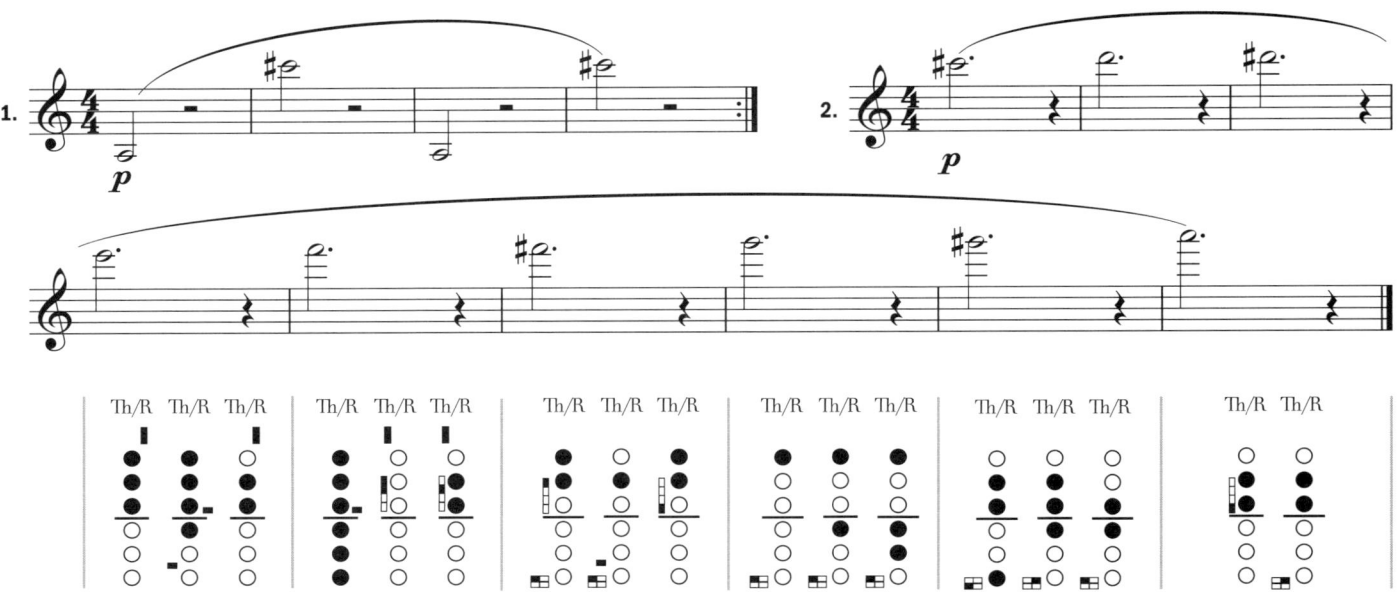

If you hear any lower harmonics (undertones), the air speed is probably too slow – don't correct this by tightening the embouchure but by employing faster air. Try this exercise (as for preparing notes in the *clarion* register):

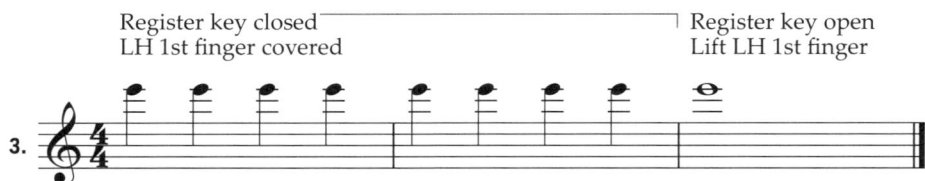

Repeat with other notes in this register as appropriate.

---

45. A harsh sound is probably the result of stimulating and combining extra and unwanted harmonics.

DEVELOPING TONE

Play the next exercise slowly and listen intently to the sound from the moment the note begins to the moment it stops. Use the GNG in preparation and take particular care not to squeeze or bite.

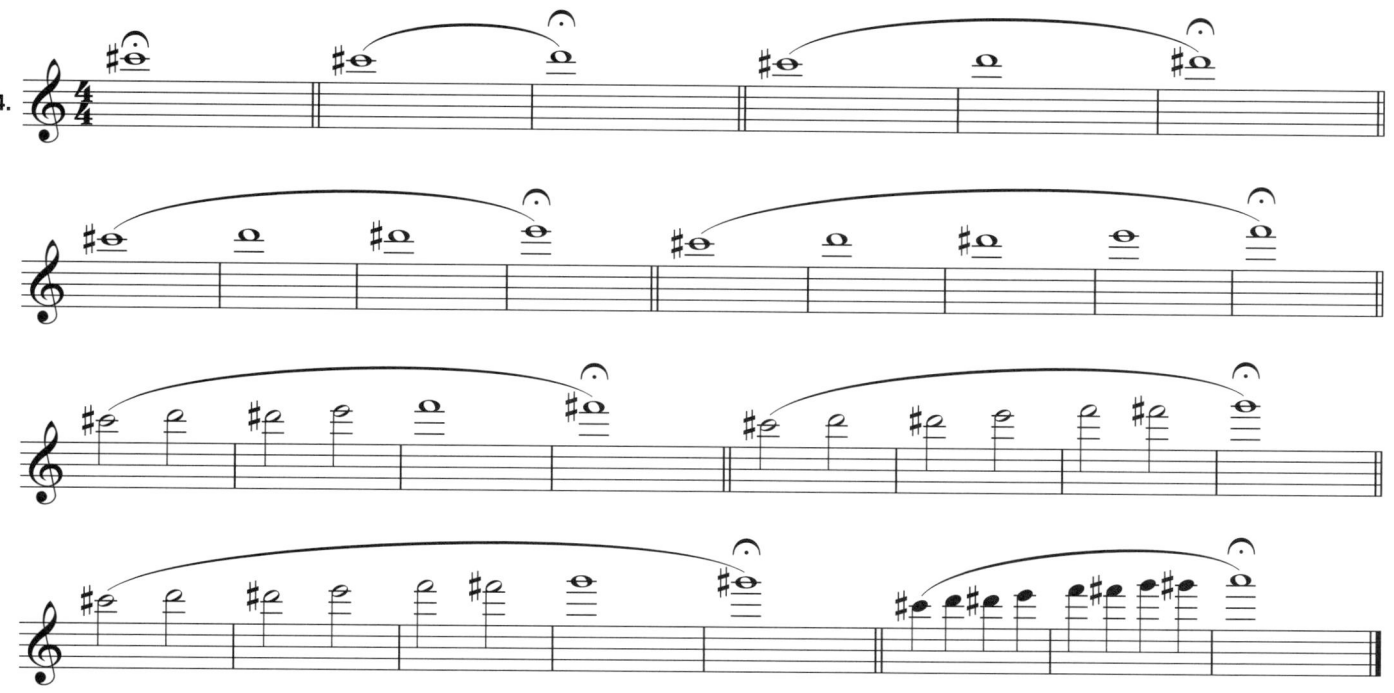

Work at these exercises at a soft dynamic as well as loudly. Ease of control at *p* in this register demonstrates a secure technique.

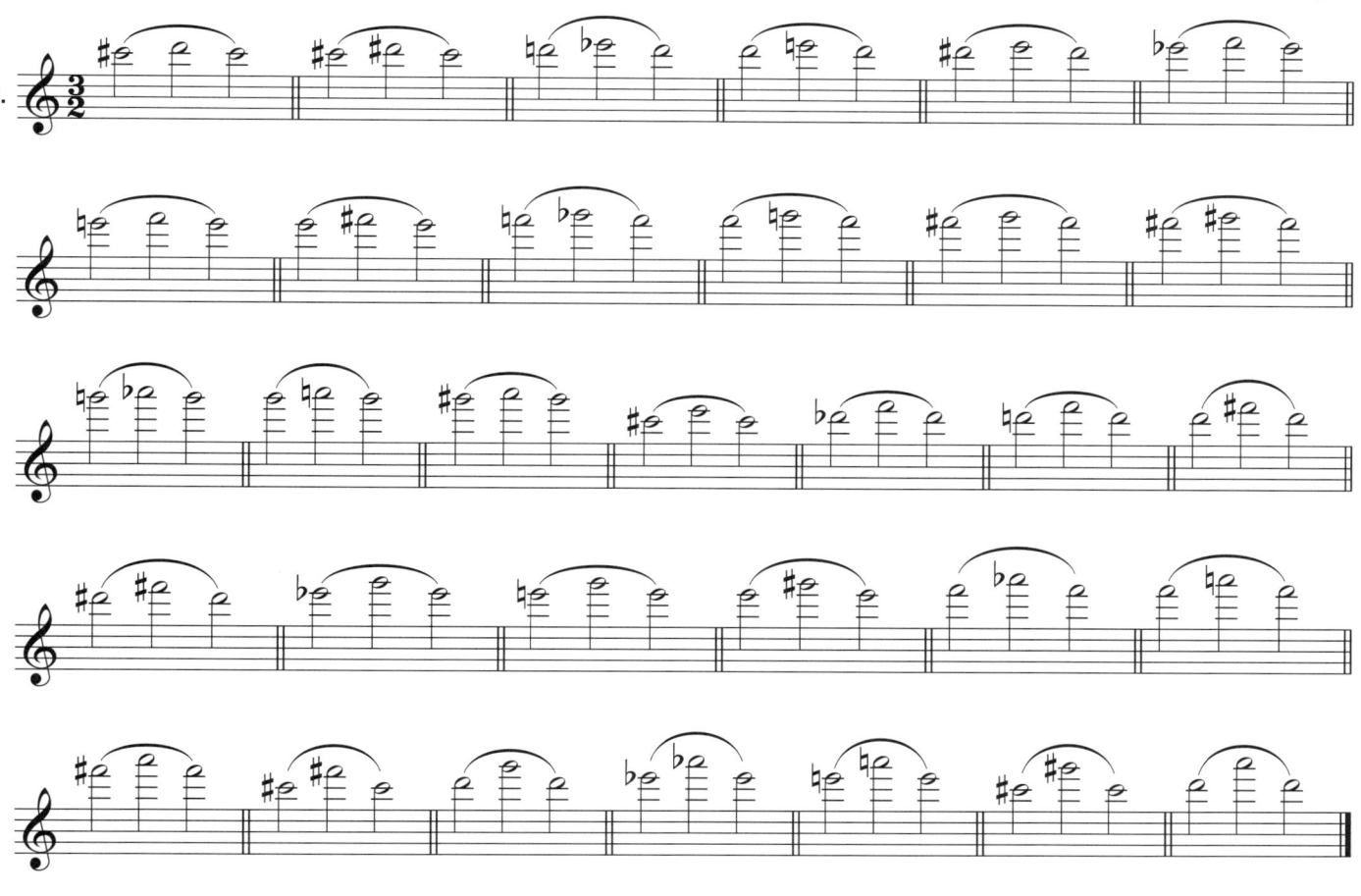

THE CLARINET

EXERCISES

Vary exercise 5 using the following patterns:

Refer to the instructions on page 69 before playing the next study.

STUDY IN THE ALTISSIMO REGISTER

DEVELOPING TONE

EXERCISES

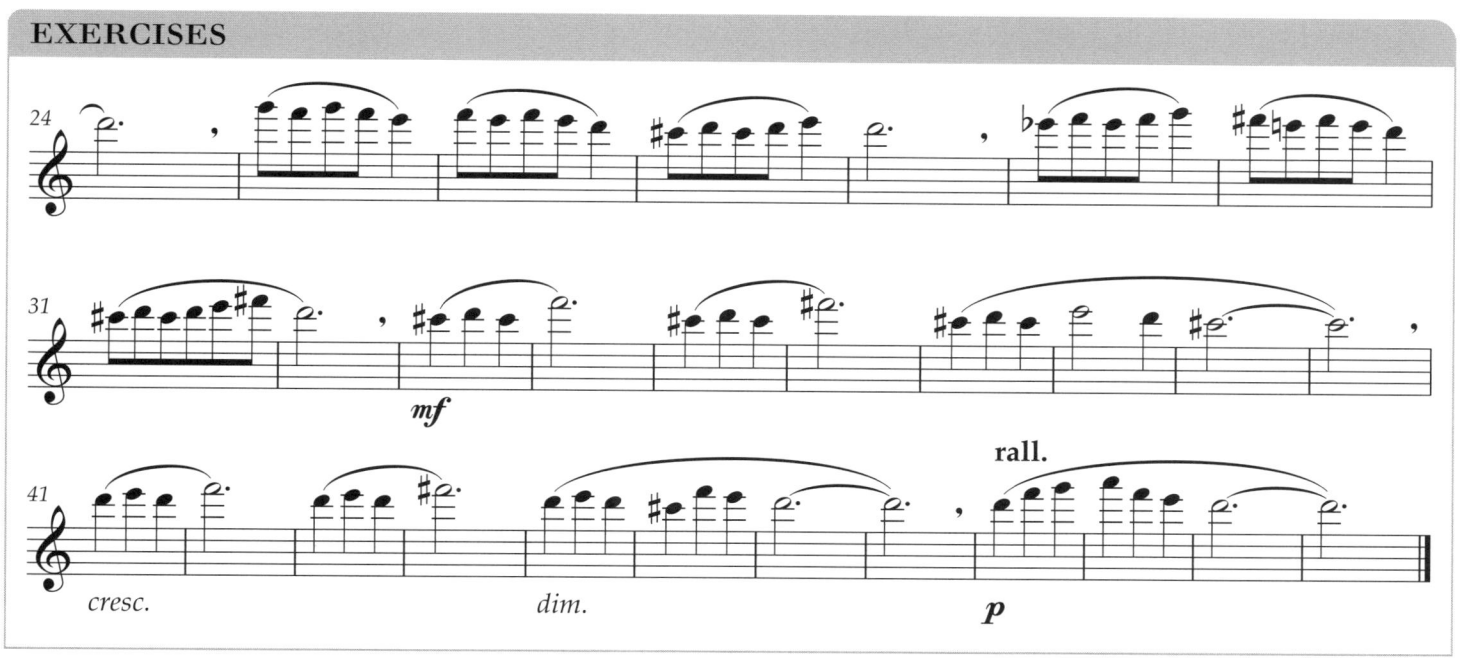

EXAMPLES FROM THE CLARINET REPERTOIRE

Here are some examples of melodic lines set in the *altissimo* register.

Copland, Concerto for Clarinet, bars 436–470

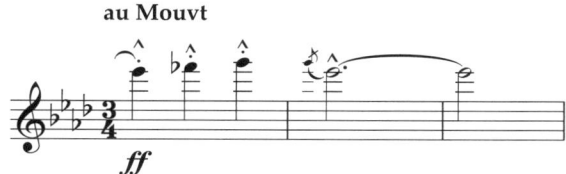

Debussy, *Première Rhapsodie*, bars 203–205

Arnold, Clarinet Concerto No. 2, III, bars 118–119

Ravel, *Daphnis et Chloé*, Clarinets I and II, bars 221–222

THE CLARINET

EXERCISES
Joining the registers

Fluent movement from one register to another requires controlled breath support, a steady embouchure and perfectly coordinated fingering. Many of the exercises in this section would benefit from playing using the GNG version first.

The first break
Play the following exercise, keeping the right-hand fingers down when you play G. Find your best sound for the first note and then try to match tone and dynamic level when you move to the second – and don't land on the lower note with a bump! Keep finger movement gentle.

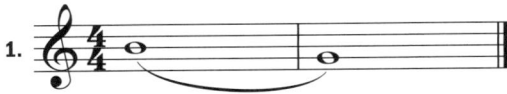

For the exercises that follow, refer to the fingerings on page 70 (*the throat register*). As before, try to keep suitable fingers (and possibly keys) held down for the second note. Economy is a good principle here. Move as few fingers as possible, taking into account intonation and matching tone. Repeat the exercises at varying dynamic levels.

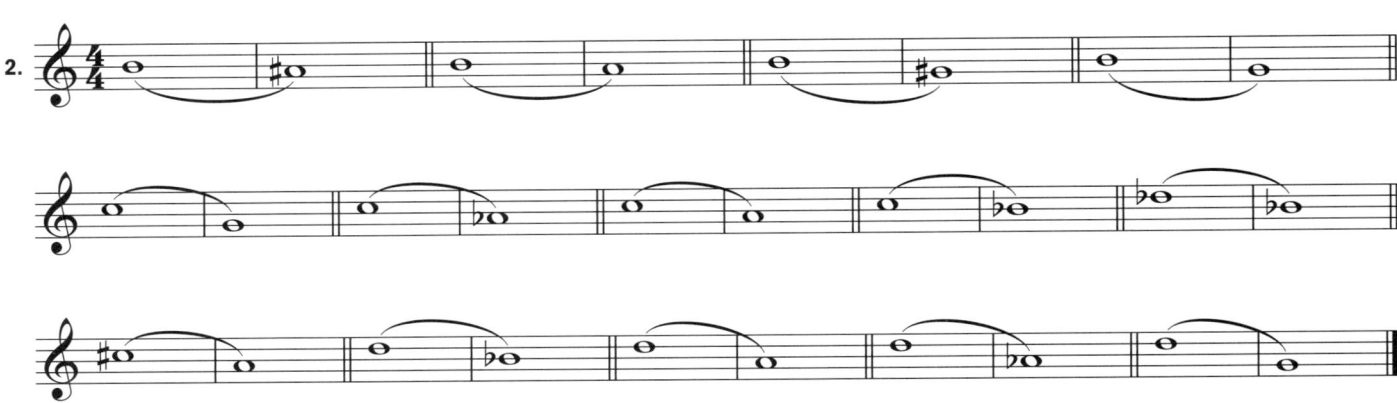

When slurring upwards, where possible, prepare for the second note in advance by placing the right-hand fingers on their respective tone holes; this is sometimes known as 'pre-fingering'. Always bear in mind, however, that this may have an effect on the intonation. Take care over the timing of the register-key movement – it must be absolutely coordinated with the other fingers.

Play each of the slurred pairs in the next exercise with a slight *crescendo* to help join the notes smoothly. Then repeat with an *imaginery crescendo*. Set up your best sound for the first note and try to match tone and dynamic levels as best you can.

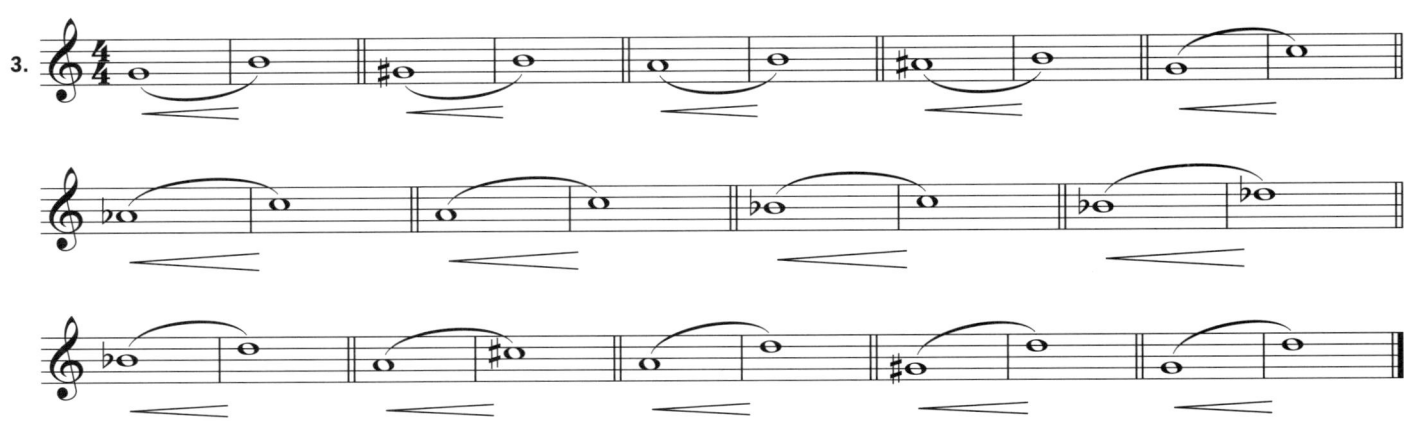

DEVELOPING TONE

Repeat the following two exercises until you achieve a perfect *legato*. Take care to maintain a stable embouchure and avoid any *tension* creeping in as you progress through each of the individual exercises.

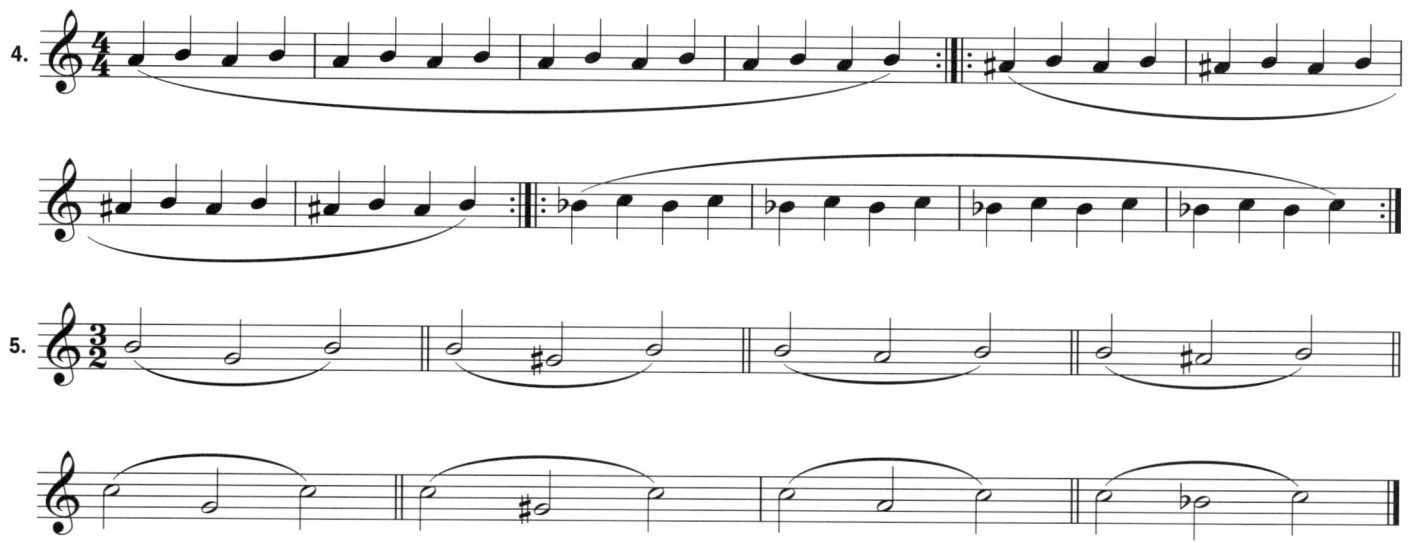

Now vary exercise 5 using the following pattern:

In the following two exercises take great care not to 'bump' from note to note. Remember to maintain air pressure and think about creating a good sense of line and direction.

85

THE CLARINET

EXAMPLES FROM THE CLARINET REPERTOIRE

Here are some examples of crossing the first break found within the clarinet repertoire:

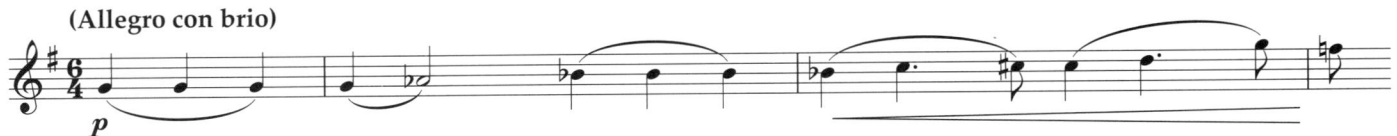

Brahms, Symphony No. 3, Op. 90, I, Clarinet I, bars 23–26

Brahms, Symphony No. 3, Op. 90, III, Clarinet I

Debussy, *Première Rhapsodie*, bars 11–14

Tchaikovsky, Symphony No. 4, I, Clarinet I, bars 115–117

Ravel, Bolero, E♭ Clarinet, bars 47–51

The second break

In all the *legato* patterns in this next section you will need to find a balance of control for each interval. Take your time, hold each note for a while and try to sense the optimum air pressure, speed and volume and embouchure control for each note. In crossing this second break, think of the resonance of the upper note as marked in preparation.

So, first set up your best upper note, then play the lower note thinking of the upper note. Then play the bar. The support will certainly need to be firm with fast air. In this register, the back of the tongue will need to be high. Thus, when moving between the notes with your optimum balance of control, you should achieve a matched tone quality with lovely *legato* in both directions and the minimum change in the oral cavity. Think about avoiding tension in the embouchure, especially when moving upwards – never bite! A sense of travel is also very helpful, as is the GNG.

You might also find the technique of *half-holing* useful. Open the register key and at the same time slightly rotate the first finger of the left hand away from you to half-open the tone hole before lifting your finger off the instrument. This technique will make a small difference to the sound, but for most it is entirely acceptable.

DEVELOPING TONE

EXERCISES

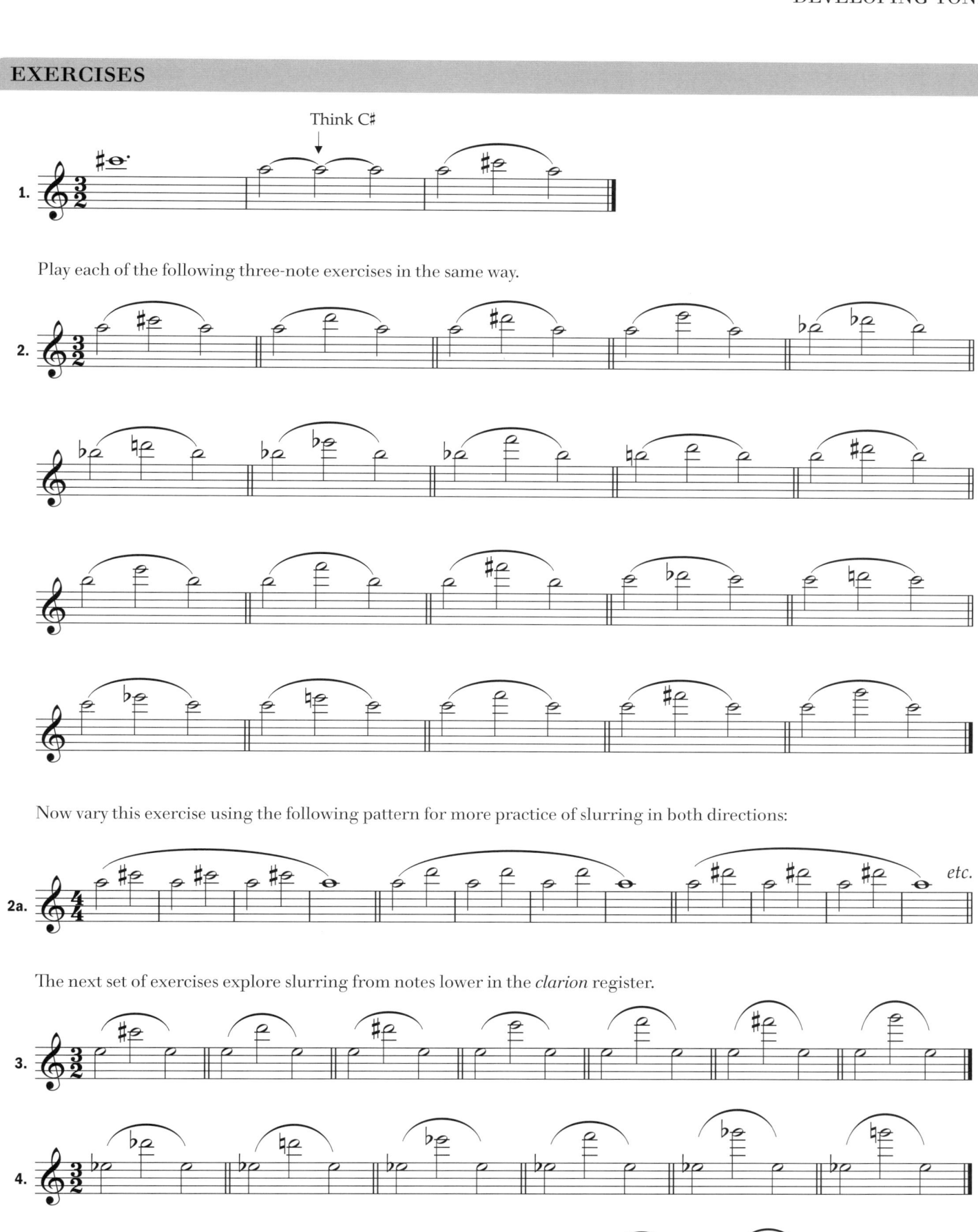

Play each of the following three-note exercises in the same way.

Now vary this exercise using the following pattern for more practice of slurring in both directions:

The next set of exercises explore slurring from notes lower in the *clarion* register.

THE CLARINET

EXERCISES

Repeat these exercises using the pattern in exercise 2a.

EXAMPLES FROM THE CLARINET REPERTOIRE

Here are some examples of crossing the second break found within the clarinet repertoire:

Debussy, *Première Rhapsodie*, bars 156–160

Ireland, Fantasy-Sonata

Busoni, Elegie in E♭ Major

Borodin, Polovtsian Dances, bars 571–576

Paul Harris, Adagio for Clarinet and Piano, bars 4–7

DEVELOPING TONE

EXERCISES

Slurring across all registers

The next exercise gives practice in slurring octaves across all registers. Particular care should be given to slurring back down into the *chalumeau* register. Aim for consistency of tone and dynamic level. This exercise will benefit from the GNG. Take care that any oral cavity adjustments, particularly in descending intervals, don't adversely affect the quality of the *legato*. Listen for small unwanted *glissando*-like sounds which may occur as the oral cavity adjusts.

Again, you will need to find a balance of control between each note for every interval. As a preliminary exercise, practise each in the following way, aiming to find the best-matched tone quality in both directions with minimum oral cavity adjustment. You'll hear if the optimum balance hasn't been achieved, if for example you get a B^3 sounding for the first note in bar 6 or for the second note in bar 7.

Extend this exercise up to C^4 if you wish.

Wider intervals

In this next series of slurs keep the embouchure still as you open the register key – avoid any temptation to squeeze with the lips or bite with the jaw. Also think about the thumb after it has done its job of opening the register key: don't allow it to lock into position or become tense, keep it relaxed.

EXERCISES

To make smooth joins between the notes in the next exercise, make sure that you maintain the tone fully, (or travel) through the lower note in each pair. Practise using the GNG first.

As you cross into the *altissimo* register you may find the half-holing technique useful (see page 86).

In the next exercise, again take care to avoid embouchure pressure or biting. Fast air is essential and oral cavity adjustment will help. Think strongly of the second note as you move through the first. From a psychological point of view, avoid thinking that the wider the interval, the more difficult it is to negotiate. Higher notes require a faster vibrating reed – just think of how you're applying the necessary energy to the reed. Half-holing may again prove helpful in some examples, depending on your *altissimo*-note fingering.

Try this Gershwin-esque preliminary exercise. Play an ascending scale from the first note to D^2 and then *glissando* from there to the upper note. This will help you find where the upper note *lives* in your side of the clarinet. Then try the exercise as written.

Slurring downwards

Slurring downwards from the *clarion* to the *chalumeau* register presents some interesting challenges. Practise the next exercise a line at a time, either going across the musical grid or downwards, sensing the slightly different responses of each interval and how those responses relate to each other as you move from one to the next. Reverse the intervals too and practise ascending. In some cases you may need to find alternative methods to effect the downward slur such as a small variation in lip or breath pressure or momentarily interrupting the vibrating reed by the lightest and swiftest glance of the tongue on the reed.

You might like to mark in the copy how each interval *feels* and *your* best way to achieve it, which will be some combination of lip, breath, tongue and oral cavity.[46]

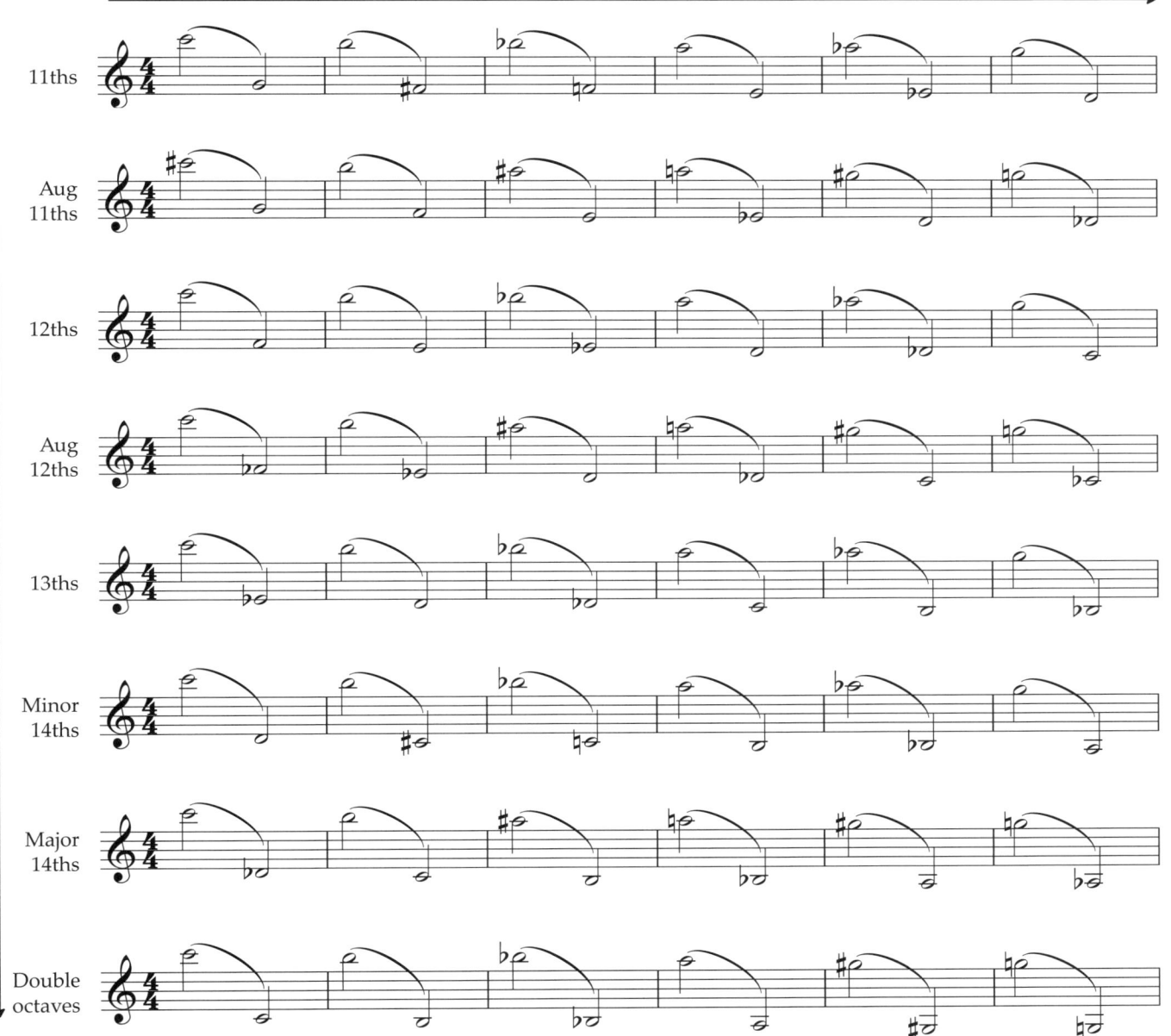

Even though much of the staple repertoire rarely uses any of the more unusual intervals in the exercise above (or they'll be articulated, which is much easier to control), mastering this will make you feel that most of what you *do* play is much simpler to negotiate.

---

46. To some extent it's all about finding a successful interaction between the vibrating air column and the vibrating reed.

THE CLARINET

EXERCISES

Notice that in this next exercise the success of the *legato* will require careful control as the intervals get smaller and the fingerings get closer.[47]

In the study that follows, the intervals are wide and sometimes dissonant. Once you are used to the unusual intervals, aim to play with a perfect *legato* and consistent quality of tone. It is important that you find the balance between each pair of notes and always maintain your breath support. Minimise oral cavity shape adjustments that may cause small *glissando* sounds and be aware of how subtle changes in lip and air pressure can assist.

As a preparation for this study, practise each interval independently as exercise 2 below. Experiment to see what will cause each interval to work smoothly and precisely. Also use the GNG.

STUDY 1: SLURRING ACROSS ALL REGISTERS

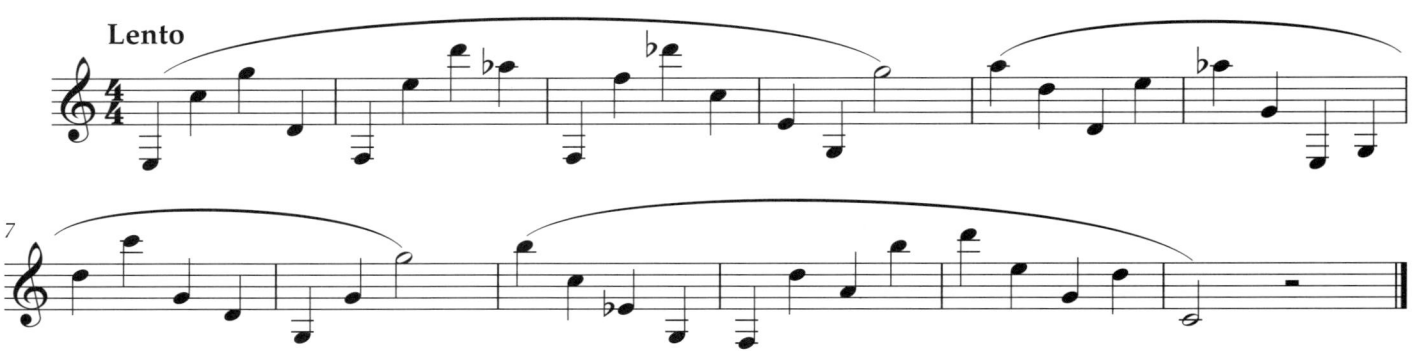

The next exercise identifies some intervals best avoided by composers who might be writing for the clarinet as they are very challenging to play! But for players, they are certainly worth mastering.

---

47. The possible reason for the increased control necessary to make these slurs work is that the pattern of vibration of the higher note becomes more present in the lower note, making it harder to effect the slur. As you practise you will begin to sense this and find a way of dampening this vibration.

DEVELOPING TONE

STUDY 2: SLURRING ACROSS ALL REGISTERS

THE CLARINET

EXAMPLES FROM THE CLARINET REPERTOIRE

Weber, Concertino for Clarinet, Op. 26, bars 15–17

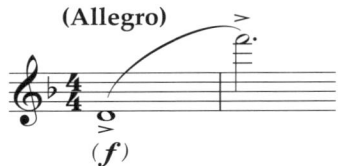

Weber, Clarinet Concerto No. 2, Op. 74, I, bars 155–156

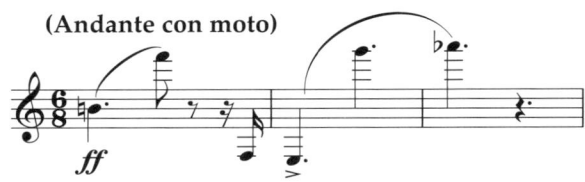

Weber, Clarinet Concerto No. 2, Op. 74, II, bars 55–57

Crusell, Clarinet Concerto No. 2, Op. 5, I, bars 122–123

Brahms, Clarinet Sonata No. 1, Op. 120, bars 5–9

Nielsen, Clarinet Concerto, Op. 57, bars 65–66

Application of tone control to playing a melodic line

When you play a melodic line it is important that your phrasing has been carefully thought out and, of course, you need to pay attention to all the aspects of technique studied so far:

- Take great care to maintain tone quality and travel
- Make sure that dynamic levels are musically appropriate and in themselves convincingly related to each other
- Make *crescendos* and *diminuendos* gradual
- Avoid undue accentuation on the first note of each phrase
- Play note lengths accurately

In speech, clarity of diction is obtained by subtleties of punctuation in addition to the breaks normally indicated by commas, full stops and so on. In some cases, words will run on smoothly, while in others greater definition is needed; such definition can be created, for instance, by the briefest period of silence between words. In just the same way, subtleties of musical 'punctuation' can be introduced to make your phrasing intelligible.

Before you play, spend some time hearing and preparing the music in your head. Imagine your ideal shaping. Sometimes, if you play without going through this process, technical considerations may take over as the prime factors in determining your interpretation and inhibit your musical ideal. As you play, seek to replicate your imagined shaping. If you do experience a technical obstacle aim to control it rather than allow it to control you.

Once prepared, practise the following extracts, listening very carefully to your playing. Try not to 'bump' as you move from one note to another and avoid any unintentional bulging. When you have mastered these examples of sustained melodic playing, there are, of course, a great many others in the clarinet repertoire that can be studied.

EXAMPLES FROM THE CLARINET REPERTOIRE

Mozart, Clarinet Quintet K. 581, II

THE CLARINET

Weber, Melody for Baermann[48]

Mendelssohn, Clarinet Sonata, II

Richard Strauss, *Duett-Concertino*, I, bars 10-22

48. This tune was written as a present for Baermann by Weber and was first published with a piano accompaniment in *Second Book of Clarinet Solos*, Faber Music Ltd.

DEVELOPING TONE

Rachmaninov, Symphony No. 2, III, Clarinet I, bars 6–28

Useful words

Words are the gateway to thoughts. Here are some words, arranged in pairs of antonyms, that are useful in thinking, talking about and describing tone and tone quality. The qualities of the second word in each pair are best avoided, though there may be occasions when such tonal colours are called for.

Bright/dull
Brilliant/dim
Centred/indistinct
Incisive/weak
Warm/cold
Sharp/blunt
Rich/thin
Pure/coarse

Refined/rough
Focussed/ill-defined
Concentrated/loose
Mellow/harsh
Intense/insipid
Vivid/lifeless
Defined/indistinct
Clear/muddy

Resonant/tinny
Thick/transparent
Ringing/muffled
Rounded/strident

Pepe Baeza

Intonation and playing in tune

Intonation challenges
Warming up the clarinet
Fine-tuning the instrument
Tuning in ensemble playing
Tuning and harmonics
Lipping up (or down)
Tuning related to the registers
Playing in tune

Intonation challenges

The clarinet's structure and the resulting acoustic characteristics set the player some interesting intonation challenges.

- As a cylindrical stopped pipe, it overblows a 12th (not an octave like other woodwind instruments) and the tuning of those 12ths is, by nature, slightly inconsistent. The tuning of the instrument by the manufacturer is, as a result, something of a compromise.[49] This means there may be a number of inbuilt intonation problems that need some understanding and control.
- Throat notes present particular tuning problems owing to the relationship between the length and diameter of the bore in that area.
- The *altissimo* register is also challenging to tune because of the complexity of the harmonics that produce the notes.

So, playing the clarinet *in tune* requires some acoustic knowledge, some particular techniques, and most importantly, a keen ear.

EXERCISES

Many players lack confidence in their ability to say whether a note is sharp or flat. The following exercises will help you to overcome this. You will need a piano or, preferably, a fellow clarinet player.

- Pull the barrel out by about 5mm (about ¼ inch). This will make all notes sound flat. Play G^2 and compare it with the appropriate sounding note on the piano (in this case, the note F) or the same note from your fellow player. The increased length of the instrument will make you sound flat. Now push the barrel slightly further in and play G^2 again. Compare. Keep pushing the barrel in until the tuning of G^2 sounds correct. Do not use any resonant fingerings when you do this exercise.
- Using a short barrel pushed right in, play G^2 again. It will be sharp, because the instrument length has decreased. This time gradually pull the barrel out and compare with the piano or your colleague until the tuning sounds correct.

Warming up the clarinet

Prior to fine-tuning, clarinets (both wooden and plastic) should be warmed up in order to reach their optimum condition. It's only then that fine-tuning the instrument will be most effective.

It is important to realise that sound isn't the result of a smooth flow of air moving through the tube, but rather the vibrations of air created by the player and the reed in the body of the clarinet. These vibrations form the soundwave. However, the temperature of the air in the tube does have a significant effect on the soundwave; the warmer the air, the higher the pitch. This settles after a few minutes of blowing: the warm-up period. In wooden instruments, the sharpening of the pitch is not in fact the result of the wood expanding as some believe. If the wood were to expand, interestingly, it is more likely to make the pitch flatter. Wooden instruments will take about five minutes to warm up and then will usually be temperature stable. Plastic instruments warm up more quickly but are slightly less temperature stable.

It's best to hold cold, wooden instruments by your side to begin the warming up. Then blow warm air gently into the instrument. Blowing straight into a cold plastic clarinet will do no harm.

Fine-tuning the instrument

As a start, it is necessary to know the pitch at which you will be expected to play. This will vary between about A = 440Hz and as much as A = 445Hz.[50]

Now test the following notes to find the right position for the barrel and middle joints. Play the notes (at not less than *mf*) and compare them with those of a well-tuned piano or electronic tuning device (see page 101). If the note is sharp, pull out the appropriate joint slightly. If flat, close it up slightly. Always warm up the instrument before tuning.

If sharp, pull out the barrel. Then slur up to …

… if sharp, pull out the middle joint.

---

49. Although today's clarinets, especially the narrower bore instruments, have virtually eliminated this compromise.
50. If you're auditioning for an orchestral position you should be told the pitch at which you will be expected to play.

When tuning to concert A (when playing with the piano or in an orchestra, for example) it's a good idea to move to your tuning note (B^2) from the note above (i.e. $C^2 - B^2$). The B^2 is likely to be truer as notes often begin slightly sharp.

Always tune your instrument carefully, both before practising and before a performance.

Using a tuning device

Regularly comparing your pitch with an electronic tuning device or app is very helpful, but should be carried out in a very particular manner. First of all, check the device is set to the appropriate A (440–445Hz) and tune your instrument as above.

Now check other notes in this way:

- Play your chosen note with your best sound and listen intently to the pitch. Really listen carefully.
- Sound the same note on your electronic tuner and make a judgement. Was your note in tune, flat or sharp?
- Switch off the electronic tuner sound and play the note again, trying your best to match it to the remembered pitch.
- After a few seconds check, using the tuner's visual display, to confirm your pitch.

In the event of a discrepancy, turn away from your tuner and try the process again as many times as necessary.

To continue, choose another note, maybe an octave or fifth away. Pre-hear the note internally, as in-tune as you can; play it and then check as above. Repeat this exercise on a regular basis, exploring intervals across the instrument.

In this way you are really developing your *ear*. If you simply check the tuning of a note with your eye (playing the note and looking to see where it is on the tuner), you will probably never improve your sense of pitch. If you repeat this exercise, even for just a minute or two each day, your sense of pitch and awareness of intonation will noticeably improve.

Tuning in ensemble playing

When playing with string instruments, it is useful to know what the strings themselves are made from. Modern strings are often made from a composite-core material and are unlikely to be affected by temperature or humidity changes. If players are using gut strings there may a tendency for them to get flatter as the temperature increases, which causes the strings to expand resulting in less tension and so a lower pitch. The clarinet will tend to get sharper with increased heat. It's therefore a good idea to retune a number of times during rehearsals and concerts.

When playing with strings, or indeed in any ensemble that doesn't include the piano (which of course is tuned to equal temperament), it's possible to explore more natural tunings (known as 'just' or 'pure' intonation) that blend to make very pure and beautiful harmony. Here is a table of adjustments to be made in cents to retune an equal-tempered note (one equal-tempered semitone is equal to 100 cents). However, this is further complicated by the fact that the adjustments in this table apply to notes in scale order. The interval of a minor third, from the sixth to the upper tonic, would need a further adjustment. In practice it would be virtually impossible to make such adjustments accurately, but using instinct, ear and musicianship, such tuning could result in creating some very special harmony and tonal blending.

Interval	*Adjustment*
Minor 2nd	Lower by 29 cents
Major 2nd	Raise by 4 cents
Minor 3rd	Raise by 16 cents
Major 3rd	Lower by 14 cents
Perfect 4th	Lower by 2 cents
Diminished 5th	Lower by 10 cents
Perfect 5th	Raise by 2 cents
Minor 6th	Raise by 14 cents
Major 6th	Lower by 16 cents
Minor 7th	Raise by 17 cents
Major 7th	Lower by 12 cents

Pianos are complicated. They tend to get flatter in extreme increased temperatures, but are very unlikely to move noticeably under normal conditions.

THE CLARINET

EXERCISES
Tuning and harmonics[51]

- Play E^1 at about *mf* and try to hear the first harmonic or overtone – the B above.

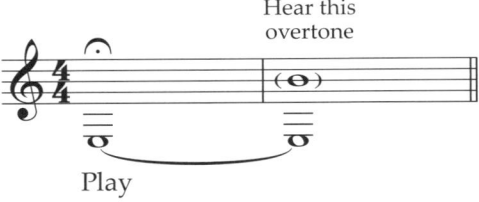

- Sometimes playing facing a wall, or into the corner of a room, will help – the walls will reflect back the sound. In time you'll be surprised at how clearly the B sounds when playing E^1.
- When you are confident in hearing the harmonic, open the register key to allow the instrument to play B^2 with its correct fingering. Was the B you heard as an overtone the same as the fingered B^2? If not, there may be a problem with the tuning of your instrument. Experiment with other notes in the *chalumeau* register.
- Now repeat the exercise and try to hear the second harmonic or overtone, the G♯.

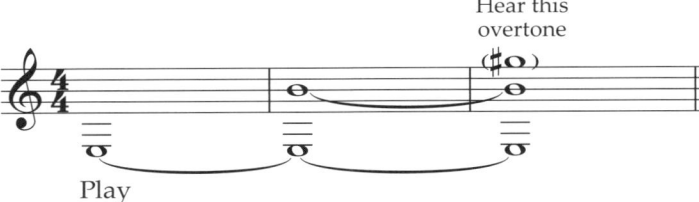

- When you can hear the G♯ clearly, compare it to the fingered G♯ in the *clarion* register. If you can't hear it at first listen to someone else playing E^1; try to steer your listening away from concentrating on the fundamental (the E). Imagine the pitch of the harmonics in your inner ear and in time they *will* become audible. Once you do 'find' them you will be surprised quite how strongly they can sound.

These exercises will help refine your ear and intonation awareness.

Lipping up (or down)

Lipping notes up or down is a practice adopted by some players. A little more lip pressure can raise notes slightly in pitch and the relaxation of the embouchure might slightly flatten the pitch. This practice is not generally advised for a number of reasons. The sharpening process may cause the player ultimately to bite or at least to tense the embouchure which will affect *legato* and the quality of tone. The flattening process will certainly have a deleterious effect on the tone quality.

As a rule, clarinet tone should always be maintained with a stable embouchure. However, there are exceptions to this. F^1, for example, may need some occasional help from the embouchure if it is particularly flat. The beginning of the first movement of Weber's Concerto No.2 is a case in point.[52]

51. The relative strength and presence of harmonics is what gives a note its timbre and character as well as its ability to project.
52. Unless you have a F^1 correction key.

Tuning related to the registers

When working through this section, you should be aware that integral tuning – how well an instrument is in tune *with itself* – will vary from one instrument to another and can also be affected by the type of mouthpiece used.

The *chalumeau* register

Notes in this register can be sharp when played softly. Avoid any undue lip pressure which is the main cause of this sharpness. Also keep the tongue low in the mouth using an 'aw' oral cavity shape and use firm breath support. The pitch may be adjusted by using certain keys and/or covering holes; for instance, to flatten A^1, B^1, or C^1 in this register, try depressing the right-hand low F or low E keys.

Sometimes, the lowest notes in this register may be flat. Moving the tongue higher in the mouth and implementing occasional embouchure adjustments can correct this, but making such adjustments whilst playing is difficult and they should only be used in extreme circumstances. If your instrument is seriously out in its integral tuning, take it to an experienced clarinet technician or replace it.[53]

The throat register

Notes in this register also tend to be sharp, particularly when played softly, and again the main cause will probably be too tight an embouchure. Closing certain keys and covering tone holes will help to correct this. The tuning of the side-key B♭ is normally better than the register-key fingering (see page 70). Oral cavity shape will also influence intonation in this register (see page 39).

The clarion register

Again, an appropriate embouchure with no undue pressure or biting, together with good breath support should ensure good tuning in this register. As you ascend each note is more prone to sharpness if there is any excessive lip or jaw pressure (or bite); B^3 and C^3 are particularly sensitive. Quiet playing in this register also tends towards sharpness that can be aided by changing oral cavity shape. B^2 and C^2 are sometimes acoustically designed to be a little sharp to avoid E^1 and F^1 being excessively flat.

The *altissimo* register

Playing in this register requires a high degree of technical control, so choose fingerings carefully considering both technical ease as well as intonation.[54] Maintain a firm embouchure, taking care not to bite as this will sharpen the pitch, and always nourish these notes with fast air but not too great a volume. A high tongue position will be necessary to achieve this. Oral cavity shape can influence tuning considerably in this register. Take particular care not to upset the delicate balance of breath and embouchure. When taking the breath, keep the top teeth on the mouthpiece and don't disturb the lower lip; lift your upper lip to allow air in. You won't wish to move lower or upper lips if you use a double-lip embouchure (see page 41); it is easier to take the breath by slightly opening the sides of the mouth.

---

53. There are specialist barrels available with differing internal tapering that might fix this problem.
54. Try to have a good book of fingerings by your side when practising: Sim, A., *505 Clarinet Fingerings & 276 Trills* (Queen's Temple Publications, 2008) and Ridenour, T., *Clarinet Fingerings: A Comprehensive Guide for the Performer and Educator* (Leblanc., 3rd ed., 1994) are strongly recommended.

THE CLARINET

EXERCISES
Playing in tune

Working through the following exercises will further help you to develop your sense of pitch. You will need the use of a tuning device or well-tuned piano.

Pre-hearing

To play accurately in tune, it is very helpful to know what a written note will sound like relative to other written notes before actually sounding it; in other words, you should be able to hear the note in your head before you play it, a technique known as 'pre-hearing'. If you have 'perfect pitch' (that is, a memory for absolute pitch) this will come naturally to you. But if, like the majority of people, you do not, you will need to work at this aspect of intonation carefully.

The following exercise, without the clarinet, will require a piano (an electronic keyboard would also work).

- Play a note towards the lower end of your vocal range on the piano, C for example. Then, with the piano C (or whatever note you have chosen) as your starting point, pre-hear and then sing a fifth above (G).[55] Immediately afterwards, check it against the piano. For example:

Play (piano)　　　　　　Pre-hear　　　　　　Sing　　　　　　Check (piano)

- Explore fourths, octaves, and thirds. Then explore tones and semitones too.
- Now pre-hear and then sing an arpeggio shape. Try singing a D♭ major arpeggio after hearing the C:

Play (piano)　　　　　　Pre-hear　　　　　　Sing　　　　　　Check (piano)

- Explore minor, diminished and augmented arpeggio patterns.
- With your clarinet, now try the following exercises. In each case, tune the first note with a tuning device (see page 101) or a piano and then play through the exercise slowly, pre-hearing every note. Finally, check the intonation of the last note against the tuner or piano.

---

55. A good consonant/vowel combination is 'dah'; 'lah' can cause tightness in the tongue.

INTONATION AND PLAYING IN TUNE

THE CLARINET

EXERCISES

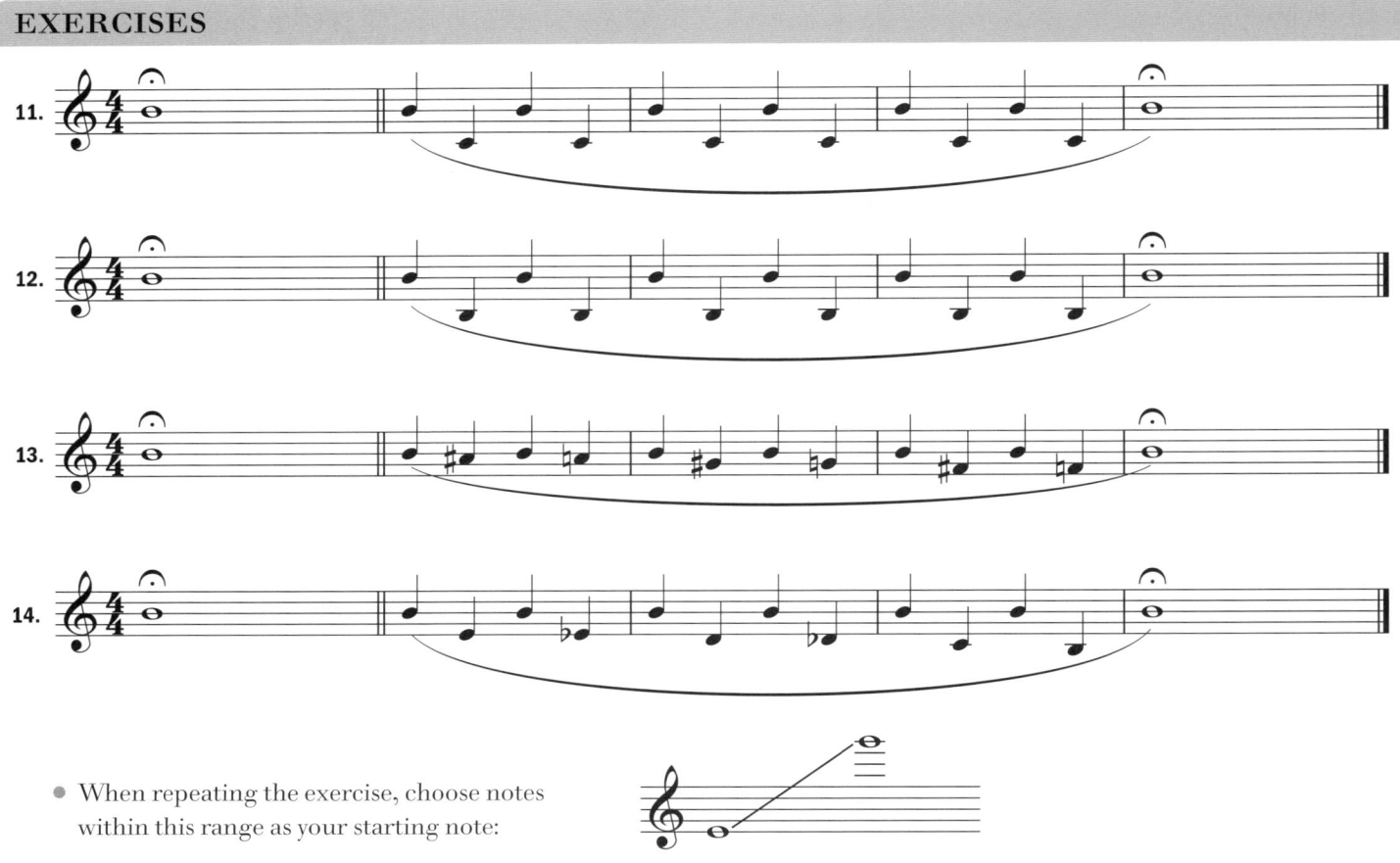

- When repeating the exercise, choose notes within this range as your starting note:

- The next exercise will require a piano.[56] Hold down the sustaining pedal and play an interval of a perfect fifth. With the piano notes still sounding, try to pre-hear first the major third and then the minor third above the lower note, and then play them on the clarinet. Check the pitch of each note you play against the piano. *Remember that the clarinet is a transposing instrument; clarinet pitches here are notated for the B♭ instrument, not at concert pitch.*

For example:

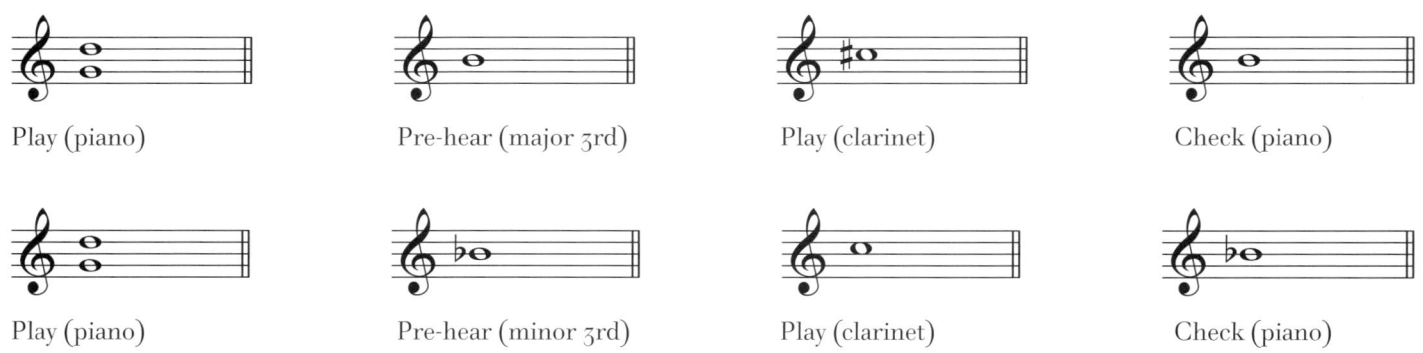

- Repeat this for other major and minor triads.

56. Acoustic pianos are best, but digital pianos will work too.

INTONATION AND PLAYING IN TUNE

Hearing 'beats'

You'll need to practise these exercises with a second player.[57]

- Choose a note in the *clarion* register and play it at **mf** maintaining as even a pitch as you can, for a few seconds. Stop playing and retain the note in your musical ear as accurately as possible. Now ask your fellow player to play the same note for a few seconds. Compare the intonation.
- Now play the note together. If the notes are of exactly the same pitch – in tune – you will hear a pure sound, as if there was just one player. If the notes differ in pitch you will hear a 'beat', a kind of audible and continuous *waa-waa-waa* pulse in the sound. This indicates that the frequency (and so the pitch) of the two notes are not the same. *One* player only must try to get in tune with the other. If you both try to make adjustments the exercise becomes counter-productive!
- The faster the 'beat' the closer you are in tune; the slower, the more out of tune you are. Using the various methods described above, adjust your note until the beat disappears. Your notes should now be perfectly in tune.
- Play a scale together agreeing on a matched dynamic level. Pause on each note until it is in tune. When you are happy indicate the next note with a small movement of the instrument (as though starting a piece). One player only should make the adjustments.

More exercises and studies

With a second player, work through scales in the following way, always listening to the intonation with great care. The second player must attempt to match the pitch of the first player and thus be the one to make any necessary adjustments. Decide on the dynamic level before you start and maintain it throughout each scale.

---

57. If a second player is unavailable, some of these exercises can be played with an electronic tuner or various *drones for tuning* websites online.

THE CLARINET

EXERCISES

In the following study, listen carefully to make sure that each octave is perfectly in tune. You may want to prepare using the GNG.

STUDY 1: OCTAVES

EXAMPLE FROM THE CLARINET REPERTOIRE

Here's a section towards the beginning of Rossini's Overture to *La Cenerentola* (Cinderella) to practise octaves with a fellow player. The lower voice needs to be a fraction stronger compared to the upper to aid a pure and clean interval. Listen very carefully to the purity of the octaves.

Rossini, Overture to *La Cenerentola*, Clarinets I and II, bars 13–20

INTONATION AND PLAYING IN TUNE

In this next study, listen to each perfect fifth for accuracy of intonation. If you have developed the ability to hear overtones (the upper harmonics) in a note, you should be able to hear the second note of each pair (an octave higher) as the harmonic of the first! This will work best for lower notes and only in the ascending fifths.

STUDY 2: FIFTHS

Articulation

Starting a note: release

Ending notes

Tongue pressure

Staccato

Tongue and finger independence

Articulation in the *altissimo* register

No-tongue (breath) articulation

Developing continuous articulation

Articulation across the registers

Developing faster tonguing

Combining slurred and articulated notes

A psychological factor

Double-, triple- and flutter-tonguing

Articulation syllables

Forms of articulation

Forms of accentuation

THE CLARINET

Articulation is all about how we begin, end and separate notes.[58]

This chapter will deal with: starting and ending notes, controlling the duration of a note, the weight and character given to a note at its initiation and developing speed and fluency in passages of continuous short notes.

The term *tonguing* is often used to describe the process of articulation. It's not a particularly helpful term as, although the tongue is certainly a central part of the process, to call it 'tonguing' gives the tongue too much prominence in the mind of the player. Let's deviate for a moment …

What are the three fundamental requirements in the act of slicing a cucumber?

- A cucumber
- Holding the cucumber steady
- An implement with which to slice it

Of the three, which is the most important? Clearly it's the cucumber. You can't slice a cucumber if you don't have a cucumber! The analogy with articulation is a good one.

- The cucumber is the air column which is the sound.
- Holding the cucumber steady is the embouchure.
- The implement that slices the cucumber (or here, the air column) into slices (notes) is the tongue.

Of the three, which is the most important? It's the air column: the sound. Without the sound there would be nothing to articulate. The embouchure and tongue are essential, but secondary to the air.

Previously we have described clarinet sound as the result of energising and moving air. We now need to look at how to start and stop that sound with precision.

EXERCISES

Starting a note: release

Think of the process of starting a note as *allowing* the note to sound – releasing it – rather than doing something to make it sound.

Try the following series of exercises to practise controlling the start of a note. In all articulation it is essential that the air is not stopped at the epiglottis (throat).

1. Without the clarinet, whisper the word 'tee' a number of times.[59] Hold the sides of your tongue against your upper back teeth to encourage independent use of the front of the tongue. Sense the action of the tongue against the alveolar ridge, that is that part of your mouth just above and behind the top teeth.

2. Now sense the part of your tongue you are using. It will be in the region of the tip and the blade. Try experimenting saying the word 'tee' using first the tip, and then towards the blade. Find your natural position. Be aware that it's just the front of your tongue that is involved in this action (the back of your tongue is independent, so you may wish still to hold it against the upper back teeth). There should be no movement of the jaw.

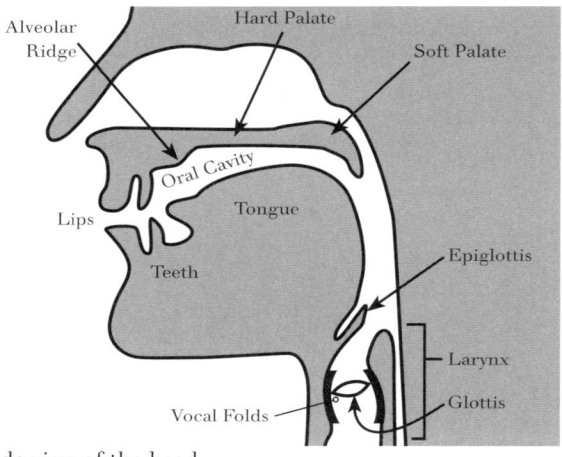

Side view of the head

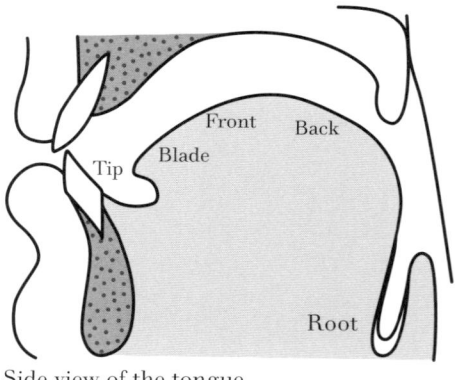

Side view of the tongue

---

58. The word 'articulation' derives from the Latin *articulus* meaning to utter distinctly, and from *articulare*, meaning to separate into joints, which both derive from *artus* meaning a joint.
59. Some players may prefer 'dee' or the slightly softer 'thee'. Remember this is not 'voiced'. Using 'tee', 'dee' or 'thee' is just to create a tongue shape and a small movement.

ARTICULATION

EXERCISES

3. Now prepare to whisper 'tee' against the alveolar ridge; with your tongue in position, energise and feel the air column ready to be released by activating the abdominal muscles. Be sure not to close the throat – the air must be held behind the tongue. Hold this position for a moment or two, sensing the air ready to release the word. Now release the word gently, concentrating more on the vowel (the 'ee') than the consonant (the 't').

4. Whisper the word again, but this time instead of allowing the sound to finish, continue hissing the 'ee' sound for a few seconds and then replace your tongue on the alveolar ridge to stop the sound. Keep blowing gently, though allow no air to escape. Feel the air column still under gentle pressure behind your tongue.

5. Repeat step four a number of times in this continuous way:

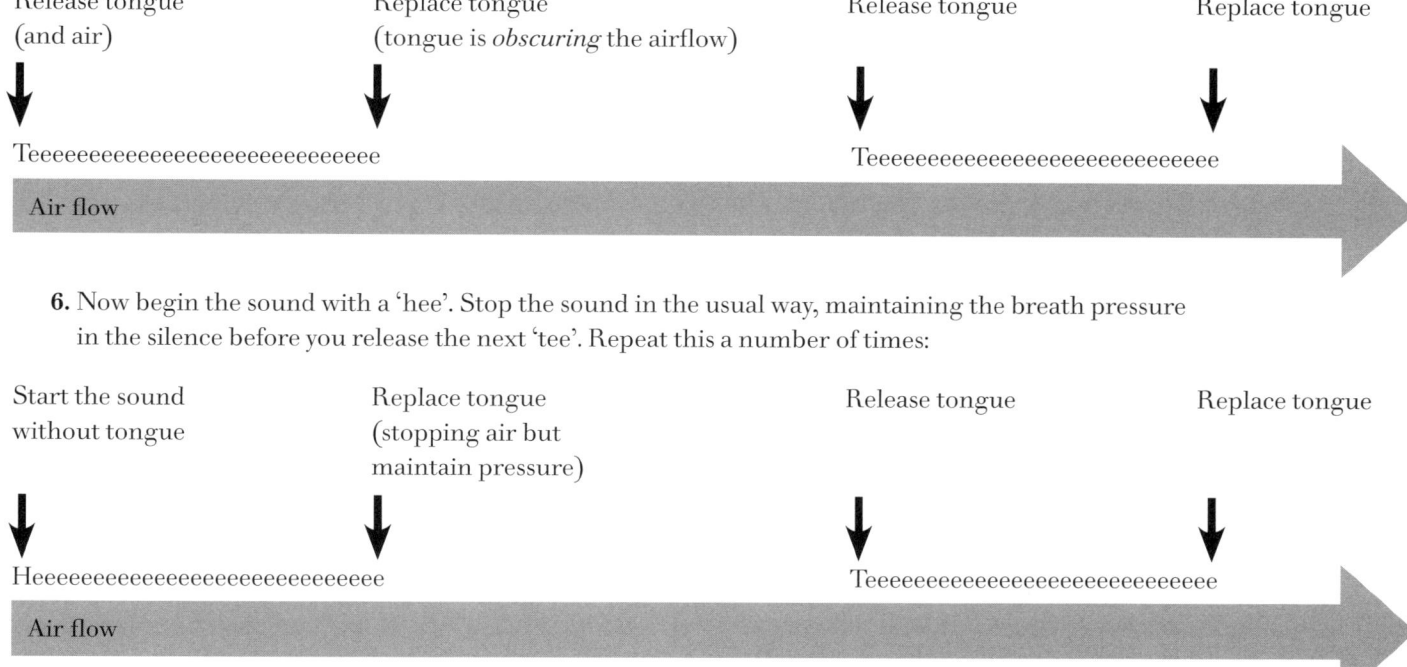

6. Now begin the sound with a 'hee'. Stop the sound in the usual way, maintaining the breath pressure in the silence before you release the next 'tee'. Repeat this a number of times:

What you have just done is very much the essence of starting and stopping a note – the basis of articulation.

7. Alternate articulating loud and soft 'tee's. Make sure each 'tee' is of the same length. Constantly feel the connection with the breathing muscles (the soft tee's will require more restraining – support – of the air column). Make sure the throat is not involved in any way and the tongue pressure on the alveolar ridge is the same for the loud and soft 'tee's.

Now, with the clarinet:

1. Form a good embouchure (see pages 41–43) and then start a long note with the air (not the tongue). E^2 is a good note for this exercise. Listen to the full and vibrant sound. Your tongue will be hovering in a position just below the reed. Now, thinking of the 'tee' position, put the tip of the tongue on the reed close to the reed tip. The reed is now taking the place of the alveolar ridge. There is no absolute rule concerning the part of the tongue to be used, however it will probably be the same part you used when saying 'tee'. There is also no precise point that you aim for on the reed. It's somewhere just away from the tip. Just try to be consistent.[60] By putting the tongue on the reed, the note will stop. Keep the tongue energised but feel no tension or stiffness. Keep the support active and the air energised, but again without any tightness. Make sure the throat is kept naturally open. Sense a feeling of 'everything is ready to begin the next note'.

---

60. Here's an exercise to promote consistency of tongue placement on the reed. Holding the clarinet with your right hand, place the first finger of the left hand firmly on the philtrum between the philtrum ridges (see diagram on page 41) and press towards the gum. Now tongue some G^2s using this as a point to aim for.

THE CLARINET

EXERCISES

2. Now release the note again. Simply move the front of the tongue downwards and slightly away from the reed thus allowing the air to move and the note to start. Avoid pushing the tongue and reed upwards before the release (i.e. towards the mouthpiece facing). It's the *same* note – a continuation of the previous note. Keep interrupting this long note, for that's really what articulation is.
3. Now you're going to begin a note with the tongue. Take a breath and at the same time as energising the support muscles and forming a good embouchure, place your tongue on the reed. You're back in that 'everything is ready to begin the next note' position. Feel that position for a few moments, then release the tongue (which will release the energised air) and you should have a perfectly articulated note.
4. Play a series of articulated notes in one breath. Start the first note by releasing the air with the tongue. Then return the tongue to the reed to interrupt the airflow, stopping the note. Maintain the air pressure between this and the start of the next note. Keep stopping and starting as many notes as you can in one breath. Keep the tongue relaxed when it is on the reed between notes. It should never be stiff or tight. Compare to the amount of tension in the tongue when you were saying 'tee'. Keep your jaw relaxed too – no biting.

The actual length of the note and the duration of the rest between notes is simply determined by when you decide to replace the tongue back on the reed. If you want a *staccato* (short) note then the tongue returns to the reed virtually as soon as it has released the note. Keep it on the reed for as long as you want the rest to be.

Clean, precise articulation is simply the result of coordinating the control of breath, embouchure and tongue.

An important thought: Don't think of an articulated note as blowing a note through the clarinet, but rather that the air, both inside the player and the clarinet, and the air around them is *energised* for the duration of that note. **An articulated note is simply energised air.**

Ending notes

So far we have been stopping the note with the tongue. Notes can also end as a result of stopping the air, which produces a slightly different sound. Notes ended with the tongue are inevitably more abrupt whereas those ended with the breath will have a certain decay, giving then them a more rounded end. It is obviously the player who will make the decision of how to stop the sound, with context and style influencing that decision. A passage requiring a sequence of accented and powerful articulated notes (like those heard in Copland's Clarinet Concerto, for example bars 150–160) would be best delivered with notes stopped with the tongue in contrast to, for example, the last note of the first phrase in the Mozart Clarinet Concerto, where the note is usually ended with the breath.

Tongue pressure

This is the amount of energy (pressure) exerted by the tongue on the reed to cause the reed to stop and start a note. The appropriate pressure is simply that which is required to stop the vibration in a particular situation.
Try this experiment:

- Play E^1, beginning the note with an air articulation, then slowly move the tongue to the reed, finally lightly touching the reed. What happens?

You should find that the note keeps sounding. To actually stop the note you'll have to press the tongue on to the reed with more pressure.

- Now play B^2 and do the same. What happens? This time the note will probably stop as soon as the tongue makes contact with the reed.

The higher you get (as the reed vibrates faster) the less pressure it takes to stop sounding a note (or stop the reed from vibrating).

ARTICULATION

As you play the notes in the next series of exercises, compare how much tongue pressure it takes to stop the reed vibrating. You'll need more in the first exercise and less as you ascend. Then try other notes in each register. As you progress higher you'll hear and feel the air is still moving between notes. This will aid ultimately in producing light and quick articulation. Play each exercise in one breath, and aim to sustain the quality through each note, taking particular care that the end of each note is vibrant and free. Always sustain an energetic and continuous airflow and try the exercises at varying dynamics beginning with ***p***. Keep the embouchure very stable and avoid any biting or squeezing.

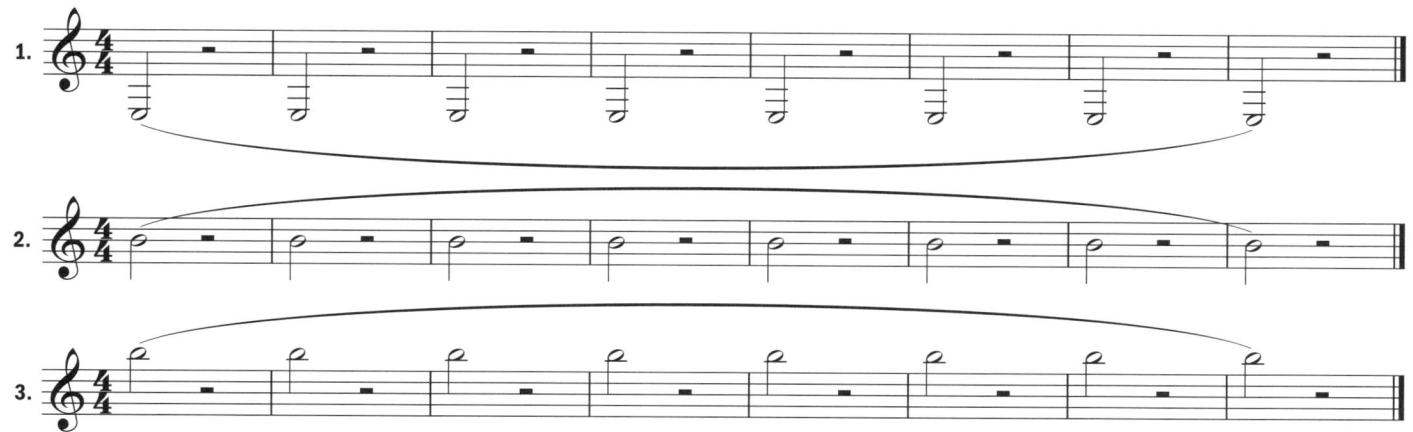

It is important to practise beginning a note accurately and at a precise moment; this will ensure clear production and accurate rhythmic placing. When articulating a note:

- Get into the habit of forming your embouchure before and not actually at the moment of articulation.
- Make sure that the embouchure is firm but never tight or tense.
- Maintain consistent embouchure pressure for the duration of each exercise.
- Remember that the aperture between the reed and the mouthpiece tip is very small; any excess tension between the lips will make this aperture too small to allow a note to sound effectively.
- Count carefully. This will help you to coordinate your reactions at the precise moment the note begins (think of the starting pistol at the beginning of a race).
- Tongue movement should be relaxed, well-directed and economical.

Play this exercise with the repeat, in one breath. Think of it as one continuous note that is being interrupted.

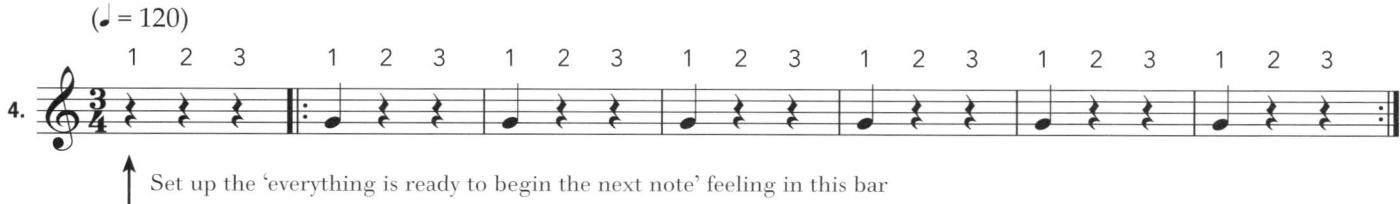

↑ Set up the 'everything is ready to begin the next note' feeling in this bar

Play the next set of exercises throughout the entire range of the instrument. Avoid any accentuation at the start or end of each note and aim for an even tone throughout. Work at precise rhythmic placing and accurate note lengths. Practise these exercises by stopping notes both with the tongue and with the breath and notice the difference in the character. For both methods take particular care over the quality of tone at the end of the note.

THE CLARINET

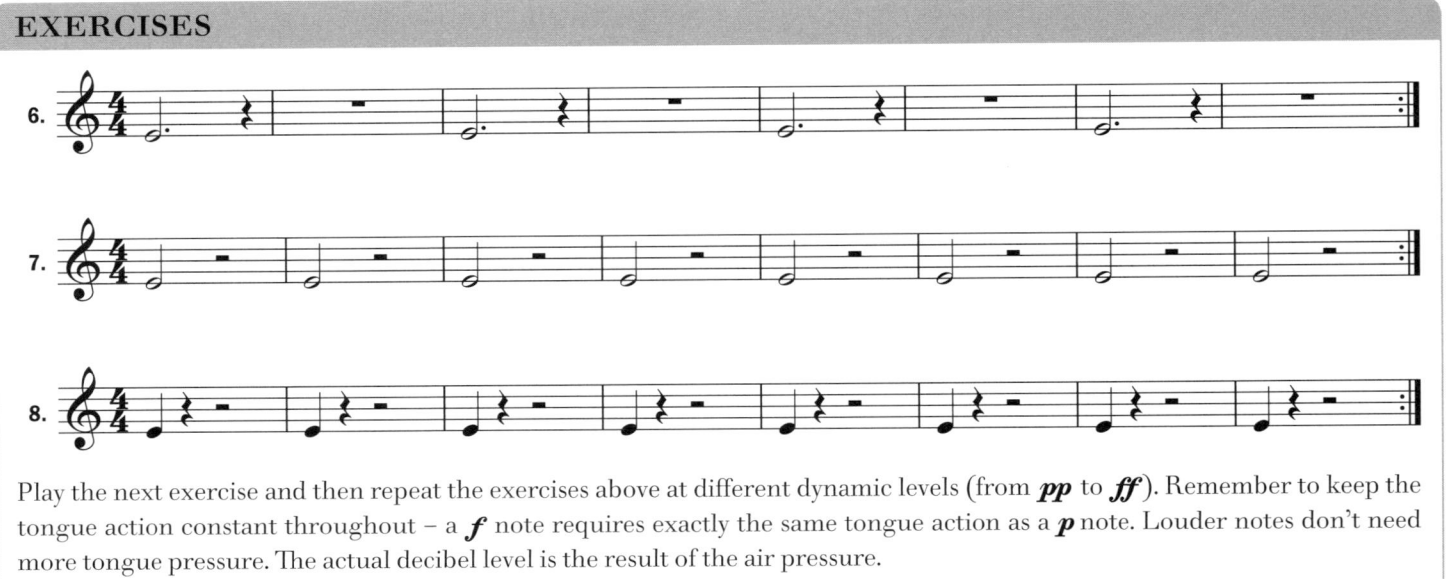

EXERCISES

Play the next exercise and then repeat the exercises above at different dynamic levels (from **pp** to **ff**). Remember to keep the tongue action constant throughout – a *f* note requires exactly the same tongue action as a *p* note. Louder notes don't need more tongue pressure. The actual decibel level is the result of the air pressure.

Staccato

The technique required for *staccato* is no different. The length of each note is determined by the tongue action. If the tongue is on the reed there will be silence, when the tongue is off the reed the note will sound. In these exercises start and stop the notes with the tongue. Keep the tongue on the reed between notes and maintain firm breath pressure without any tension or force. Tongue movement must always remain relaxed, well directed and economical.

When playing *staccato*, again try to be really consistent in your tongue action – both in the amount of tongue energy used and exactly where it strikes the reed.

EXERCISE

Try this exercise: sitting down, prepare to play G^2 and rest the clarinet on your knees. Cover your ears with your hands. Now play exercise 1 above again (this time, playing G^2). What you hear will help you concentrate on tongue action, energy and placement on the reed. Aim for real consistency on each of these points.

Tongue and finger independence

An important technique in *staccato* playing is to move your fingers independently from your tongue.

EXERCISES

Play the following scale, consciously and precisely preparing (fingering) the next note in the rest.
Come back to this exercise regularly, gradually increasing the tempo.

In the next study, each crotchet (quarter note) must be accurate in duration; end each note precisely at the beginning of the second beat. Maintain an even dynamic level throughout. Move fingers (i.e. prepare the next note) in the rests. Practise ending notes both with the tongue and with the breath. Listen carefully to the sound.

STUDY

Vary the study with the following note values. Again, explore ending the note with the tongue and then with the breath. What are the differences in colour, character and energy?

Articulation in the *altissimo* register

Success when articulating notes in the *altissimo* register is generally dependent on four considerations (assuming you have an appropriate, well-balanced and responsive mouthpiece and reed):

- The avoidance of biting with the jaw or tensing the embouchure;
- Maintaining a fast air flow;
- Maintaining a neutral and relaxed throat;
- Using appropriate tongue pressure: less pressure is required to stop higher notes due to the faster vibration of the reed.

As we move into the higher notes there is a natural tendency to tense the embouchure. This has the effect of reducing both the aperture and the reed's ability to vibrate freely. If notes will sound at all, they will probably be thin, lacking in resonance and out of tune. Instead, keep the embouchure firm but relaxed. Make sure the airflow is fast. Good quality support is needed to keep the tone refined – too great a volume of air will result in a harsh sound. Use a 'hheee' shape to keep the tongue high in the mouth.

It is also important to consider the amount of mouthpiece in the mouth. Either too much or too little will impede the success of these notes.

EXERCISES

Play the exercise below, starting the notes alternately with the air and the tongue. Notice how notes started with the air will speak easily. Aim to find the same ease of production with the tongue-articulated notes:

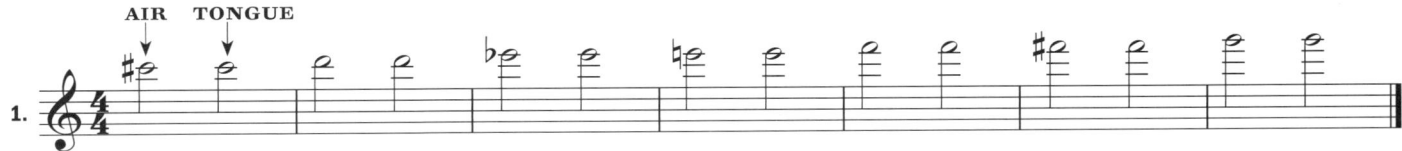

Continue in the same way up to C^4 and beyond if you wish.

Consider the points above when playing the next exercises. Play each in a single breath, as a single continuous musical thought. Go as high as you wish. Remember that the embouchure plays no part in stopping and starting the notes.

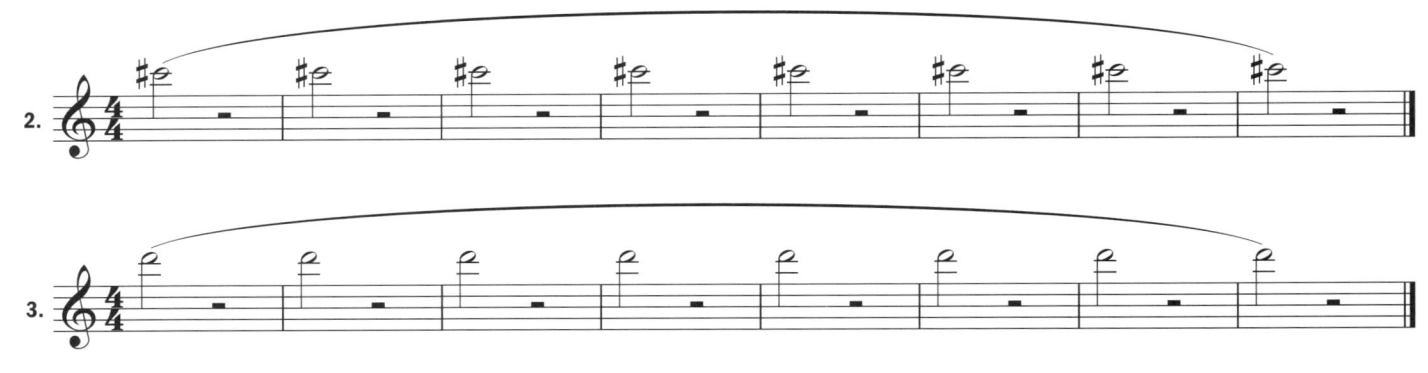

No-tongue (breath) articulation

Breath articulation is the starting of a note with the breath, without the use of the tongue, and is a very useful technique. Successful breath articulation is the result of being able to move the airflow at the appropriate speed from its inception. Take care not to hold the air at the throat. Feel the connection between the breath and the embouchure.

- For an imperceptible start to a note, begin it by gradually increasing the breath pressure.
- For a conventional start (such as you'll find at the opening of Weber's Concertino or Brahms' Sonata Op. 120, No. 2) find the balance between airflow and embouchure at the desired dynamic level.
- For a forceful attack, start the note with a sudden push from the abdominal muscles.

The great German player, Karl Leister (among others), often recommends using a no-tongue articulation to start slurred phrases or passages that don't require repeated notes or rapid continuous articulation.[61] Of course, it's up to you whether you employ the tongue or not, and each decision must be made based on the context.

EXERCISES

Developing continuous articulation

The next series of exercises will help you develop the technique of continuous articulation. In playing them, feel that each note is released. Remember that starting an articulated note is not about *doing* something *to* the reed with the tongue, but using the tongue to *release* the reed and air column and thus create the note.

- Feel that the tip of your tongue travels in small upwards and downwards movements (not forwards and backwards).
- Feel the independence of the front of the tongue (doing the work) and the back.
- The movements should be rapid, relaxed and light.
- Take care to avoid accenting notes and keep the tone even throughout.

- Remember that when you are articulating continuously, the length of a note is controlled by the return of the tongue to the reed.
- Ensure no biting or squeezing of the embouchure.
- Always maintain a steady supply of airflow, as though you are playing a long note. This is the basis of effective continuous articulation.

Begin in the *chalumeau* register and play each of the next set of three exercises in one breath (breathe in the rest if you need to) and at different dynamic levels. Aim to maintain the quality of tone throughout, imagining with each exercise that you are continuously interrupting a single long note. The gap between notes should be hardly noticeable.[62] Sufficient tongue pressure will be needed to stop the low notes in this register. Explore all other notes up to Bb^2.

Tongue pressure will be lighter in the *clarion* register. Explore all notes up to C^3.

---

61. For example, there are a great many opportunities for no-tongue articulation in the first movement of Brahms' Sonata Op. 120, No. 2.
62. This is often termed *legato tonguing*.

THE CLARINET

EXERCISES

In the *altissimo* register, maintain fast air speed throughout. Take special care not to bite or squeeze with the embouchure and keep the throat neutral and relaxed with the tongue pressure light. Extend to higher notes as you wish.

Play the following exercises using notes across all registers. Watch yourself playing in a mirror. If all is well controlled you shouldn't see any movement in the jaw, the chin or the throat and neck area. Vary the dynamic levels and tempo, gradually increasing the speed by very small increments over time.

Here's an exercise to contrast *legato* tonguing with *staccato*. Repeat the exercises above, playing bars 2 and 4, then bars 1 and 3 *staccato* as follows:

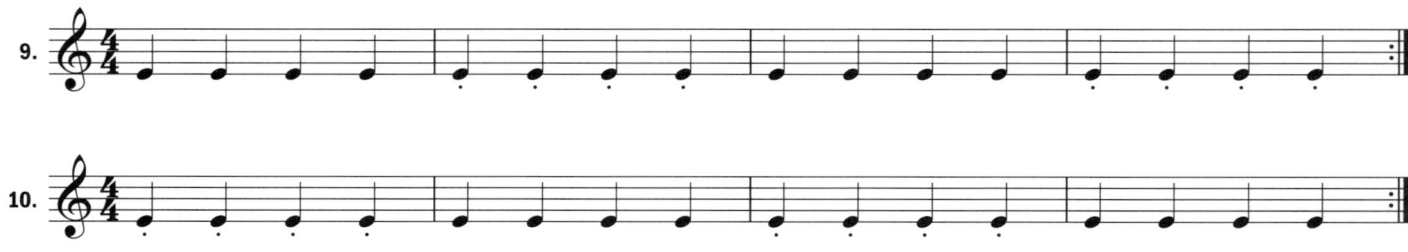

ARTICULATION

The next set of 24 single-bar exercises will further develop your continuous articulation technique. Practise them regularly and repeat each one a number of times. To derive full benefit from them, you should practise over a fairly broad band of tempi (from ♩ = 90 to about ♩ = 160) and over the full range of the instrument.

There are a number of ways to play these exercises:

- *Legato tonguing*: where the tongue release is synchronised with the start of each note. The sound will be virtually continuous.
- *Staccato*: where each note is clearly stopped and the duration is about half the written length.
- *An articulation between the two*: this is sometimes called *non-staccato*, which is like a longer *staccato*, giving a clear definition to the rhythm.

Remember that you're stopping each note and then releasing the next – have this in your mind as you're playing. The use of a metronome is recommended.

Can you recognise any of the above from famous symphonies or film scores?

THE CLARINET

EXERCISES

Articulation across the registers

This section will develop the ability to articulate across the registers with control, ease and speed.

Set 1: The first break[63]

Keep the tongue action light, don't bite or squeeze with the embouchure and maintain air pressure. Listen carefully to the start of the Bs. There should be no delay at the beginning of the note. If there is, consider airflow and embouchure pressure. You may feel a change of resistance when moving to B; make sure you don't react with any tension in the embouchure. Ensure air speed is sufficiently fast for both notes.

Similarly, listen and be aware of the 'feel' of the response in the next two exercises.

Aim for an even and consistent start to all notes in the following exercises.

EXAMPLE FROM THE CLARINET REPERTOIRE

Mendelssohn, *Scherzo* from 'A Midsummer Night's Dream'

---

63. Make sure your instrument is in good working order. Any pads that are not covering properly will limit the success of these exercises.

Set 2: The second break

Keep the tongue action light, don't bite or squeeze with the embouchure and maintain a fast air speed. Feel the airflow in the rests – remember that the tongue doesn't need to push the reed right onto the mouthpiece facing to stop the notes. Listen for undertones in the notes. Often they are the result of insufficient air speed or biting with the embouchure.[64]

Aim for an even and consistent start to all notes in the next exercises.

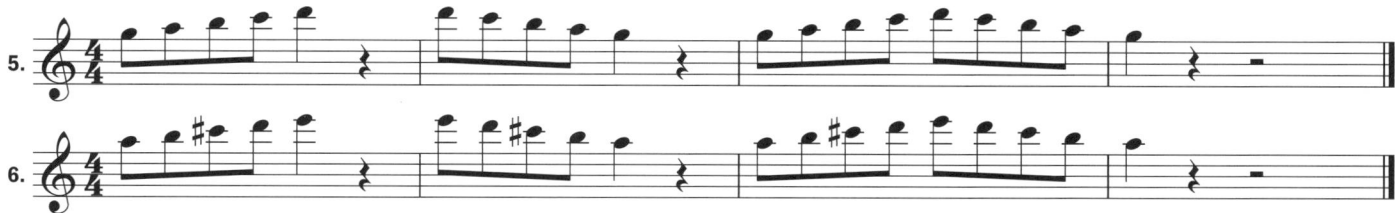

The next set of exercises further explore articulation in the *altissimo* register. Aim to play each in one breath. Maintain embouchure control, taking care not to bite or squeeze. You'll hear and feel some air movement during the rests. Keep the throat neutral and relaxed. Also consider tongue pressure; very little is needed to stop notes in this register.

64. They may also be caused by a reed that is too soft (or at least a reed that doesn't set up the optimum resistance with the mouthpiece).

THE CLARINET

EXERCISES

Set 3: Wider leaps

Think about all the considerations given (tongue pressure, airflow and embouchure) in playing the following exercises. Begin at a slow tempo and gradually speed up over a period of weeks and months. The higher you play, the more responsive and sensitive notes become to tongue pressure, but as you begin to negotiate faster tempi you will have to find a compromise as the restricted time between notes may not be sufficient to make any significant adjustment.

Now continue using all notes chromatically up to F^2/C^3 (see the next exercise below). As you ascend make sure the lower note is played with sufficient air speed to prepare for the upper note to sound easily. In descending, take care over the embouchure – any bite on the upper notes will impede the production of the lower notes.

Crossing the second break will require fast air. As usual, don't bite or squeeze the embouchure.

Continue with all notes chromatically up to:

The next set of exercises take you across all three registers. Avoid any tension in the embouchure.

Extend this series further if you wish (adding the side B♭ key for $F\sharp^4/G\flat^4$, for example).

ARTICULATION

Here are some exercises that span the entire compass. Find a good compromise of embouchure and, as always, never bite or squeeze. Repeat the following exercises using higher pitches as you wish.

At slower speeds you will be able to consciously think about tongue pressure. As you get faster just be instinctive in the two exercises that follow.

Repeat the following exercise going as high as you wish.

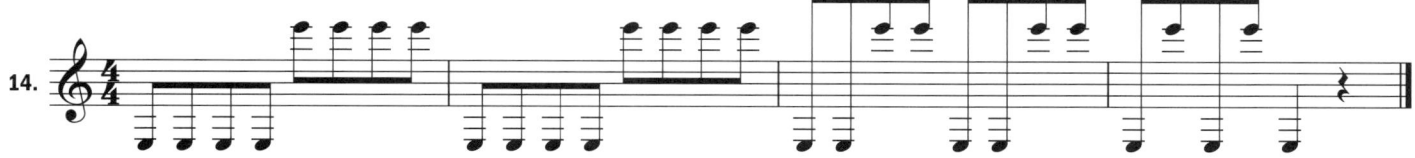

EXAMPLES FROM THE CLARINET REPERTOIRE

Here are two examples of articulation in wide leaps from Franz Tausch's Concerto in E Flat Major. If you have worked through the exercises above, they should cause no problems.

Tausch, Clarinet Concerto No. 3

THE CLARINET

EXERCISES

Tausch, Clarinet Concerto No. 3

Occasionally there may be instances where you might vary the articulation between tongue and breath in the two notes of a leap. In the following example from Mozart's Clarinet Concerto, try articulating the D^3 with the breath:

Mozart, Clarinet Concerto K. 622, II, bars 41–42

Play the next study to explore articulation in a more musical context. First play *non-staccato* and then *staccato*.

ARTICULATION STUDY

Developing faster tonguing

The tongue is a muscle that will strengthen with regular workouts. Aim to develop your tongue speed gradually; this is not just a matter of developing the muscle but also developing *tongue intelligence*. Think of this as learning to *control* the movement of the tongue. The brain needs to learn *how* it moves the tongue. Success in fast, precise tonguing is just as much the brain knowing how to do it as in the development of the muscle itself.

To begin, play the next exercise and develop more of your own in a similar style. Give the tongue *lots of rest* between each repeat as you start the process of increasing your tongue speed. At first, choose a fast but manageable speed and very gradually increase the tempo over a period of days and weeks. Use a metronome to keep track of your progress. As you're playing this exercise, be aware precisely of what you're doing and how you're doing it. Keep the tongue relaxed and remember that you're playing a phrase, not a lot of single notes. Listen intently to every nuance.

Here's another exercise to warm up and develop the tongue muscle. Start at a very comfortable tempo (again, note the metronome mark) and very gradually increase the speed over a period of weeks and months. Keep your tongue and jaw muscles relaxed. For best results practice *f*. Remember that it's the air pressure that produces the dynamic, not the tongue. Come back to this exercise regularly and choose a different note each time.

For the following exercise, play each rhythm on a single pitch continuing for as long as you can. Practise at a variety of tempi. As you become more proficient, don't neglect to practise at slower tempi; the tongue needs to be skilled at all speeds.

THE CLARINET

EXERCISES

Play scales and arpeggios using the patterns from exercise 3. For example:

Coordinating faster tonguing with finger movement

Play this exercise at a comfortable speed. Be aware of your finger movement – make it economical and relaxed. Gradually increase the speed and repeat on other notes and using other intervals.

Work at the next three exercises as a set, with very little break between them. Be aware of the slight increase in tongue pressure required when descending to the lower notes but make sure you don't change the position of the back of the tongue. Also, lighten the tongue pressure when ascending into the upper register to achieve the desired effect (see *Tongue pressure*, page 114).

Use this basic idea in all sorts of other ways when practising scales:

- Ascending and then descending
- In all other keys
- Across two and three octaves

ARTICULATION

Here is another exercise to develop scale patterns. Aim to keep the tongue action light, the fingers relaxed, and a fast air speed.

Repeat this exercise often. You may notice the first few bars can be played at increasingly fast tempi. So you can articulate quickly! Always keep your tongue, embouchure and mind relaxed and, in time, you will be able to play more and more bars at ever increasing speeds. Also, repeat the exercise in all keys, particularly those of pieces you are studying. Once you are comfortable with a tempo, increase the metronome mark by a small increment.

Here's a famous passage from the opening of the last movement of Beethoven's 4th symphony. Keep the tongue pressure light. Some players add slurs, but practise it without.

Beethoven Symphony No. 4, Op. 60, IV, bars 297–302

Combining slurred and articulated notes

Most clarinet music continually combines articulated and slurred notes. Moving from one to the other must be managed with natural and controlled precision so that the tone quality remains constant throughout any passage. As long as nothing changes in embouchure and breath control, this should present no difficulties. Often a change in tone quality is heard, with articulated notes sounding poorer than the slurred notes that might precede or succeed them. Work through these exercises and this problem should disappear.

Begin by playing G^2 as a long note. The next set of exercises are simply that same long note but with 'interruptions'. Play them slowly, and be aware when you first stop the note – the tongue is both ending that note and preparing to restart it. Embouchure, back of the tongue position and airflow should remain constant throughout each of the exercises (1–4).

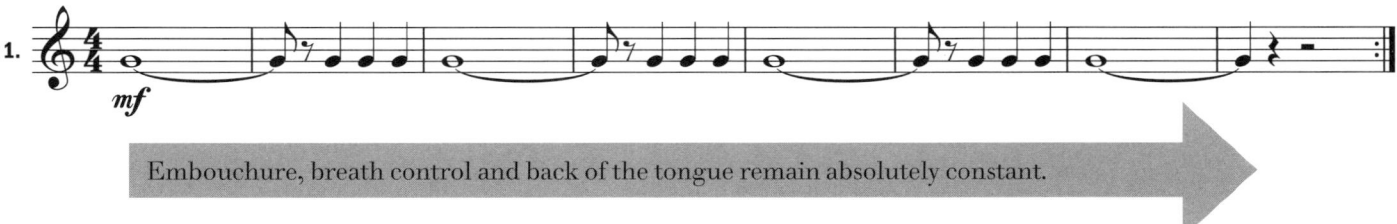

Embouchure, breath control and back of the tongue remain absolutely constant.

In this exercise, the tongue action ends the first note and begins the second without a break. Think of it as releasing the next note, rather than *tonguing* it.

THE CLARINET

EXERCISES

The same control is required here with the addition of some finger movement.

This next exercise requires exactly the same tongue control as exercises 2 and 3.

Repeat the four exercises above at a faster tempo.

You should now be ready to combine slurred and articulated notes with ease and perfect control. Take care not to exert any unnecessary jaw pressure (biting) in the next exercises. They are designed to ensure that the air is continuous throughout as you change from *legato* to articulated notes, and are eventually to be played without a break. Maintain a good airflow and light tongue action.

A psychological factor

Some players occasionally find it challenging to articulate a note after a sequence of slurred short notes. There is no difficulty here at all – it's simply like articulating longer adjacent notes. Each 'longer' note just happens to include a number of slurred notes before the next articulation.

Here is a way to develop this ability using a phrase from the opening of the Mozart Concerto.[65] In the first three exercises, ensure the articulated notes are placed very rhythmically. When these are accurate and easily controlled, go on to the final exercise to play the original passage.

Always think of, and prepare other similar passages in the same way if necessary.

---

65. Other editions may have different slurring, but it's the principle that we are concerned with here.

Double-, triple- and flutter-tonguing

Double- and triple-tonguing are techniques for the articulation of very fast duple and triple groupings. Many players today develop their single-tonguing such that these techniques are not necessary in the standard repertoire, but for some music it is certainly a useful technique. Ravel's *Introduction and Allegro*, and the solo towards the end of the fourth movement of Beethoven's 4th Symphony are often played with double-tonguing.

Double-tonguing

Double-tonguing consists of alternating a front (tip) of the tongue articulation with a back of the tongue articulation by forming the syllables 'tee-gee' or 'tee-kee'.[66] The 'tee' is articulated with the front of the tongue and the 'gee' or 'kee' with the back. It will probably depend to some extent on the shape of your hard palate as to the best second syllable; experiment to find what is best for you. Each will affect, to some degree, the airflow, articulation quality and intonation. 'Tee' is possibly the most helpful first syllable as it will keep your tongue high in the mouth, but also experiment with 'dee'. A firm embouchure and constant airflow are essential.

You will feel a change in pressure in the oral cavity when articulating 'kee' or 'gee', where the back of the tongue lifts and presses against the hard palate. Be sure to maintain firm breath support and minimise this change. This will require very precise control of the second syllable, both in its speed and positioning.

Begin practice with just the mouthpiece and a fairly soft reed. Coordinate the articulation with changing pitch as soon as possible. Sometimes reverse the syllable order and practise 'kee-tee' or 'gee-tee'. It will take time for your double-tonguing tone quality to get close to your single-tonguing tone quality, so be patient. Practise slowly to begin and when you feel there is virtually no distinction between the 'tee' and 'gee', then begin to speed up and move into the higher registers.

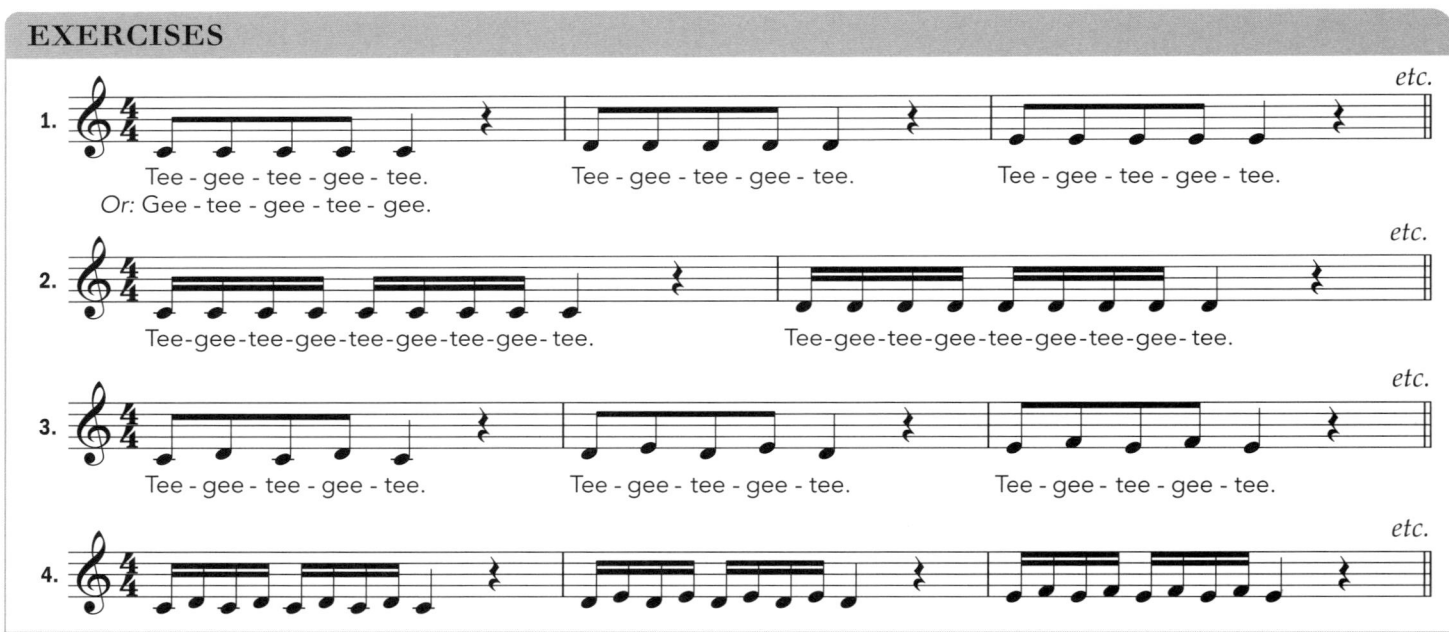

EXAMPLE FROM THE CLARINET REPERTOIRE

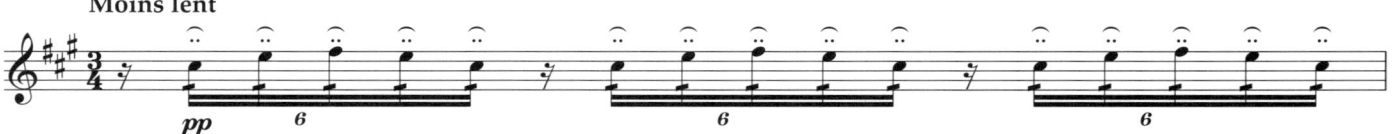

Ravel, Introduction and Allegro, bar 13

---

66. There are, of course, other possible syllables and you should experiment to find what suits you most effectively. Here are some alternatives: 'dee-gee', 'dee-kee', 'tu-ku', 'du-gu', 'nuh-guh'.

ARTICULATION

Triple-tonguing

When triple-tonguing, form the syllables 'tee-kee-tee' or 'tee-gee-tee'. The articulation at the back of the tongue, 'kee' or 'gee', requires considerable breath support.

The following exercises should be practised slowly at first. Use a metronome and build up the speed gradually.

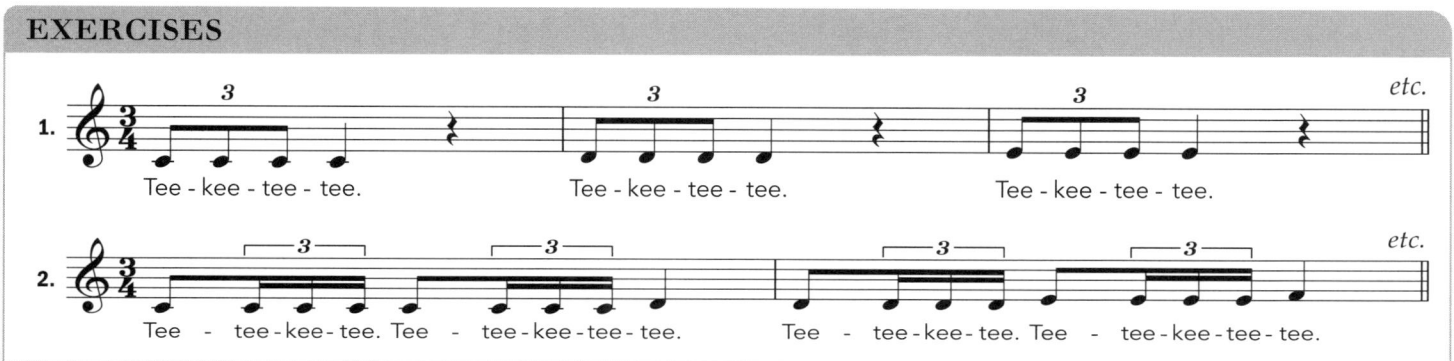

Flutter-tonguing

Most people can learn to flutter-tongue – it is not genetic!

In flutter-tonguing, the tongue itself needs to be very relaxed and must not touch the reed at any time. Think of it like a flag flapping in the wind! Produce a well-supported airflow and then try to roll your 'r's. A firm embouchure is essential.

For soft flutter-tonguing, place the tip of your tongue behind your upper teeth and, with firm breath support, roll your 'r's.

For a harder (more distorted) effect, hold the flattened part of your tongue firmly against the front of your palate; blow forcefully and your tongue will vibrate. Alternatively, start by forming the sound 'h', then follow it by a roll of the tongue. (This method, however, can cause a sore throat and should be avoided if possible.)

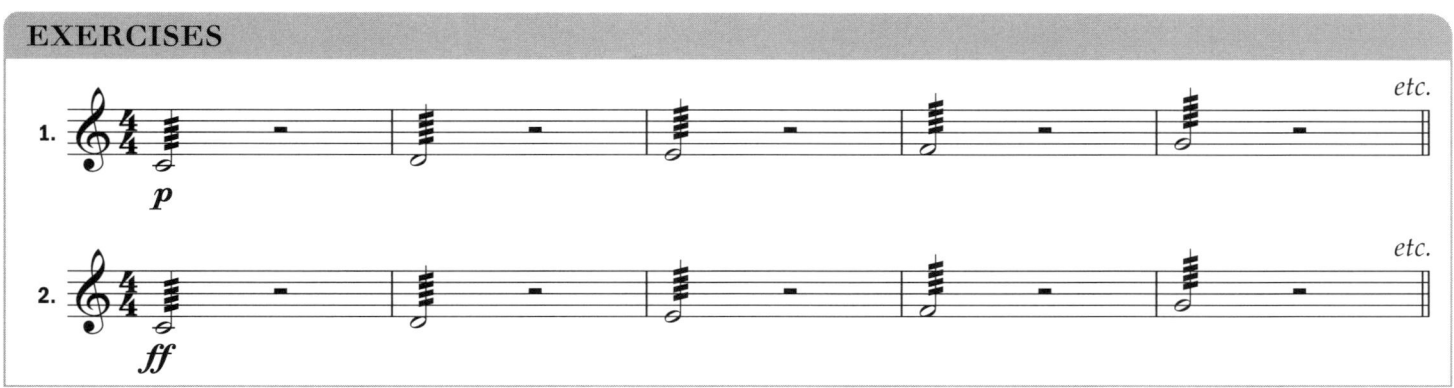

EXAMPLE FROM THE CLARINET REPERTOIRE

Berg, *Vier Stücke* Op. 5, III, bars 6–8

Flutter-tonguing could be used tastefully to add effect in some folk-inspired works such as *Dances from Korond* by László Draskóczy. See also bar two of Peter Maxwell Davies' *Hymnos*.

THE CLARINET

Anchor-tonguing

In anchor-tonguing the tip of the tongue is held lightly behind the lower teeth, and the tongue is then pushed forward. Technically it will be the blade of the tongue that will strike the reed. Some aspects of playing will be more difficult to develop, including speed and lightness of articulation, but all are possible.

If you are anchor-tonguing and have the sound and all the control you wish then there would be no reason to change. If you are frustrated in any of these areas, it will take some time to change but it is entirely possible to do so.

Articulation syllables

Articulation syllables combine articulation with voicing, such as 'ta', 'da', 'tu' and 'tee'. They are used by some players to help create the character and definition of an articulation or rhythm. Often just thinking these different syllables will help create the effect psychologically. They can bring phrases to life and give more expression.

The following examples will give you some ideas. They are just suggestions – it is most important that you experiment extensively.

Remember that once the tongue has left the reed the sound is controlled by the air and voicing. Varying articulation shapes may also help with tuning.

EXAMPLES FROM THE CLARINET REPERTOIRE

Mozart, Clarinet Concerto K. 622, I, bars 57–58

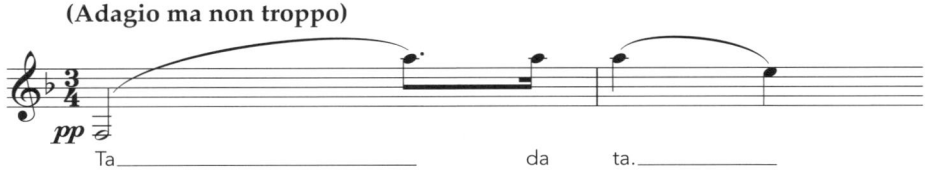

Weber, Concertino for Clarinet Op. 26, bars 16–17

Brahms, Sonata No. 2, Op. 120, III, bars 28–30

Forms of articulation

A range of symbols are used to indicate different forms of articulation and accentuation. To interpret them musically and effectively, it is helpful to have some knowledge of:

- The composer's style and intentions;
- The character of the music;
- The style of the period in which the piece was written;
- The specific instrument for which the piece was written.

The following comments and examples are intended as a guide to the interpretation of these symbols. It is not an exhaustive survey. Always remember that the meaning of a symbol is not always consistent from one period to another and from one composer to another.

Playing clarinet music from different periods
When playing early clarinet music, it is helpful to have some awareness of the differences between instruments of the period and those of today. These differences relate to fingering, tone production and quality, and range. Also, on early instruments the reed was usually placed on top of the mouthpiece rather than below, which had quite a significant influence on what was possible and will have produced a different sound from that of the modern clarinet. Because the modern instrument is more powerful, you may prefer to play early music with gentler articulation and a lighter tone. Composers up to and including Weber usually left all aspects of articulation to the taste and experience of the performer. Most of the markings found in modern publications of early music are those of editors or performers, so allow yourself some freedom in interpretation.

Forms of *staccato*

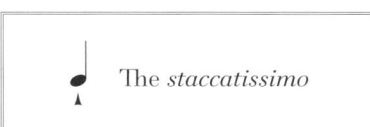

The *staccatissimo*

In early clarinet music, the wedge indicates that a note should be played with a small accent and slightly shorter than its full written value. Thomas Willman, in his clarinet method of 1848, suggested playing notes so marked with 'promptitude and vigour'.[67]

STACCATISSMO STUDY 1
In this study, interpret the *staccatissimo* in an 18th- or 19th-century manner.

67. Willman, T., *A Complete Instruction Book for the Clarinet*, 1848.

THE CLARINET

EXAMPLES FROM THE CLARINET REPERTOIRE

Lefèvre, Sonata No. 1, Op. 12, I, bars 12–13

Brahms, Clarinet Quintet Op. 115, I, bars 32–34

STACCATISSIMO STUDY 2

In 20th-century music, a wedge generally indicates that a note should have an accent and be considerably shortened. In this study, interpret the *staccatissimo* in a 20th- or 21st-century manner.

Caprice Español

ARTICULATION

EXAMPLES FROM THE CLARINET REPERTOIRE

Reger, Sonata Op. 107, II

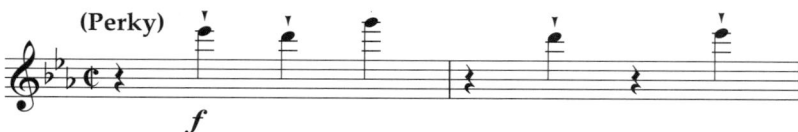

Copland, Clarinet Concerto, bars 155–156

The *staccato*

Notes marked with a dot should be played lightly and without accent. Their length depends on the tempo, character and style of the music. It is worth being aware that *staccato* notes tend to sound longer at loud dynamics than at soft ones, so when a *crescendo* or *diminuendo* occurs in a *staccato* passage, you may have to compensate by making your *staccato* gradually shorter as you grow louder and longer as you grow softer.

Be aware of any potential changes in oral cavity shape when playing descending *staccato* passages. If there is a tendency for its shape to assume a more 'aw' formation as notes descend, the throat will open and so more air will be required to sustain the tone. It is best to avoid this to help keep the lower notes in tune too. This passage, usually played *staccato*, from the first movement of the Mozart Concerto is a good example:

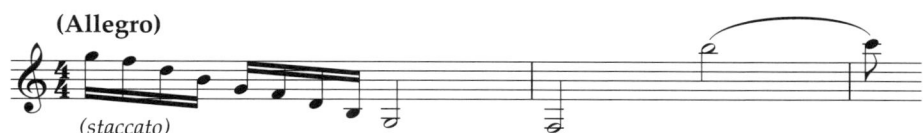

Mozart, Clarinet Concerto K. 622, I, bars 69–71

Aim to maintain the relative values of *staccato* notes. For example, in the second of the following studies, the *staccato* crotchets (quarter notes) must be proportionally longer than *staccato* quavers (eighth notes).

STACCATO STUDY 1

THE CLARINET

STACCATO STUDY 2

EXAMPLES FROM THE CLARINET REPERTOIRE

Mozart Clarinet Concerto K. 622, I, bars 57–58

Brahms, Sonata No. 1, Op. 120, IV, bars 184–185

Copland, Clarinet Concerto, bar 348

Weber, Clarinet Concerto No. 1, Op. 73, I, bars 134–137

ARTICULATION

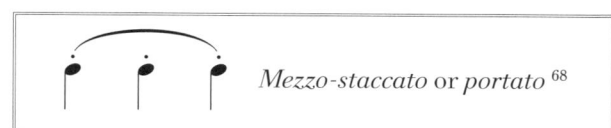
Mezzo-staccato or *portato* [68]

Mezzo-staccato notes should be gently articulated without interrupting the flow of the music (or the air stream) giving a smooth, pulsing effect. Your tongue should be in contact with the reed for the minimum period of time. The weight of tongue action is not different from other forms of articulation but there is some extra breath support behind each note. The result is that each note is given more expression and clarity compared with simply playing *legato*. Exploring different articulation syllables may be useful here.

MEZZO-STACCATO STUDY 1

MEZZO-STACCATO STUDY 2

---

68. From the Italian *portare* meaning 'to carry'.

THE CLARINET

EXAMPLES FROM THE CLARINET REPERTOIRE

Mozart, Clarinet Concerto K. 622, I, bars 70–72

Brahms, Clarinet Sonata No. 1, Op. 120, IV, bars 198–199

Finzi, Five Bagatelles Op. 23, Fughetta, bar 27

Beethoven, Symphony No. 6, Op. 68, Clarinet I, V

When playing *mezzo-staccato* in the *altissimo* register keep the tongue action light – just touching the reed will cause it to stop vibrating and the sound to stop briefly. Keep the air flowing continuously. Here's a famous example from the Debussy *Rhapsodie*:

Debussy, *Première Rhapsodie*, bar 26

ARTICULATION

This rather ambiguous symbol (the dot implies *staccato* – short and light, and the line implies *tenuto* – hold the note) is probably best interpreted as playing with gentle emphasis and very slight shortening of the note. Generally speaking, if composers use it, they probably just wish that note to be a bit special! Give notes so marked a little extra warmth and projection.

STUDY

EXAMPLES FROM THE CLARINET REPERTOIRE

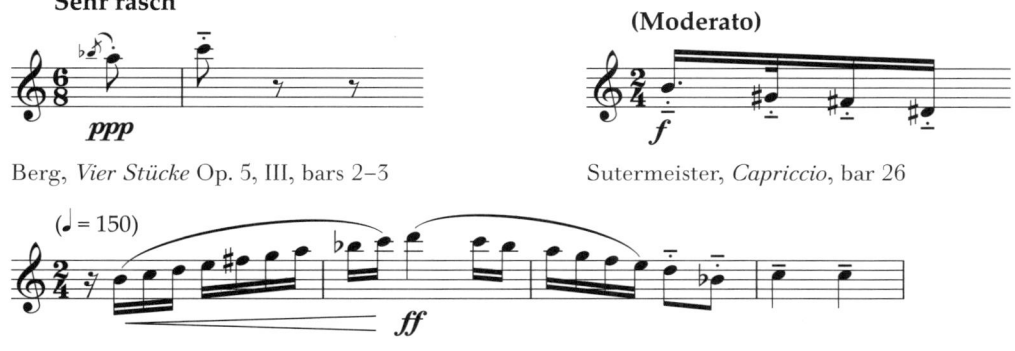

Berg, *Vier Stücke* Op. 5, III, bars 2–3

Sutermeister, *Capriccio*, bar 26

Bartók, Contrasts, III, bars 113–116

Examples may also be found in the first movement of Lutosławski's Dance Preludes (bar 62) and the renowned Clarinet Sonata by Archduke Rudolph of Austria (see page 143).

THE CLARINET

> Marking the final note in a phrase with a dot indicates a slightly abrupt and 'lifted' ending. Play this note for about half of its written value. Remember that for this to be effective, it is important to maintain the tonal level throughout the duration of the note.

STUDY 1

STUDY 2

ARTICULATION

EXAMPLES FROM THE CLARINET REPERTOIRE

Weber, Grand Duo Concertant Op. 48, III, bars 42–43

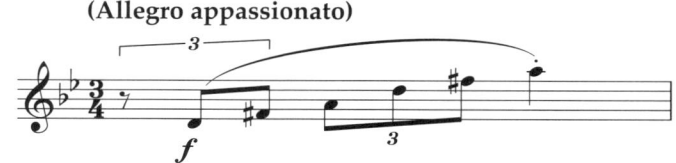

Brahms, Sonata No. 1, Op. 120, I, bar 29

Saint-Saëns, Clarinet Sonata Op. 167, II, bar 12

Arnold, Divertimento For Two Clarinets Op. 135, V, Clarinet I, bars 17–20

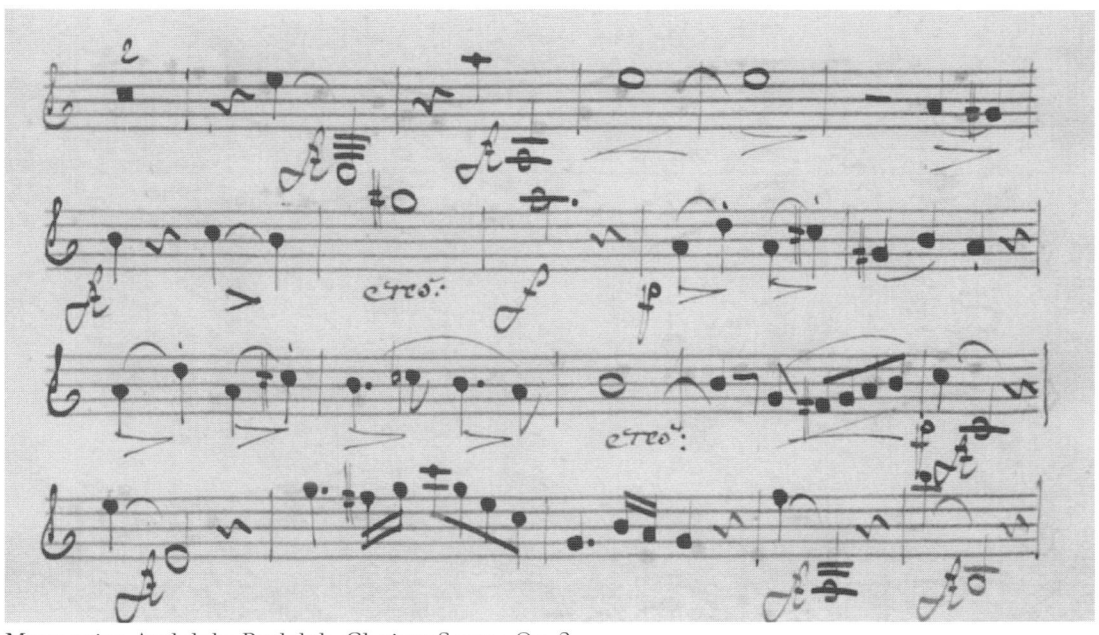

Manuscript: Archduke Rudolph, Clarinet Sonata Op. 2

THE CLARINET

MULTI-STACCATO STUDY
The following study contains examples of all the *staccato* symbols. Take care to differentiate clearly between each symbol.

ARTICULATION

Forms of accentuation

Accents are used to indicate moments of heightened and more intense expression, to clarify the metric structure of a phrase or to elicit more energy. It is important to have a good understanding of the style and character of the piece when interpreting these symbols.

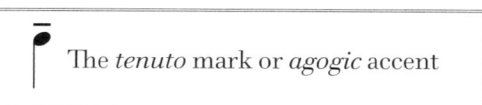

The *tenuto* mark or *agogic* accent

This notation has two elements. Notes marked with this symbol should have both a slight but maintained stress, and be held for their full written value but played with the smallest amount of separation. In the example below from Saint-Saëns, the marked note comes within a *legato* slur so the duration is non-negotiable; it simply requires a slight, maintained and expressive stress. In the example from Puccini, the notes so marked that occur under the slur would be played with particular intensity and any separation would be virtually negligible.

EXAMPLES FROM THE CLARINET REPERTOIRE

Hindemith, Sonata, I, bars 56–57

Finzi, Five Bagatelles Op. 23, Prelude, bars 8–9

Saint-Saëns, Clarinet Sonata Op. 167, I

Puccini, *Tosca*, Act III, bars 181–185

Elgar, 'Enigma' Variations, No. 10, Clarinet II, bars 2–5

THE CLARINET

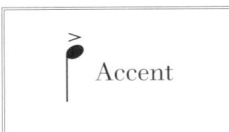

This mark (usually known simply as an accent) indicates that a note should begin with a degree of intensity greater than the prevailing dynamic level. Many German players interpret it as an *espressivo* sign meaning the note is given a more expressive emphasis rather than a harder or significantly louder sound. This is a particularly helpful interpretation if the accent falls within a slur.

EXAMPLES FROM THE CLARINET REPERTOIRE

Spohr, Clarinet Concerto No. 1, III, bars 100–101

Crusell, Concerto for Clarinet No. 2, Op. 5, III, bars 203–206

Elgar, 'Enigma' Variations, No. 4, Clarinets I and II, bars 15–20

Tchaikovsky, Symphony No. 6, Op. 74, III, Clarinet I, bars 202–213

On a note of longer duration, the interpretation is about when to return to the original marked dynamic level. In German music, it's considered appropriate to maintain the louder accented tone for quite a lengthy portion of its full duration. In the example from Weber, maybe half the note length maintains a stronger dynamic before tapering back to f. Ultimately, in each case, it is important to use one's musical instinct when finally deciding how to interpret these markings.

Tchaikovsky, Symphony No. 6, Op. 74, III, Clarinet I, bars 242–250

ARTICULATION

Weber, Grand Duo Concertant Op. 48, I, bars 13–14

Schumann, *Fantasiestücke* Op. 73, III, bars 33–34

Gade, *Vier Fantasiestücke* Op. 43, bars 47–49

Here's an interesting example from the second movement of Stanford's Sonata where there are accents at the start of slurs, within slurs, on individual notes and attached to notes of various lengths.

Stanford, Sonata No. 2, Caoine, bars 42–47

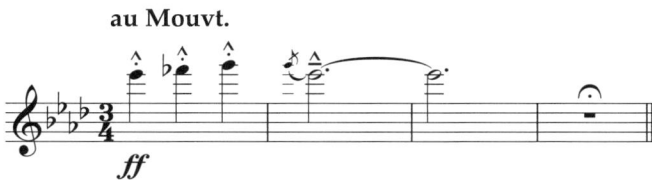

Marcato

This marking (which is less common than the accent) indicates a heavier and more intense accentuation.

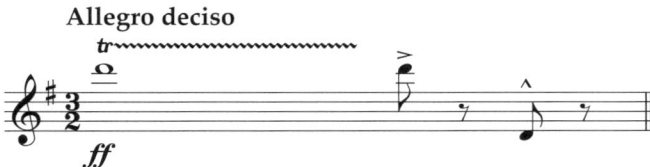

Debussy, *Première Rhapsodie*, bars 203–206

This excerpt from Finzi's Five Bagatelles uses both accents:

Finzi, Five Bagatelles Op. 23, Prelude, bar 96

THE CLARINET

These symbols indicate a sudden increase in volume. The degree of loudness depends on the dynamic level of other notes in the passage.

EXAMPLES FROM THE CLARINET REPERTOIRE

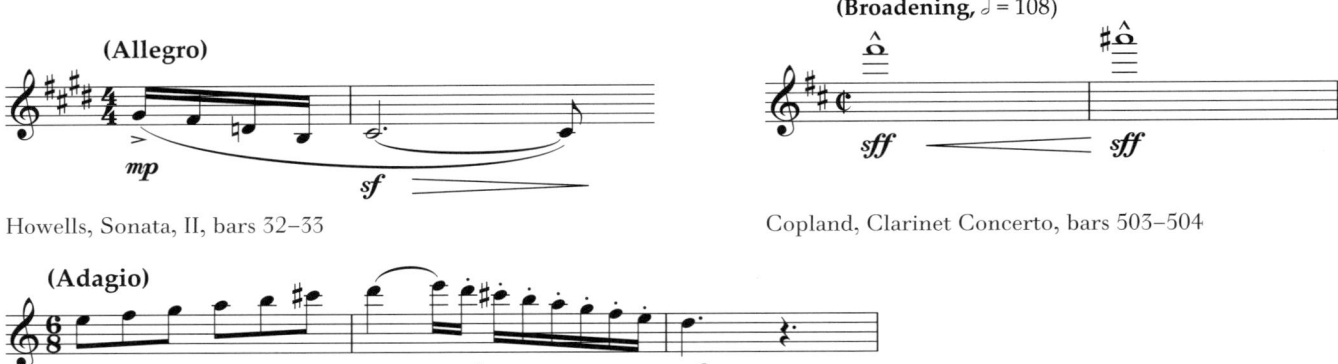

Howells, Sonata, II, bars 32–33

Copland, Clarinet Concerto, bars 503–504

Berlioz, *Symphonie Fantastique* Op. 14, III, Clarinet I, bars 127–129

The *fz* (*forzando* or *forced*) is less commonly found but requires the same interpretation as *sf* and *sff* markings.

(Allegro con brio)

Dvořák, Symphony No. 8, I, bars 76–80

ARTICULATION

> The **rf** symbol literally means 'reinforced' – allow the note to emerge from the texture expressively.

EXAMPLE FROM THE CLARINET REPERTOIRE

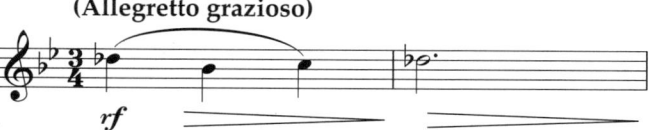

Brahms Sonata No. 1, Op. 120, III, bars 68–69

> The expression **fp** indicates a short but distinct **f** that changes quickly to **p**.
> Leopold Mozart calls this 'a forceful expression mark'.[69] The change to **p** may be
> played abruptly or as a rapid *diminuendo*, depending on context.

Try the following exercise in both ways:

EXAMPLES FROM THE CLARINET REPERTOIRE

(Zart und mit Ausdruck)

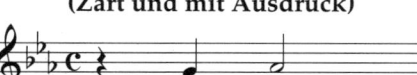

Schumann, *Fantasiestücke* Op. 73, I, bar 24

(Sostenuto ed espressivo)

Brahms, Sonata No. 1, Op. 120, I, bar 214

> Musical notation is not a science and cannot give an exact
> indication of composers' (or indeed editors') intentions. Therefore,
> your interpretation of these symbols will ultimately depend
> on your understanding of the style, character and expressive
> intensity of the notes or passages concerned, taking into account
> contemporary musical fashion, the evolution of notation, what you
> think the composer was probably intending, and the acoustic of
> the space in which you are playing.
>
> You might like to apply all the different forms of articulation and
> accentuation to scales and arpeggios (see pages 164–177) when you
> practise them.

---

69. Mozart, L., *A Treatise on the Fundamental Principles of Violin Playing*, 1756. Even though it was
written in 1756, it is full of fascinating thoughts that players (of all instruments) can learn much from.

Finger-work and dexterity

Finger movement

Correct location of fingers over tone holes and keys

Finger pressure

Fingerings are not all they seem

Finger strengthening

Developing control of keywork

Changing fingers on the same note

Tips for using scales and arpeggios to develop finger technique

Scale and arpeggio exercises

Developing fast playing

Developing finger independence and agility

Finger movement

All players ultimately desire fluent, fast, economical, precise and well-coordinated finger movement. This is very much part of the artistry of playing. The actual movement and velocity of the fingers contribute to the very sound you make.

But let's begin by looking at how fingers work. It may surprise you to learn that fingers do not contain muscles. Finger-moving muscles and tendons are actually located in your palms and forearms. You can see these moving if you hold your hand palm facing downwards: wiggle your fingers and watch for the movement under the skin at the back of your hand, wrist and forearm.

Before working at any aspect of finger technique, ensure fingers, wrists and forearms are warm. If they are cold, it suggests there is not enough blood circulating in these areas and they simply won't work efficiently.

What drives finger movement?

It's the brain – not muscles in the fingers (there are none!) – coupled with a very strong feel for rhythm and pulse. In developing finger movement always remember that fingers respond to messages sent from the brain, and these messages should always be rhythmic. The more rhythmic they are, the more precise your finger-work will become.

> *Always try to remember to feel an internal pulse when working at finger technique and connect each movement to a brain-generated rhythmic impulse.*

Use a metronome from time to time, and sense strongly the connection with the pulse that it is generating. Don't just have it on as background noise to which you pay only limited attention. Ultimately, you will develop a strong internal sense of pulse and sub-division that will drive your finger movement.

Back swing and mental preparation

Before tennis players hit the ball, they will normally swing their arm and racket back giving them the necessary control and energy to make their shot. We can also employ a back swing technique to get control of the fingers before their downward movement. This is about preparing the move just before you make it. If you have any awkward movements to make (or even simple ones) occasionally engage and energise the fingers *in your mind*, then swing them back a small amount before their downward movement onto the instrument.

This can also be done in reverse. Engage the fingers to be moved *upwards* very deliberately in your mind before you move them. The principle is, prior to making a movement: think about the particular movement – get mental control of the fingers first. This will connect the brain with the fingers for longer and is very effective in making practice more efficient. This is a particularly useful technique when employing *slow motion* practice (see page 193). When you can employ this kind of mental back swing, it will aid, ultimately, in even more precise and economical movement.

Speed of movement

Whether you are playing fast- or slow-moving music, your fingers should move from one position to the next efficiently but without *excessive* speed. Often players move their fingers too fast and too heavily which disrupts the air column and will adversely affect the flow of the sound. Observe the speed of your finger movement in front of a mirror occasionally.

Efficient speed of movement is the product of good all-round finger technique (position, direction and control), rhythmic clarity and musical understanding. Once all these are coordinated, mentally and physically, then your fingers should accommodate virtually anything you desire.

Coordinated movement

The technique of moving combinations of fingers will develop in time and practising all arpeggio shapes and scales in thirds, fourths etc. is highly recommended.[70] There is much profit in practising these patterns often and at a slow tempo. As you increase the tempo, be very rhythmical.

---

70. Carl Baermann's *Tägliche Studien* Op. 63 is an invaluable aid for this kind of technical work.

Correct location of fingers over tone holes and keys

- Hold your arms by your side and shake out any tensions, one at the time.
- Look at the hand's natural shape and you'll notice gently curved fingers. Now bring the hand to the instrument from the elbow, being careful to retain the same natural shape. Be careful that in maintaining this shape you don't inadvertently create tension. Don't *lock* them in this shape. Try to maintain this same hand shape when placing the fingers on the instrument.
- Finger F^1. Your fingers will be slightly curved, with the fingertip toward the upper half of your finger's top joint, covering the appropriate tone holes. Movement is made from the knuckle joint thus maintaining the natural curved shape of the fingers.
- Now slowly lift all your fingers simultaneously from the tone holes and keys to finger G^2. Your fingers should be held the smallest possible distance from the instrument to allow for adequate venting. Relax the fingers back on to their tone holes and pick them up again. Do this a few times and ensure no tension creeps in.

Of course, there are exceptions to every rule and those with smaller hands, some young players, or those who may have arthritis or have suffered some damage to the hands, may need to experiment with slight adjustments to this position to see what will work best. A neck strap or harness is always worth considering, especially for those who play a lot. It will take virtually all the pressure off the right-hand thumb and allow for a more effective hand position.

EXERCISES

Play the following exercises at approximately ♩ = 50. Move your fingers slowly and gently up from the tone hole or key and similarly downward again.[71] Keep them well placed above their appropriate tone holes for the duration. Repeat often.

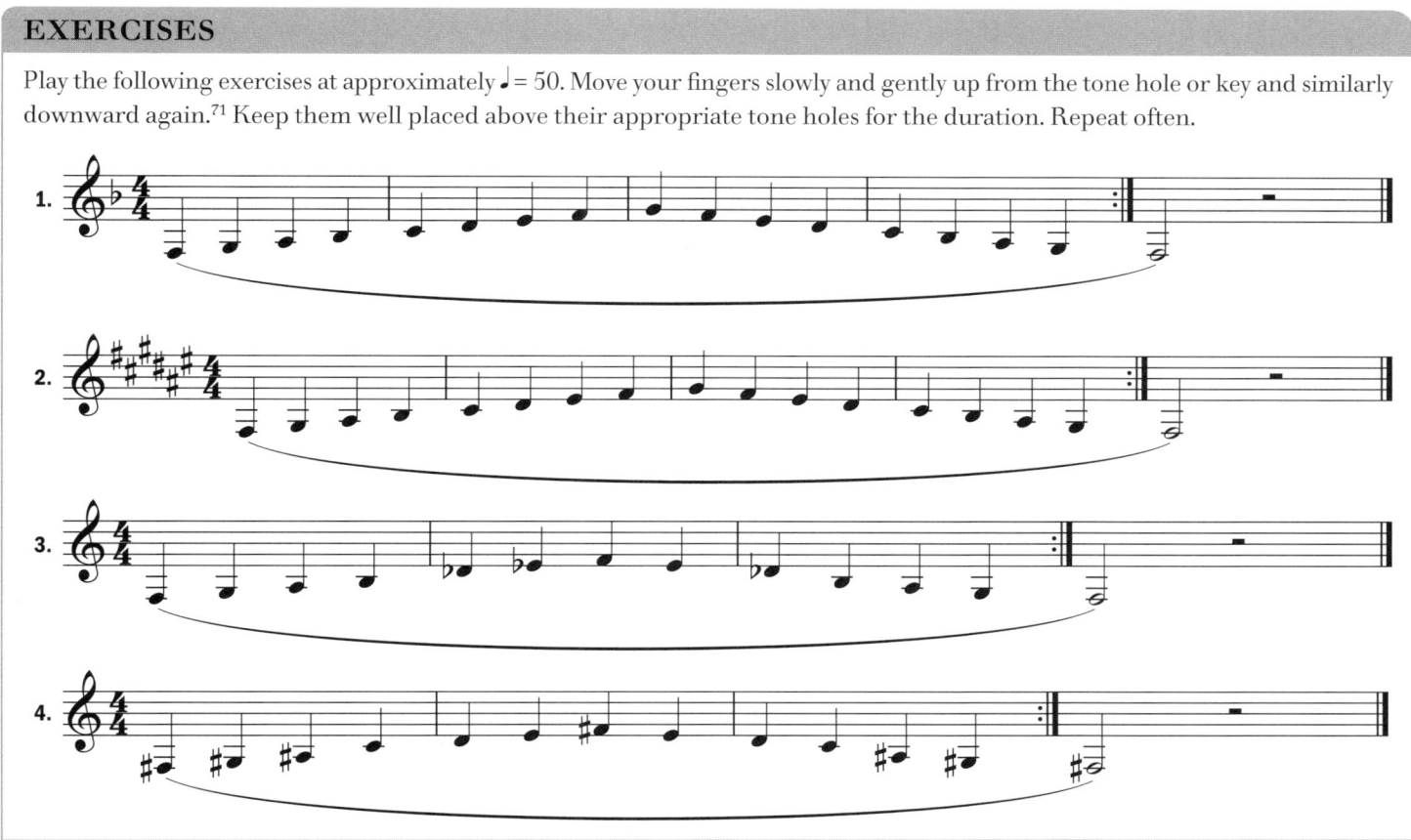

71. The diameter of tone holes increases as notes descend, so for those with thinner fingers more precision is necessary.

Finger pressure

Finger pressure is an area rarely thought about by many players, but it's an interesting and important aspect of technique and may well contribute significantly to your playing.

> **EXERCISES**
>
> Repeat exercises 1–4 on page 153, this time thinking about the amount of force or pressure you are using in the movements. Experiment and find the optimum amount of finger pressure sufficient to carry out the movements successfully. This is essential in developing a beautiful *legato* as excessive finger velocity (speed, force and direction of motion) can produce a distracting 'pop' sound as the air is 'slapped'. Players often move their fingers with too much unnecessary force. Finger movement that moves the instrument or disturbs the embouchure should be avoided.[72]
>
> Occasionally, however, a little finger noise may add to the character and expression. In these slurred pairs a little finger sound as you alight onto the second note brings some extra energy and colour to the music. Too little pressure, which can affect tone and intonation, and the quality of *legato*, is also undesirable.
>
>
>
> Paul Harris, Sonata da Camera, I, bars 20–23

Fingerings are not all they seem

What is the fingering for C^1? Tutor books, manuals and fingering charts tell us that it uses the left-hand thumb plus fingers 1, 2 and 3, but if you are moving to C^1 from say A^1, to finger the C you actually lift right-hand fingers 1 and 2. Fingerings given in charts show where we need to place our fingers to sound the particular note. The actual *fingering* of a note is dependent on the preceding note. It's the movement necessary between the note you're playing and the arrival note. The reason for making this point is that fingering becomes an active ratherthan a passive concept. The manner in which we move from one note to the next suddenly becomes more vibrant.

---

72. This will also help to maintain good finger health.

EXERCISES
Finger strengthening

Trills

Practising trills is a good way to develop finger strength and control.

- Aim to keep the rhythm and tone even.
- Choose different dynamic levels.
- Move your fingers quickly and lightly without lifting them too high.
- Always aim for economical finger movement.
- Consider particularly the upward movement of the finger – so often when playing a trill, we concentrate and are more aware of the downward movement.
- Be aware of any tension emerging in the trill finger itself, other fingers, wrist, forearm or elbow as a trill proceeds.

Don't suddenly do a lot of trill practice – work up incrementally (as you would in anything). If your soft tissues are prepared, trained and 'conditioned' for the task, there should be no problem. Problems only arise when people do a lot of something they are not used to, or overload a system that is close to working at capacity.

Here is an exercise to help keep all contributing muscles tension free. As you practise trills, with the elbow of the trill hand, simultaneously make small circles in the air through a combination of wrist and shoulder movement whilst aiming to trill evenly.

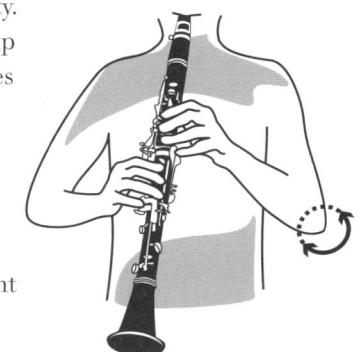

Play the following exercise slowly. The movement of the first finger of the left hand should be consistent, precise and rhythmical. Aim for an even tone.

Practise the following exercises in the same way as part of your daily routine. Keep the breath flow generous and experiment with a small surge of pressure at the start of the trill.

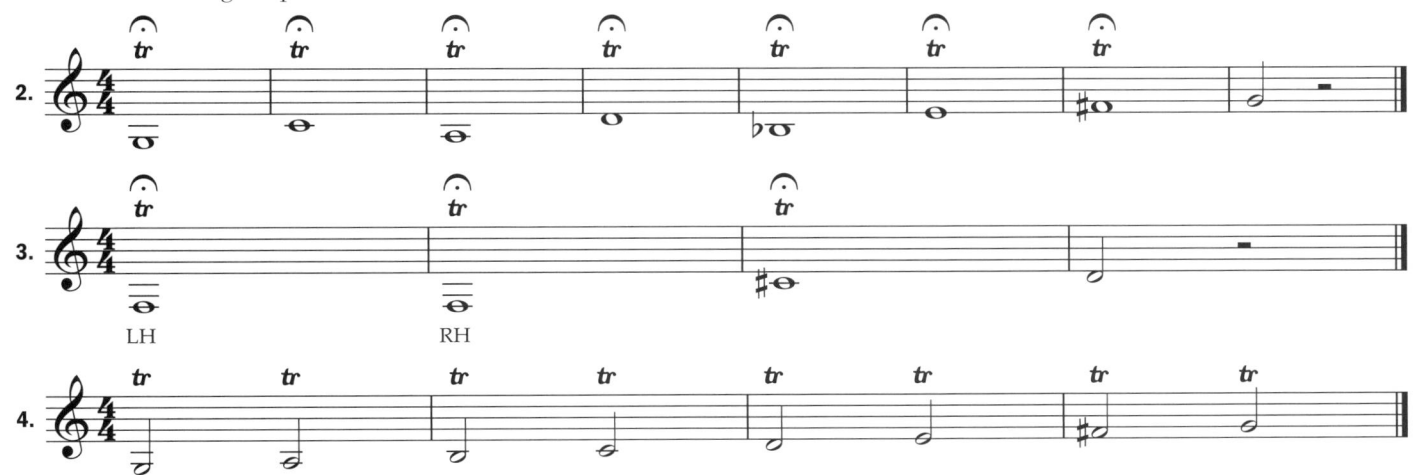

THE CLARINET

EXERCISES

Choose and work at one or two of the following in a practice session.

FINGER-WORK AND DEXTERITY

Individual finger exercises for strengthening and independence

Though these next two exercises develop the independence and strength of *each* finger, they are particularly good for exercising the right and left hand's third and fourth fingers. These anatomically share a flexor tendon[73] so contraction of one inevitably causes a slight contraction in the other. Practise them both carefully.

1. Finger $A\flat^1$ and then play a slow trill with the right-hand third finger. Keep all other fingers (including the fourth finger) relaxed but firmly holding their position. Increase the speed as you gradually develop more strength. Repeat with the second and finally the first finger.

2. Now finger $C\sharp^1$ and play a slow trill with the left-hand third finger. As above keep the other fingers of the left hand relaxed but firmly holding their position. Repeat with the second and then the first fingers.

The little fingers

SET 1: THE RIGHT-HAND LITTLE FINGER

Repeat each of the following many times always beginning at a slow tempo. Gradually increase the tempo over a period of weeks and months. Keep the hand still (though not locked) and make sure it is the little finger that is doing the work. Keep your wrist and forearm as relaxed and still as possible.

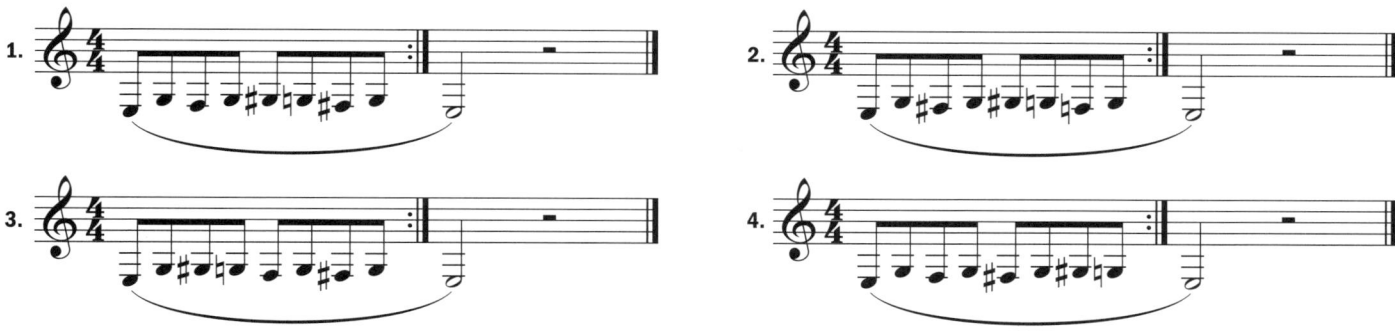

Extend these exercises as follows. On each subsequent repeat, replace the bracketed notes with any note up to E^2.

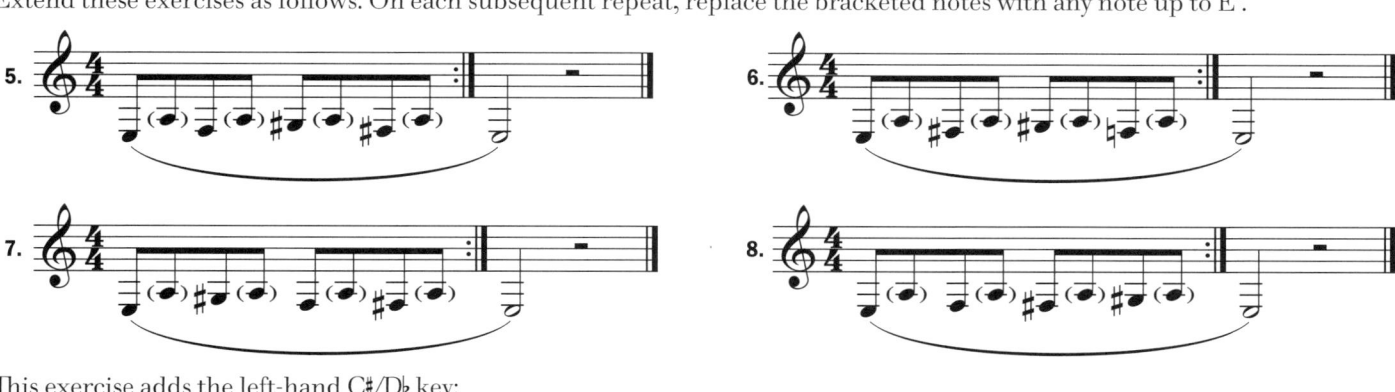

This exercise adds the left-hand C♯/D♭ key:

73. Flexor tendons are smooth and strong cords that connect the fingers.

EXERCISES

SET 2: THE LEFT-HAND LITTLE FINGER

10.

11.

12.

13.

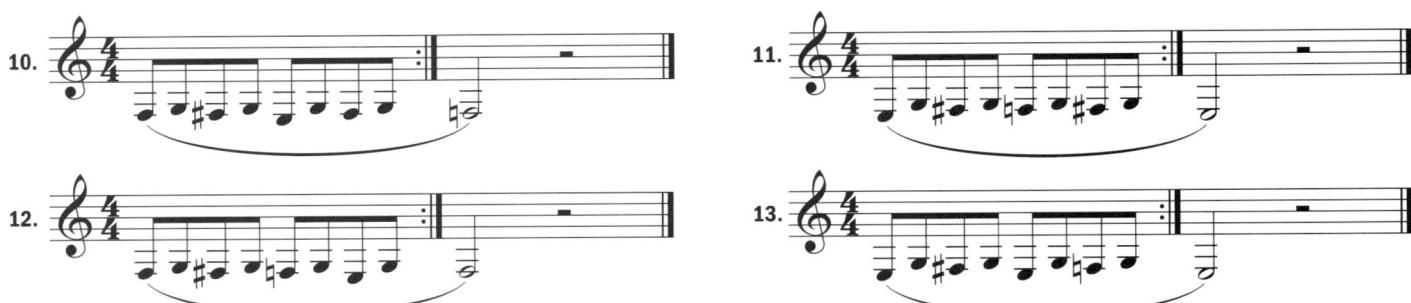

Add G♯ to exercises 10–13 if your instrument has the appropriate extra key. Then extend these exercises as follows. On each subsequent repeat, replace the bracketed noted with any note up to E² (but missing out C♯¹).

14.

15.

16.

17.

18.

19.

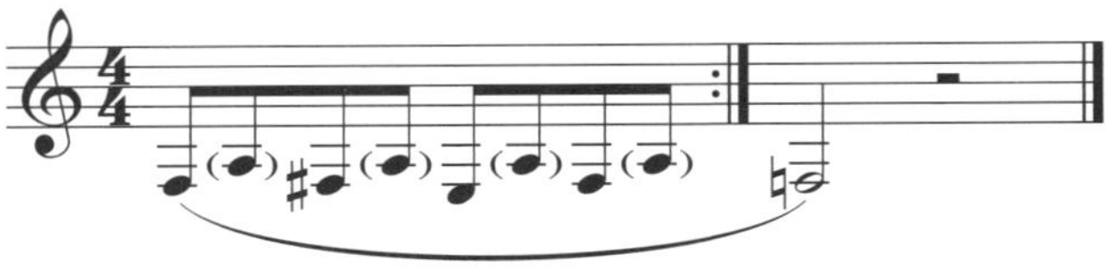

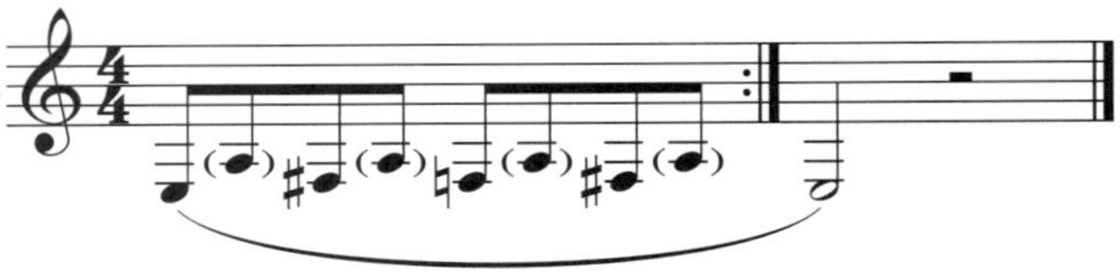

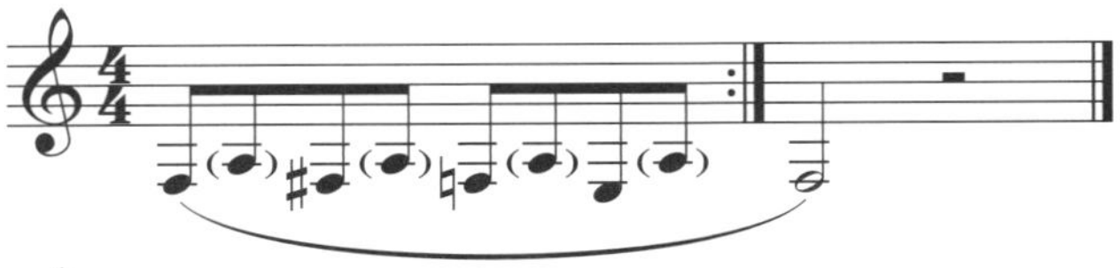

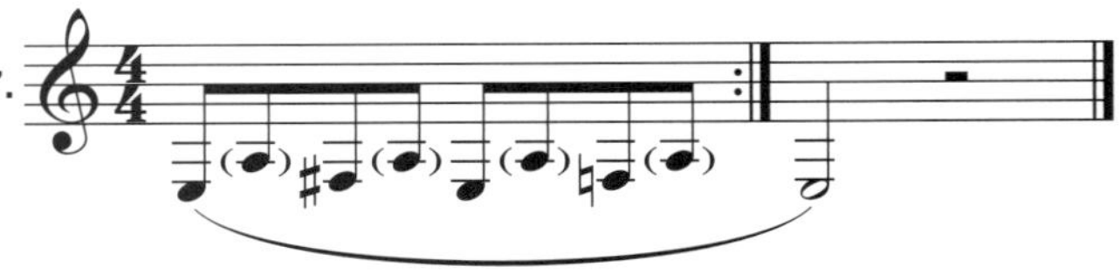

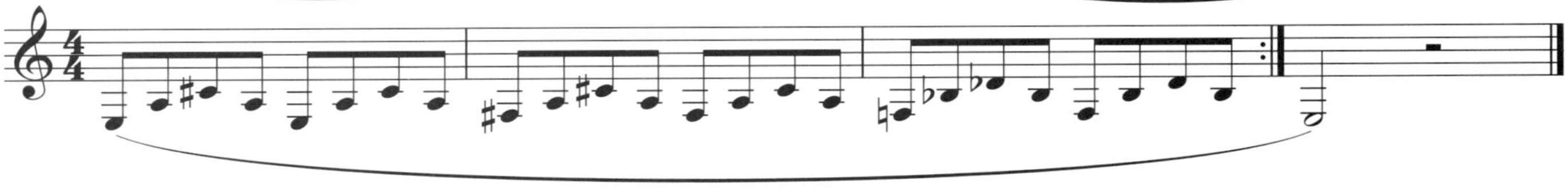

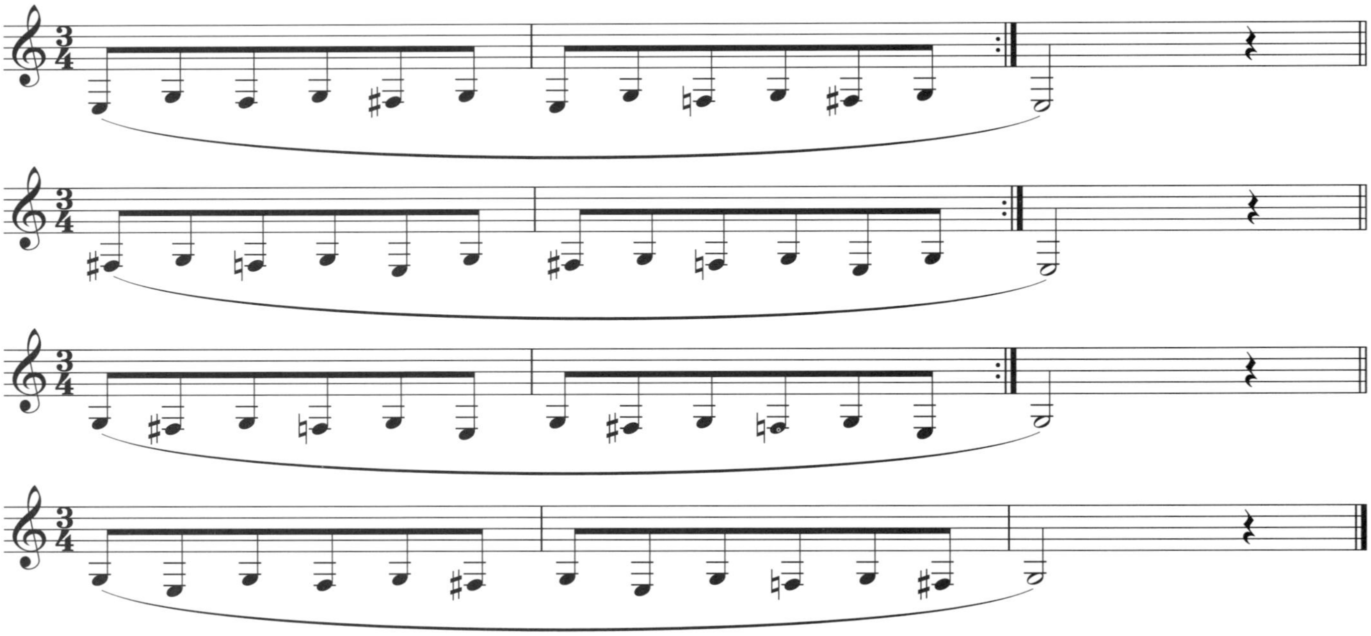

Extend exercise 19 by replacing G¹ with any note up to E² (except C♯¹).

FINGER-WORK AND DEXTERITY

Developing control of keywork

The A² key

The A² key is operated by rolling the index finger of the left hand onto the edge of the key. Make sure the other fingers are held above their respective tone holes and just slightly away from the instrument to allow for adequate venting. This will ensure that the fingers are always in the correct position. Avoid 'jumping' onto the A key in exercise 1 (i.e. taking the finger completely off the instrument while moving to the key), which is both inefficient and will sound the G between notes. Don't rotate the wrist and avoid sliding further up the A key once you're there!

To develop the most efficient movement of the left-hand first finger, practise opening the A key keeping the F♯ tone hole covered. Repeat often.

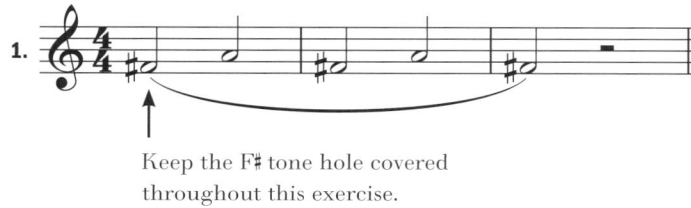

Keep the F♯ tone hole covered throughout this exercise.

Practise the following exercises slowly. Use a mirror to observe your finger movement.

The first finger is 'hovering' when approaching A² from either G² or F². Try to land on the same part of the A key, and with the same part of the finger as above. In the next two exercises, F♯ will set up the correct position of the first finger. Play the exercises slowly and consider carefully the finger's position.

THE CLARINET

EXERCISES

The register key

The register (speaker) key is operated with the side of the left-hand thumb, using a rolling movement onto the edge of the key. To play B♭, use the register key and the A key as described on page 159. Remember to keep your other fingers located directly above their respective tone holes. Play the following exercises slowly.

Play this next exercise slowly and prepare the first finger and thumb carefully for travel onto their respective keys.

Practise this interval from the opening of Brahms's Sonata Op. 120, No. 2:

Think of keeping the first finger and thumb 'soft' and relaxed as you move from B♭2 to E2.

The G♯/A♭ key

Operate this key by turning in the second joint of your left-hand index finger against the main face of the key.

To develop the most efficient movement of the left-hand first finger, practise the following exercise, opening the G♯ key keeping the F♯ tone hole covered. As with the A key, avoid excessive wrist movement. Repeat this exercise often.

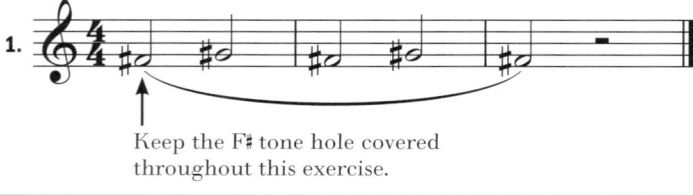

Keep the F♯ tone hole covered throughout this exercise.

FINGER-WORK AND DEXTERITY

Remember to keep your other fingers located directly above their respective tone holes. Practise the following exercises slowly.

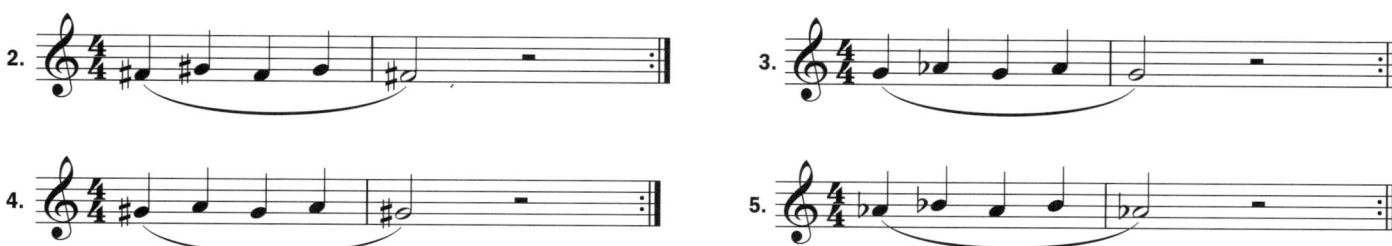

The next group of exercises make use of all the keys studied so far. Practise each one carefully, first slowly then at progressively faster speeds. These are the musical equivalent of tongue-twisters!

The side E♭ key

The commonly used side E♭ key is usually controlled with the part of your right-hand index finger just below the second joint, though this depends a little on the length of the finger. In the next preliminary exercise, cover the B♭ tone hole with the right-hand first finger throughout to develop the most efficient use of the finger. Don't expect much quality in tone for the E♭.

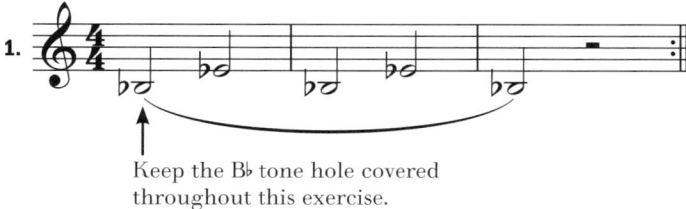

Keep the B♭ tone hole covered throughout this exercise.

THE CLARINET

EXERCISES

Keep your fingers located directly above their respective tone holes throughout the following exercises.

Work carefully at the movement of both first fingers in these next two exercises. Repeat each exercise multiple times.

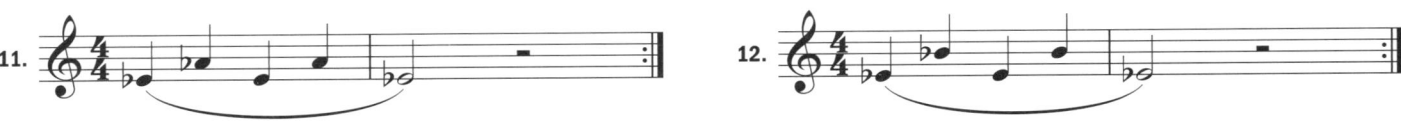

The side B♭ key

The side B♭ key is played with the right-hand index finger, about halfway down the second finger joint. The tone quality is often better compared with the register-key fingering owing to the larger tone hole. It's rarely a practical fingering if preceded or succeeded by a higher note. Try to limit the movement of your wrist and forearm when using this fingering. Again, ensure that other fingers are located as near as possible to their respective tone holes throughout the following exercises. This fingering, though useful, can be non-ergonomic and should only be used with discretion.

Changing fingers on the same note

Because of the technical limitations of the instrument, it is sometimes difficult to maintain a *legato* in certain passages.[74] Changing fingers while playing the same note will often help. The finger change must be quick and precise. Exercises 3–5 will develop your general coordination and precision of the little fingers. Play them slowly at first and gradually increase the tempo, always ensuring that the sounding note is absolutely continuous as you change fingers.

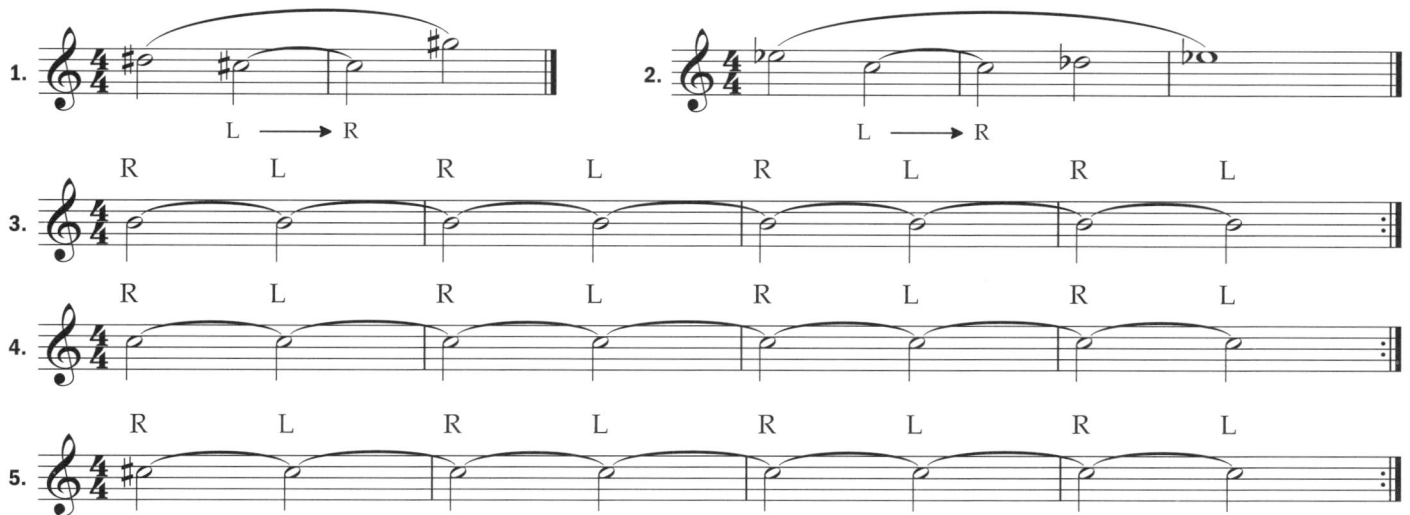

Add E♭ if you have a left-hand E♭ key.

EXAMPLES FROM THE CLARINET REPERTOIRE

Saint-Saëns, Sonata Op. 167, II, bars 57–59

Brahms, Clarinet Sonata Op. 120, I, bars 106–113

Avoid sliding your fingers from one key to another, unless it is absolutely necessary. For example, in the following extract (unless you have extra keys on your instrument), you may like to slide either the little finger of your right or left hand before articulating the D♯.

Finzi, Five Bagatelles Op. 23, *Forlana*, bars 19–20

Weber, Grand Duo Concertant Op. 48, I, bars 133–135

74. Specifically resulting from the lack of a left-hand G♯/E♭ key on some (not all) models.

Tips for using scales and arpeggios to develop finger technique

- Practise scales and arpeggios slowly and in time using a metronome. Only increase the tempo when you can play a scale perfectly at a slower speed. Drive your finger movement with very clear rhythmic thinking generated by your sense of pulse and sub-division.
- Always aim to play scales with your most beautiful sound. A scale should be played musically with a lot of care and concern.
- Be aware of finger pressure. Occasionally, practise scales and arpeggios in front of a mirror and watch the way your fingers move. Keep fingers relaxed as you cross the breaks. Excessive force should always be avoided.
- Use the full range of the instrument; for example, begin C major on E^1 and play up to E^4 or G^4.
- Play scales, still over a two- or three-octave range, beginning on notes other than the keynote, e.g. play G major beginning and ending on A as below.

- Play scales descending and then ascending.
- Occasionally think of the name of each note as you play it. This will help you to develop your ability to identify notes easily.
- Silent practice is also valuable; that is, sometimes practise scales without blowing to allow you to concentrate solely on your finger movement.
- Occasionally practise them with the tip of the reed placed well beyond the lip of the mouthpiece; you will only hear the movement of the air. Listen intently to the air sound. This exercise will make you more aware of voicing and so the part played by the oral cavity.
- Practise maintaining *one dynamic level* throughout. Be guided by your ear – listen intently for any *crescendo* or *diminuendo* – let your breath control be determined by what you hear.
- Practise scales with varying dynamic levels, rhythms and articulations. The following models will give you some idea of the wide range of possibilities.

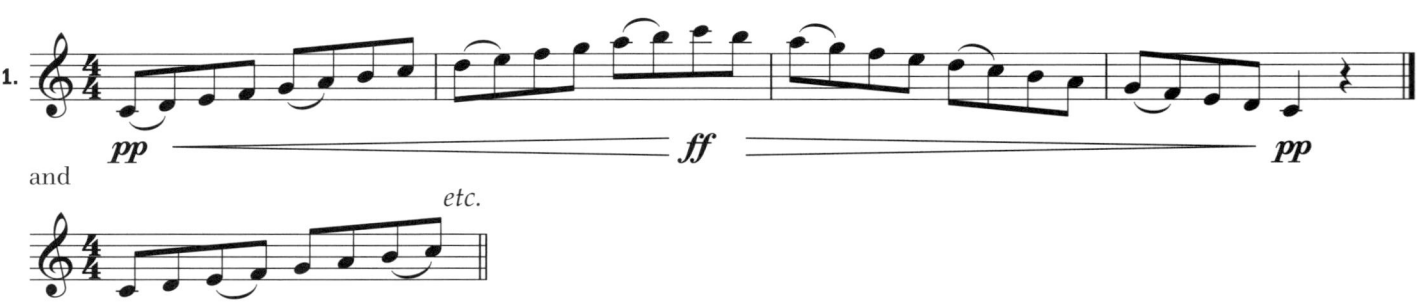

FINGER-WORK AND DEXTERITY

The following rhythmic patterns can also be applied:

Remember that a beautiful tone should always be your primary aim. All other technical considerations, though important, are secondary.

Never allow yourself to play any note with a tone you consider less than beautiful (unless the character of the piece demands some compromise in the quality).

THE CLARINET

EXERCISES

Scale and arpeggio exercises

The following exercises will help you overcome certain technical features found in particular scales and arpeggios. Use them in your practice, in conjunction with the scale or arpeggio concerned. When playing pieces in these keys, use these exercises as warm-ups.

Play them at different dynamic levels (make connections with the pieces you are studying), varying the tempo and articulation. Play each exercise at least twice and end by repeating the first note as shown below.

Each of the following exercises will have certain intervals boxed – work at these particular intervals carefully, especially at finger coordination. Then add the proceeding note and perfect the three-note pattern. Some have additional comments to clarify certain technical details. Once you get into this routine you'll probably find other intervals that need practice in relation to your own particular needs. As you play the patterns, the boxes will also alert you to those moments where concentration needs to be at its highest levels to achieve the best results.

C MAJOR

A MINOR

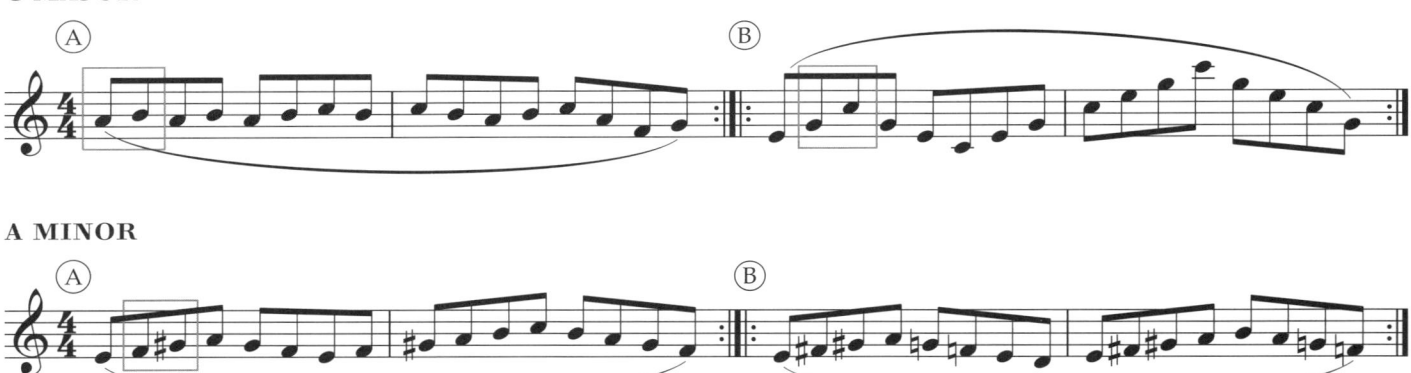

Ⓐ Ⓑ When fingering in the throat register, keep your wrist as still as possible.
Ⓔ When moving from A^2 down to E^2 keep the pads of the left-hand first finger and thumb as close as possible to their appropriate tone holes; the movement should be quick and precise.

FINGER-WORK AND DEXTERITY

G MAJOR

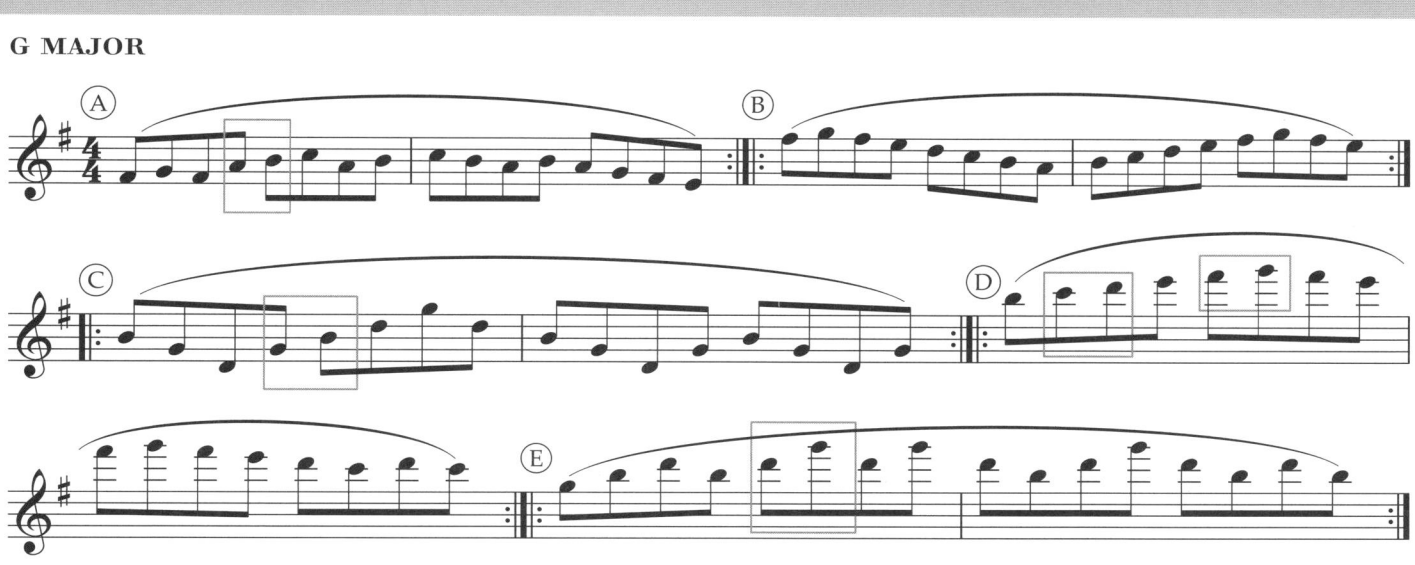

Ⓔ Think carefully about your oral cavity and tongue position when moving up and down from D^3 to G^4. In addition, take care over the intonation of these notes.

E MINOR

Ⓒ Note if you have any contact between your third and fourth fingers when moving from E^3 to $D\#^2$ (or visa versa). This will not be possible for smaller hands but is not to be considered inappropriate, and may help in coordinating these fingers.
Ⓔ In concluding the arpeggio and starting the repeat, the movement of the fourth finger must be quick and vigorous.

THE CLARINET

EXERCISES

D MAJOR

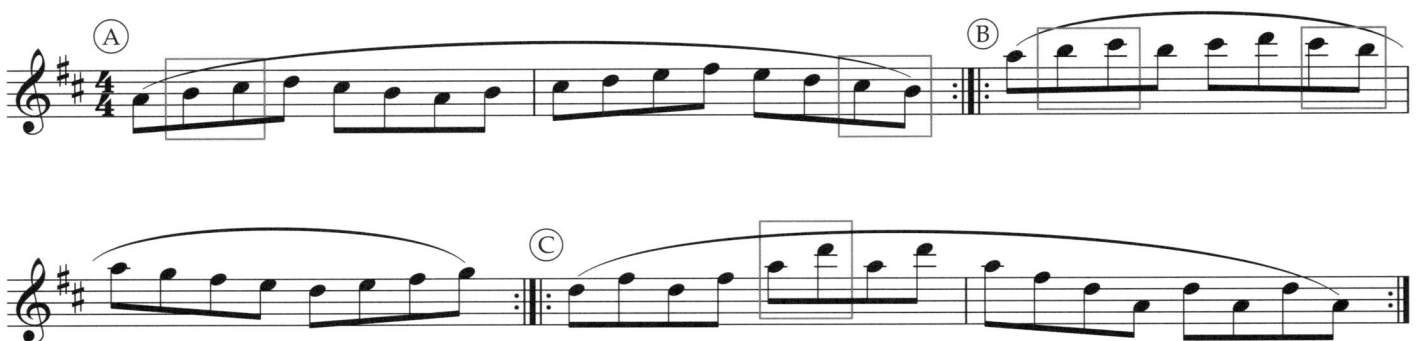

B In moving from C#^{3} back to B^3, put the left-hand first finger down with a quick and accurate movement.
C When moving between A^3 and D^3, concentrate on the placing of the right-hand first finger and the left-hand third finger while lifting the left-hand first finger.

B MINOR

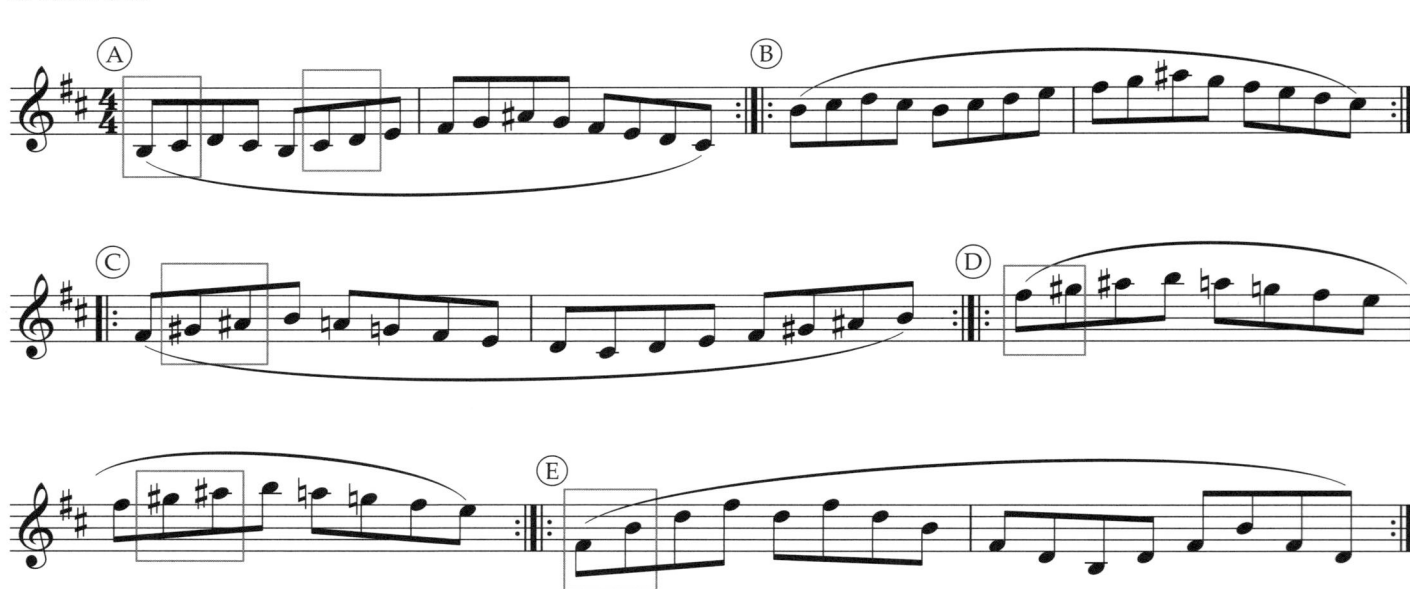

A Note (as in the E minor exercise) if you have any contact between your third and fourth fingers in moving from C#^{1} to D^1. As before, this will not be possible for smaller hands but is not to be considered inappropriate, and may help in coordinating these fingers.
C Work carefully at limiting your wrist movement.

FINGER-WORK AND DEXTERITY

A MAJOR

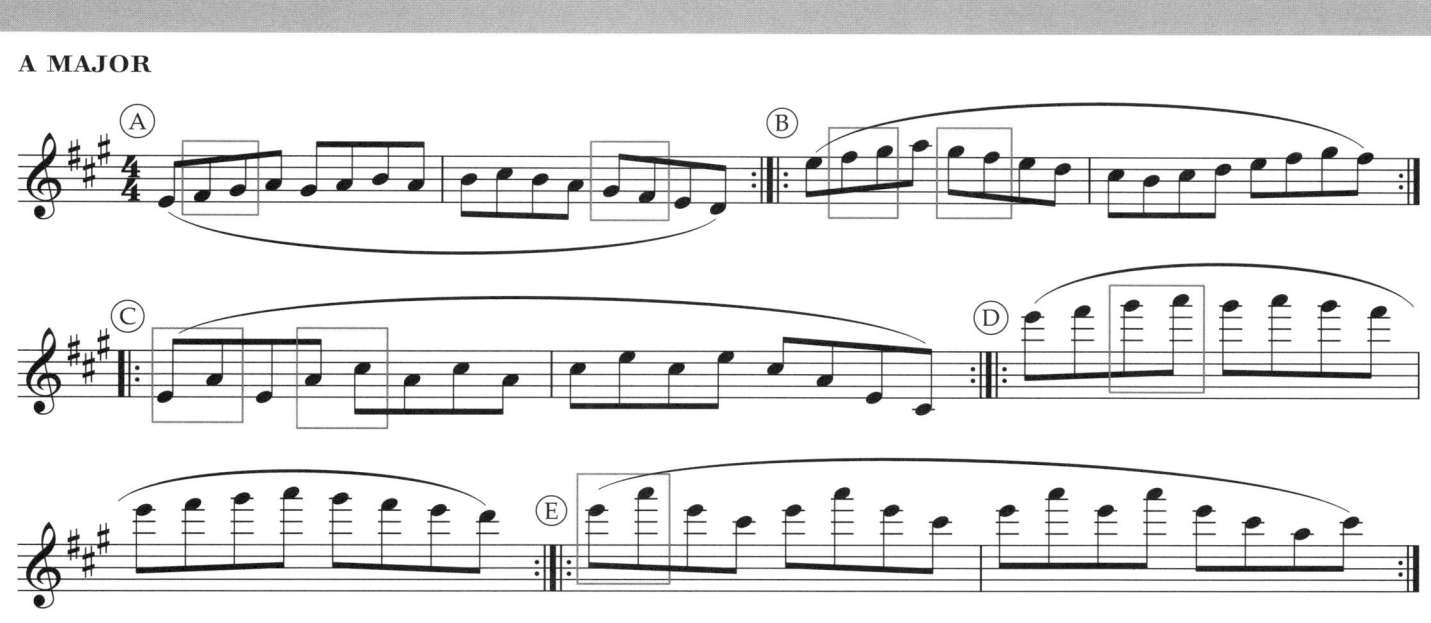

Ⓔ This secton is quite a challenge. Play it tongued many times first. Then work at helping the *legato* across the harmonics with adjustments in the oral cavity (see *Sounding good*, page 39) and lip pressure.

F SHARP MINOR

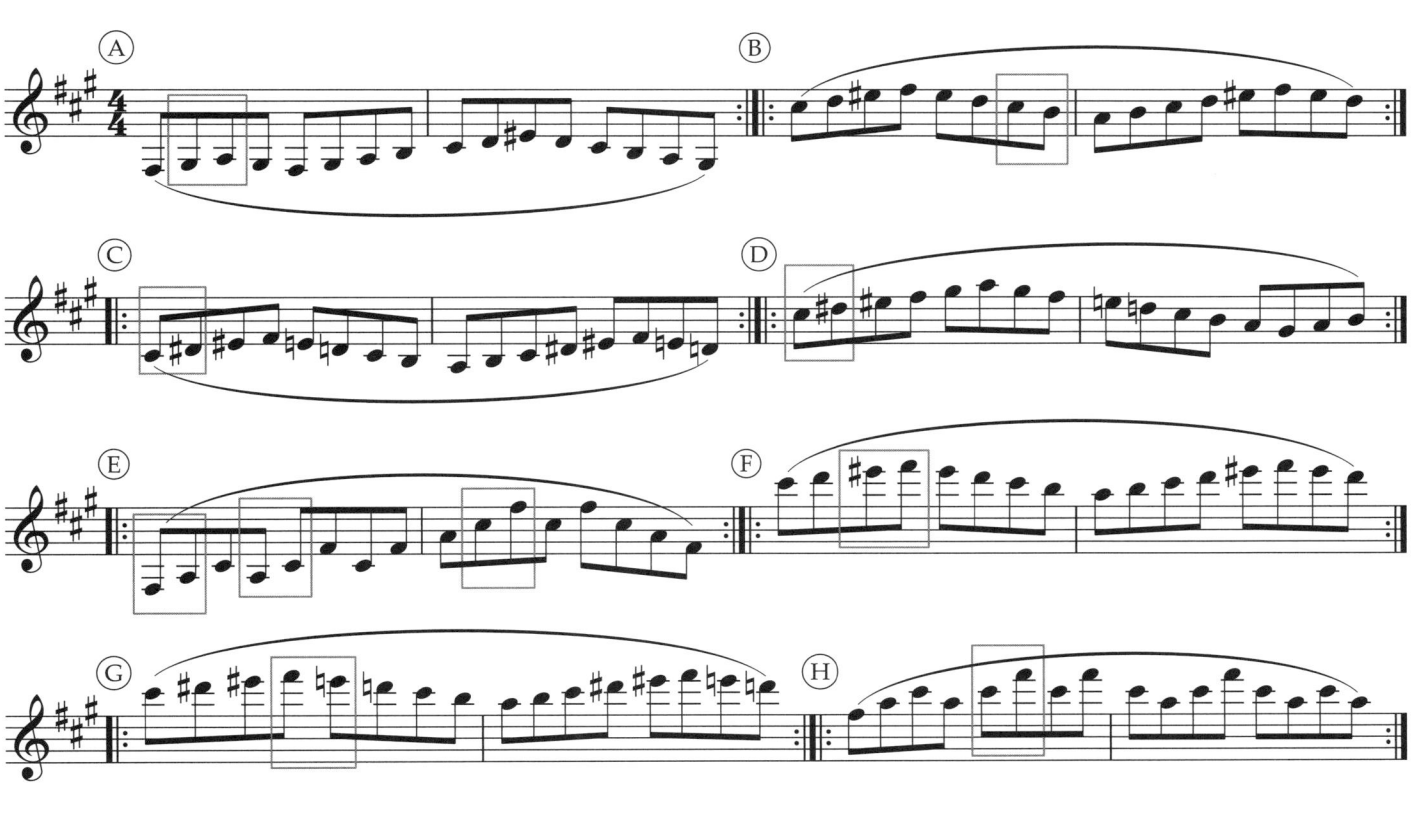

THE CLARINET

EXERCISES

E MAJOR

Ⓒ To join G#^{2} to B^2 across the break, ensure that the pad of the left-hand first finger is held as near as possible to the tone hole. In moving to B, coordinate all fingers carefully.

C SHARP MINOR

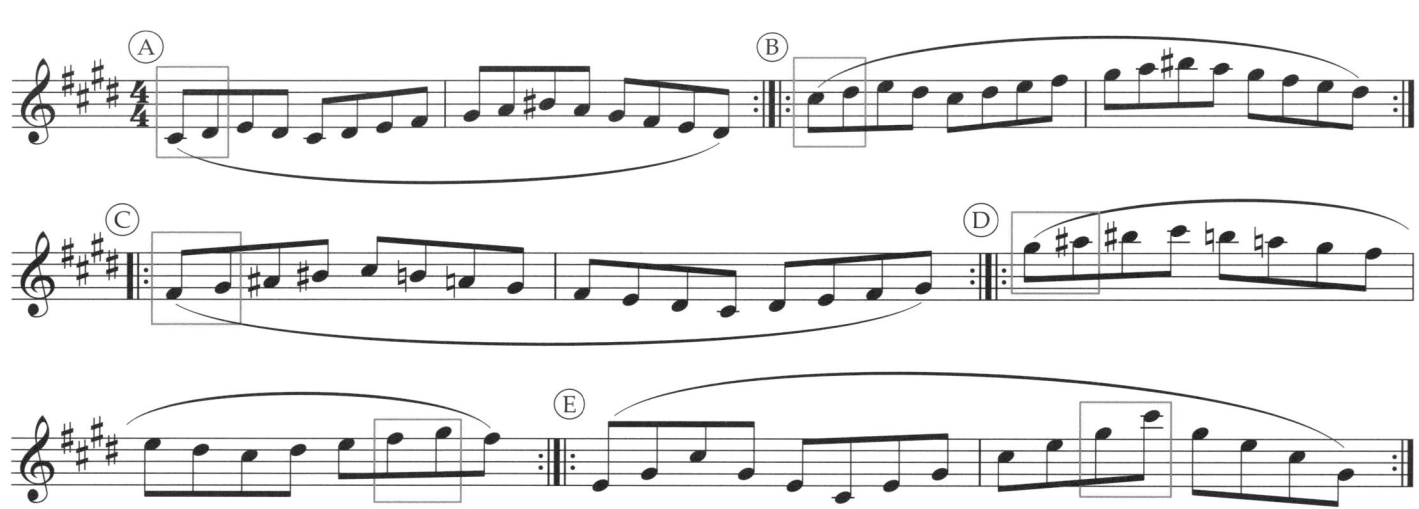

Ⓔ Moving from G#^{3} to C#^{3} across the top break is complex. The first and second fingers of the right hand must be put down precisely as left-hand's first and fourth fingers are lifted; practise this slowly at first. Use the trill fingering for C#^{3} if it's well-regulated on your clarinet.

FINGER-WORK AND DEXTERITY

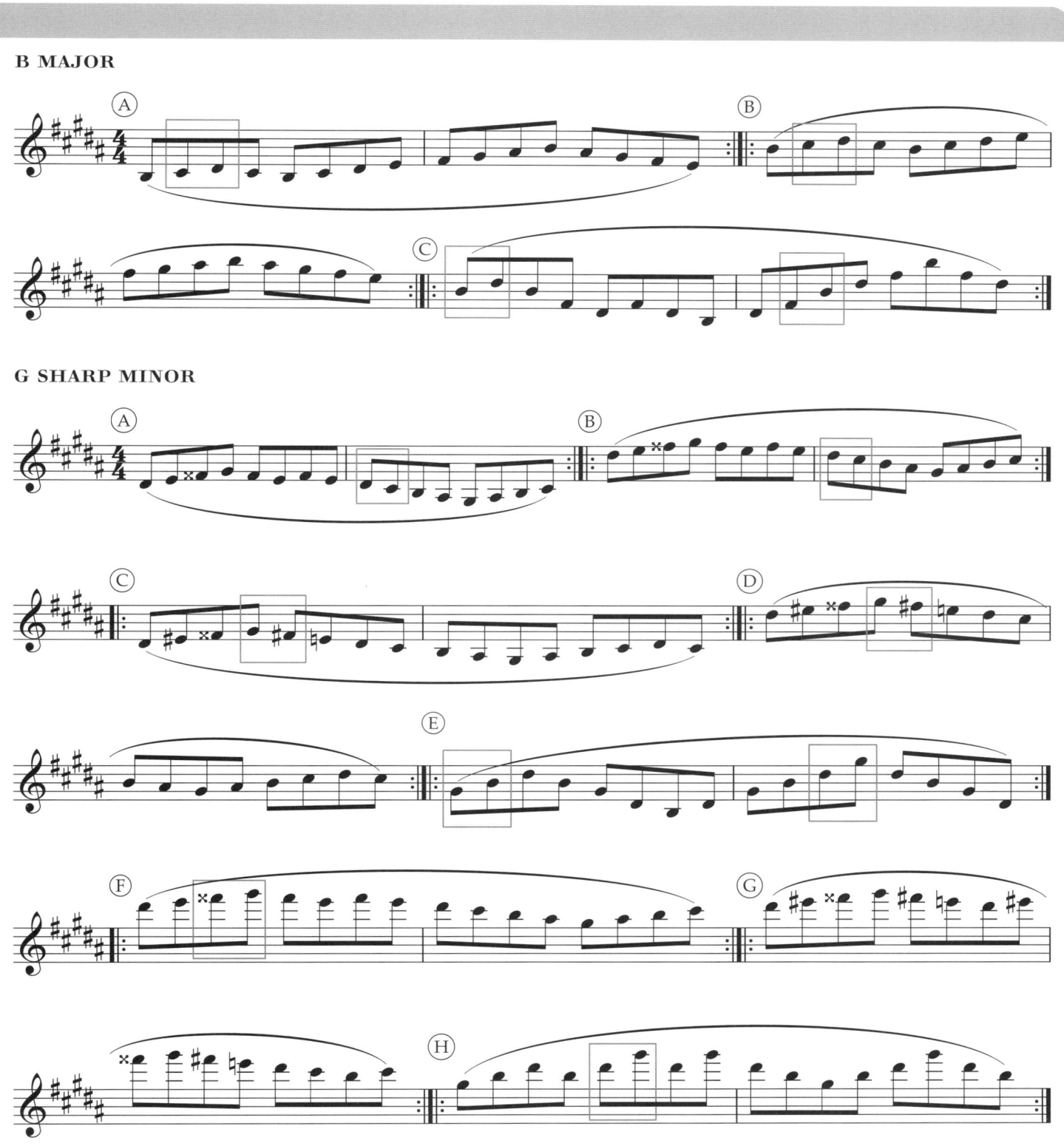

Ⓔ In returning from the G#^{3} to D#^{2}, make sure you replace your fingers precisely and coordinate this action with lifting the left-hand fourth finger.

THE CLARINET

EXERCISES

F SHARP MAJOR

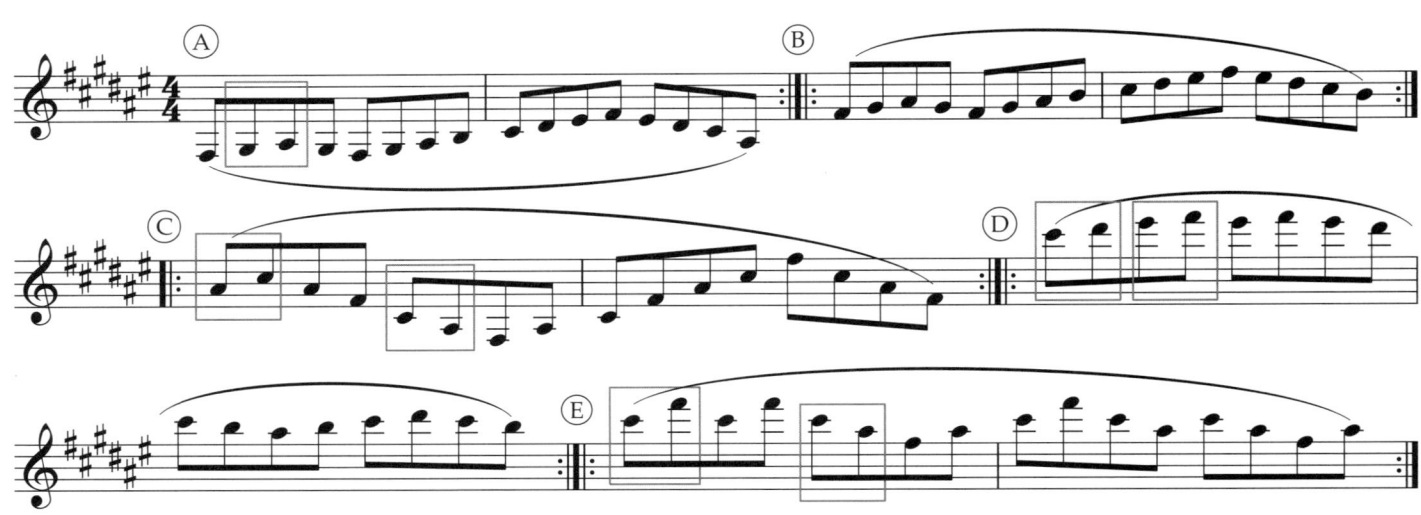

Ⓒ Moving from A#2 to C#2 across the break will require careful study. Prepare to finger the C#2 while you are playing the A#2, holding all fingers ready above the appropriate tone holes.

E FLAT MINOR

Ⓐ Experiment with both the left-hand first finger and the right-hand trill fingering for G♭2.

172

FINGER-WORK AND DEXTERITY

D FLAT MAJOR

Ⓒ In moving from D♭2 to F3 take care to keep the fourth finger well positioned in relation to the other fingers. Don't lift it more than is necessary. In fingering F3 back to D♭2, 'lead' with your fourth finger in order to achieve a clean leap. It should not have far to travel if the former movement was well set up.

B FLAT MINOR

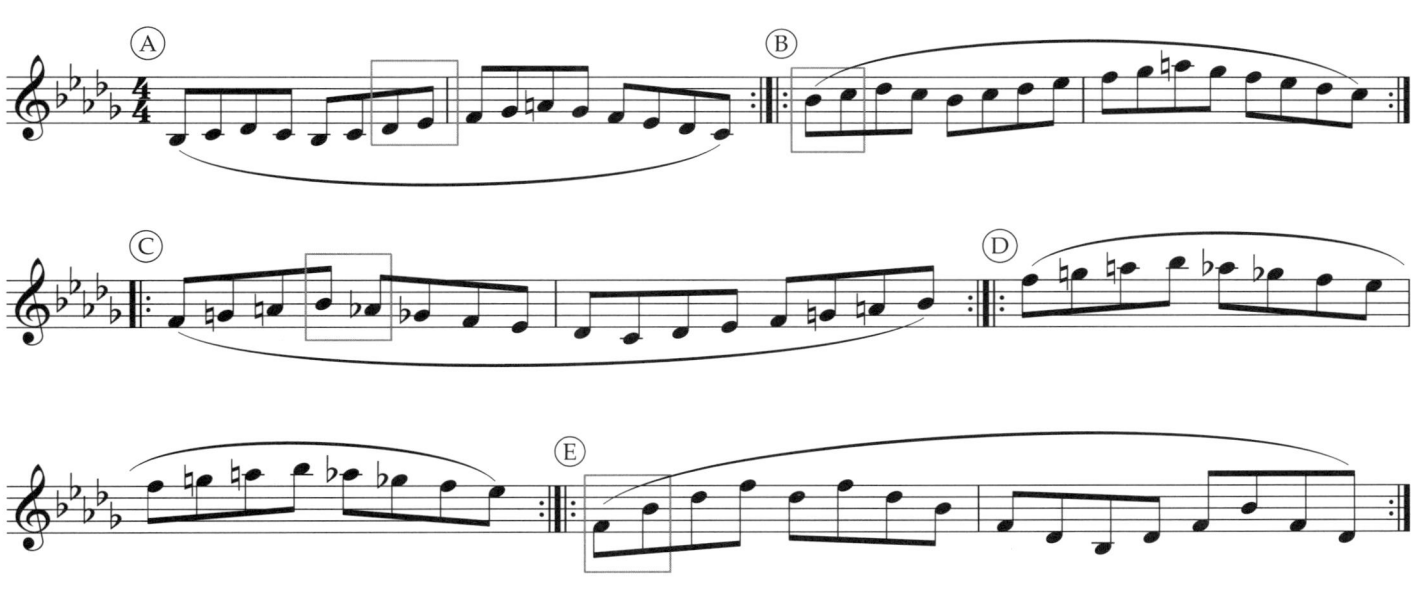

THE CLARINET

EXERCISES

A FLAT MAJOR

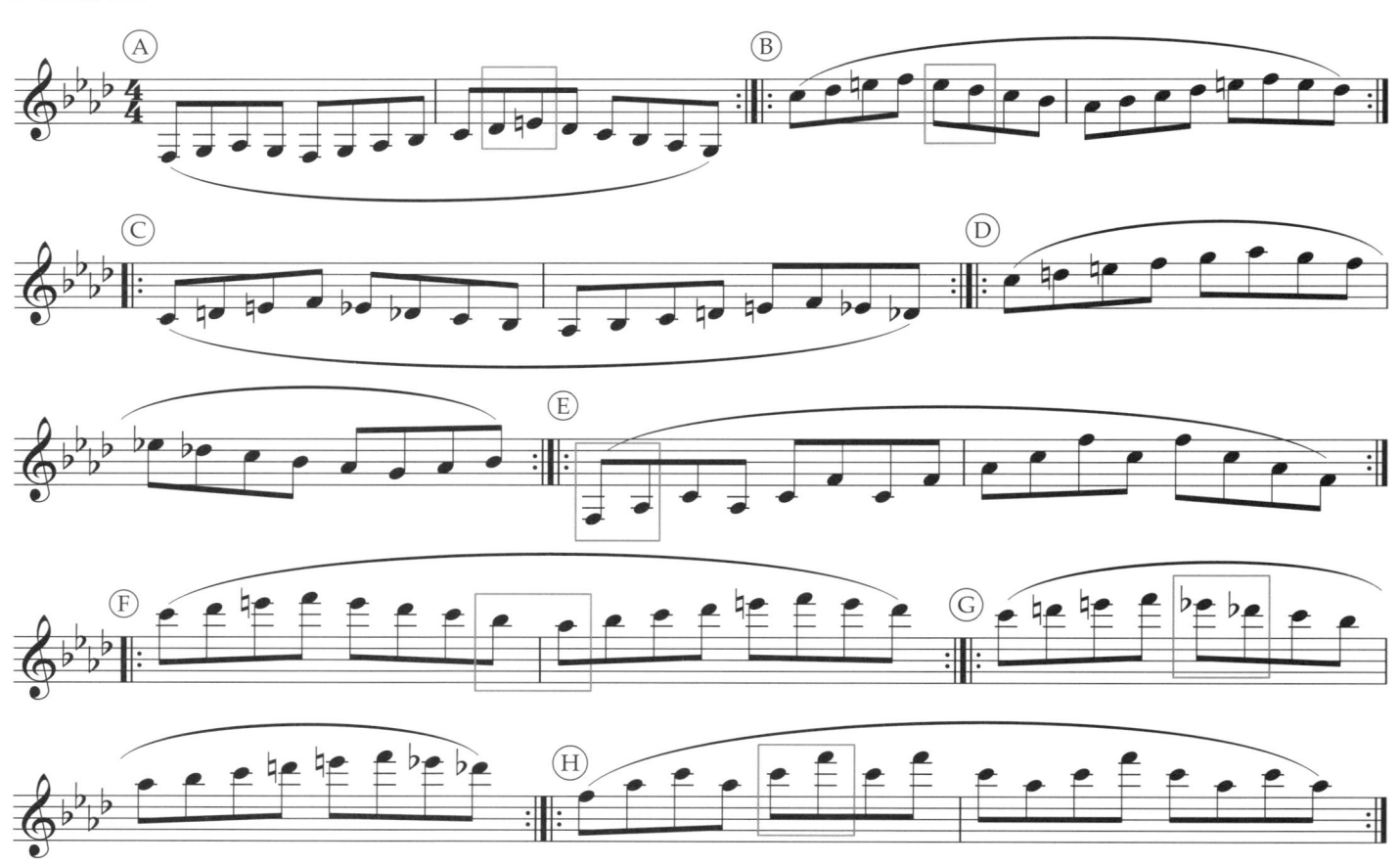

Ⓒ Avoid excessive wrist movement when moving from $E\flat^1$ to $A\flat^2$ and from $A\flat^2$ to C^2.
Ⓔ Find a fingering for $A\flat^4$ that doesn't involve any sliding.

F MINOR

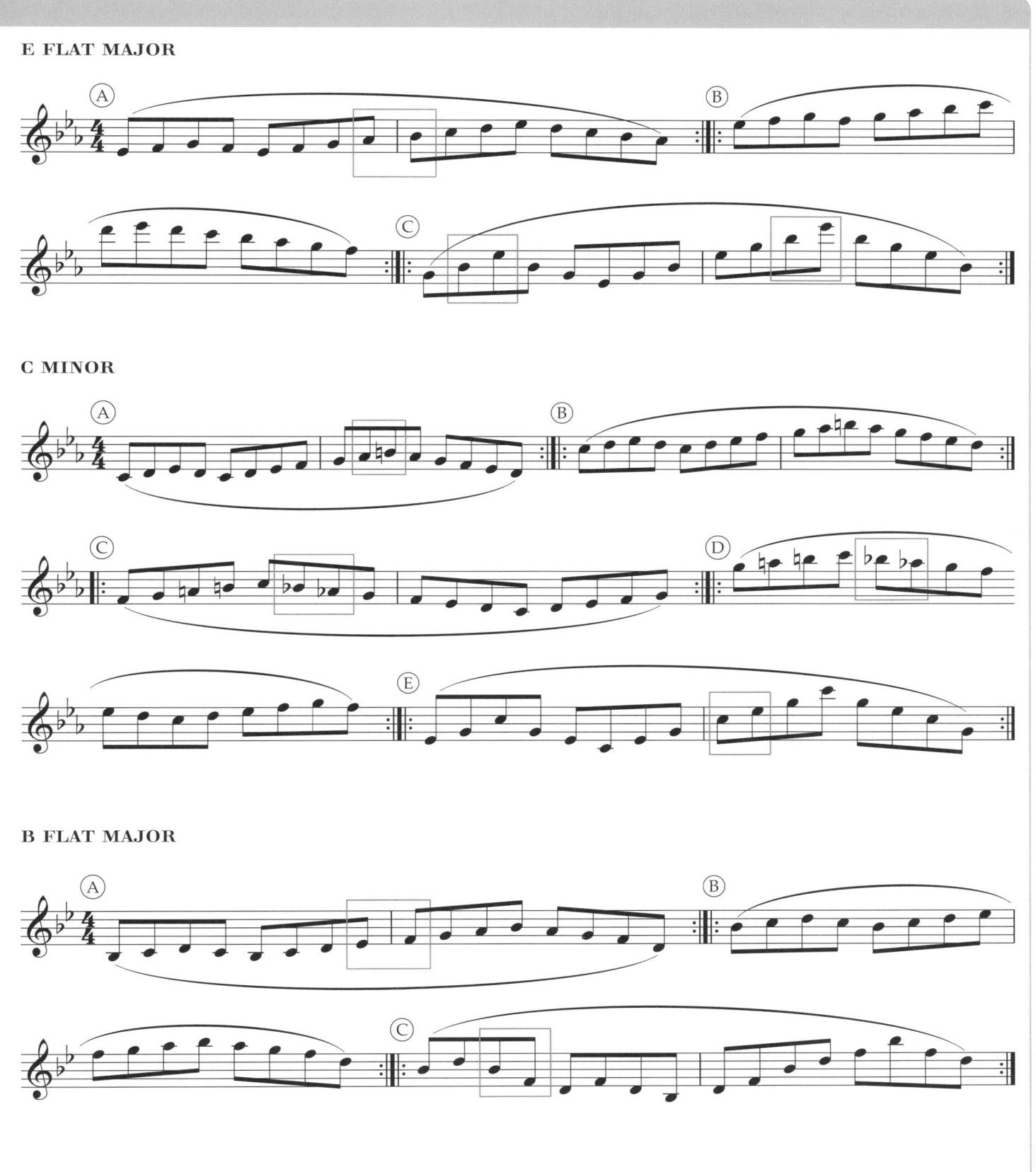

THE CLARINET

EXERCISES

G MINOR

E Take care to give the first B♭ in the second bar its full value – the change of fingering from D^2 to B♭^{2} can sometimes lead to rhythmic unevenness.

FINGER-WORK AND DEXTERITY

F MAJOR

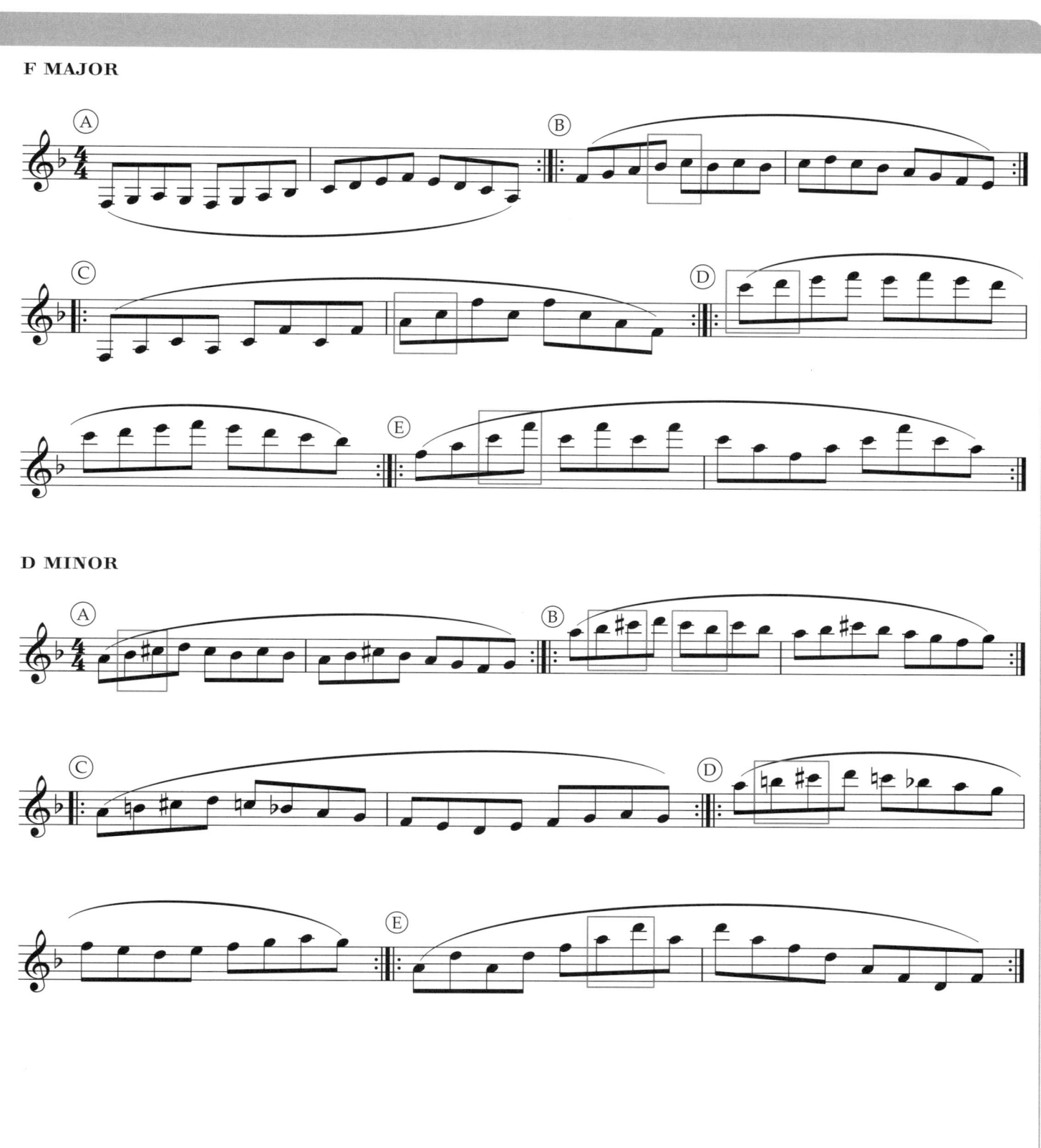

THE CLARINET

Developing fast playing

If asked what makes fast music sound fast, many will answer that it's your fingers moving fast! Certainly in playing trills you are moving your fingers rapidly, but in most cases this is not the reason. 'Fast' music usually means short note values and lots of them played in a short space of time. The 'faster' the music, the sooner the next note is played. So fast music is often not about fast fingers but rather about the (short) gap between each finger movement.

The ideal manner in which to prepare 'fast' music is to practise slowly, 'programming' each movement carefully into your memory. Work at each interval meticulously, thinking about:

1. Which fingers move
2. How they move
3. Any coordination issues
4. Use of oral cavity (voicing) and/or embouchure

Then work at moving from one note to the next as efficiently as possible. Always begin at a very comfortable speed where the finger movements are clean and efficient. Never play the next note until you are able to do so with complete control. At some point you will feel the gap between the notes can be shortened. Never feel out of control.

Here are some phrases that are normally considered 'challenges'. However, if practised slowly and carefully they can be programmed scrupulously into the brain, ultimately making them comfortable to play. With patience, you will be able to place and control the next note sooner, finally achieving the appropriate speed and accuracy.

Crusell, Clarinet Concerto No. 2, Op. 5, III, bars 224–234

Debussy, *Première Rhapsodie*, bars 114–115

Spohr, Clarinet Concerto No. 2, Op. 57, I, bars 83–87

Nielsen, Clarinet Concerto Op. 57, I, bars 196–305

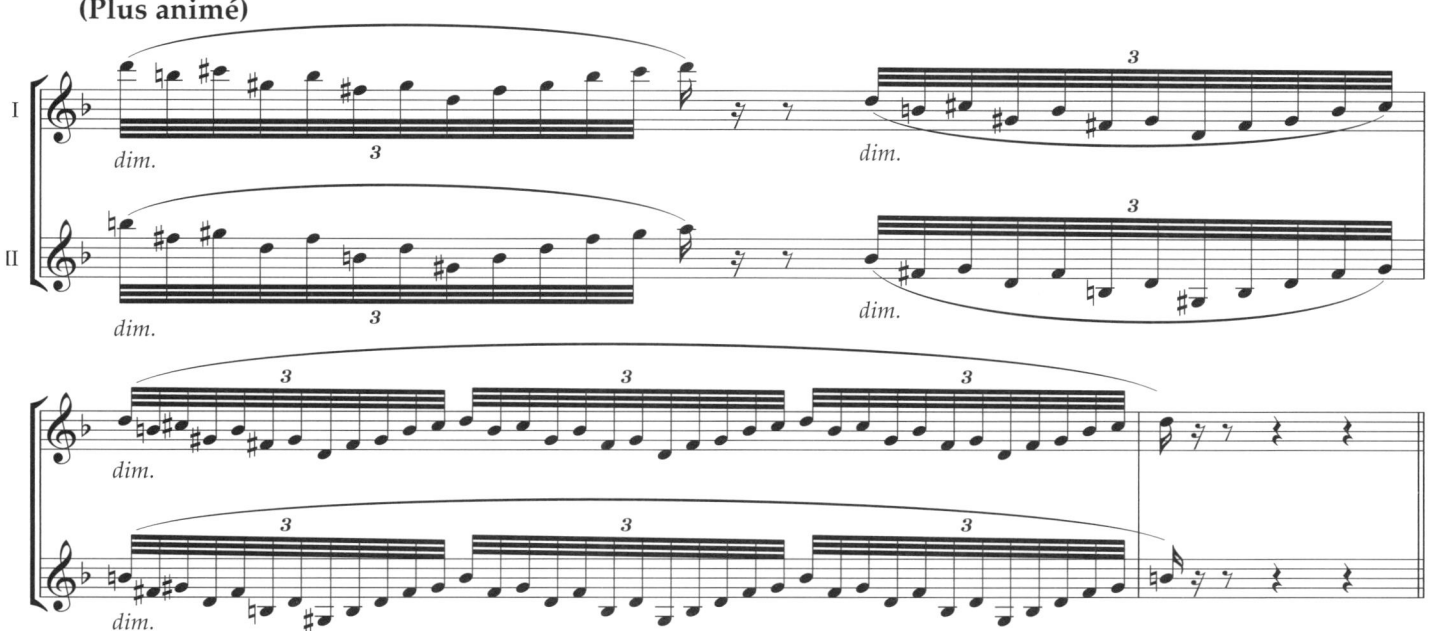

Ravel, *Daphnis et Chloé*, Clarinets I and II, bars 162–164

THE CLARINET

EXERCISES
Developing finger independence and agility

Play the following exercise slowly. Your finger movements should be precise and rhythmical. Make sure you maintain an even tone.

Now repeat the exercise somewhat faster but at a tempo where you still have complete control.

All the following one-bar exercises should be played as in the above example. Practise them *legato* and with varying articulation patterns. Also explore varying dynamic levels. Don't forget to pay attention to intonation as well as fingering. Mastery of all the exercises will lead to a very strong finger technique. Play a few at each practice session.

Repeat the above patterns with the register key open (i.e. using the *clarion* register).

Where throat notes appear in the following patterns, take care to keep the wrist relaxed and to minimise any wrist movement.

Keep your mind relaxed when playing these exercises. Be especially aware of your fourth fingers when they're used in the next sequence – they have a tendency to become tense. Send relaxing messages from your brain to your fingers whilst playing, or stop for a few moments.

FINGER-WORK AND DEXTERITY

Repeat the exercise above with the register key open.

Again, be aware of your wrist in exercise 5.

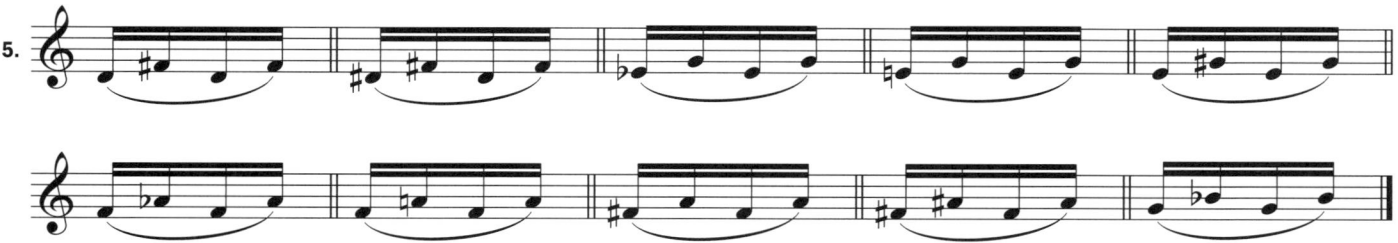

The following sequence crosses the break. Ensure steady and firm breath pressure.

Remember to consider finger pressure in the next exercise.

Repeat the exercise above with the register key open.

THE CLARINET

EXERCISES

9.

Repeat with the register key open.

10.

11.

Repeat with the register key open.

12.

13.

Repeat with the register key open.

FINGER-WORK AND DEXTERITY

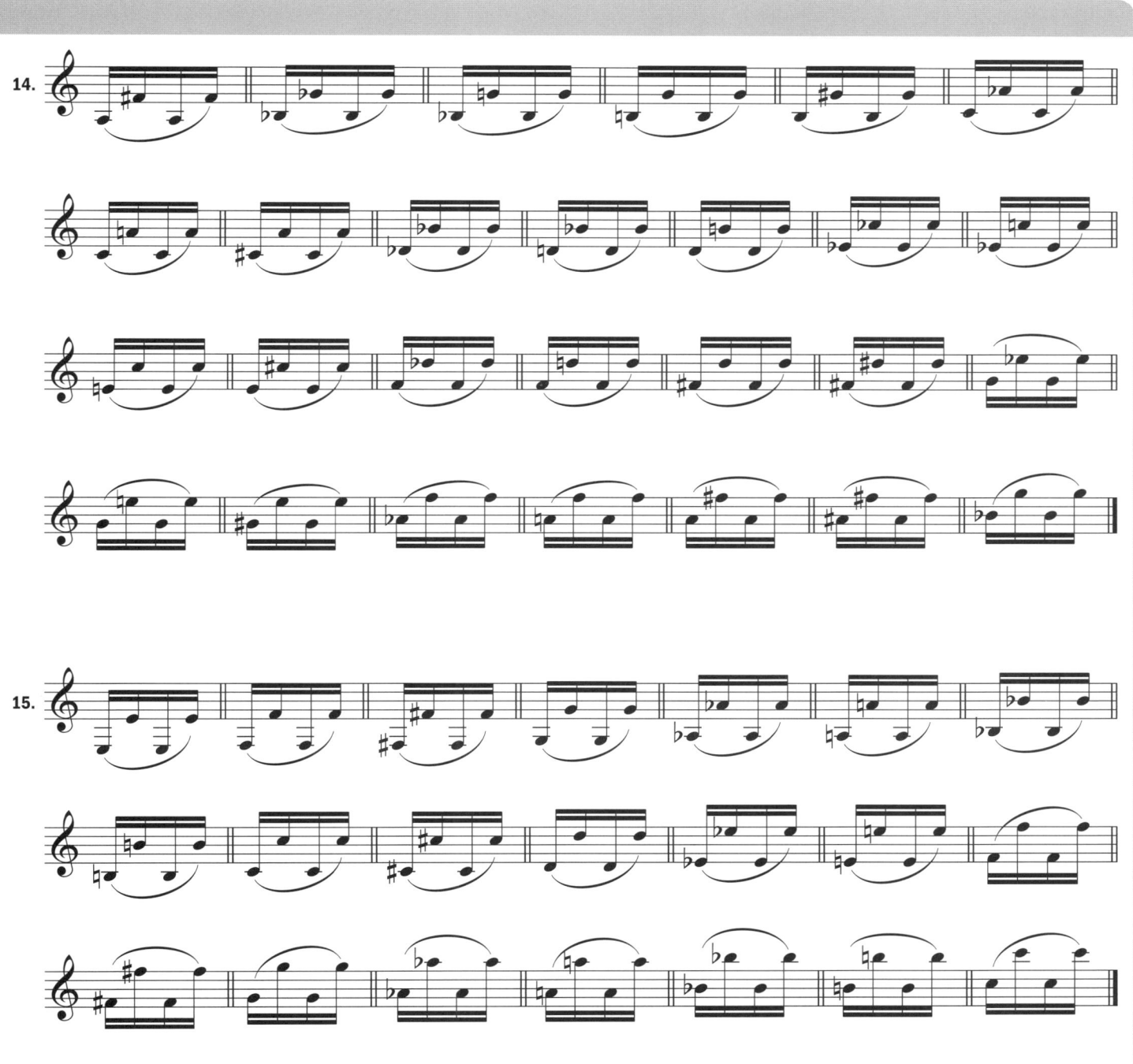

THE CLARINET

EXERCISES

The next sequences of exercises (16 and 17) make use of all possible combinations of keywork.
If necessary, mark in the fingering.

16.

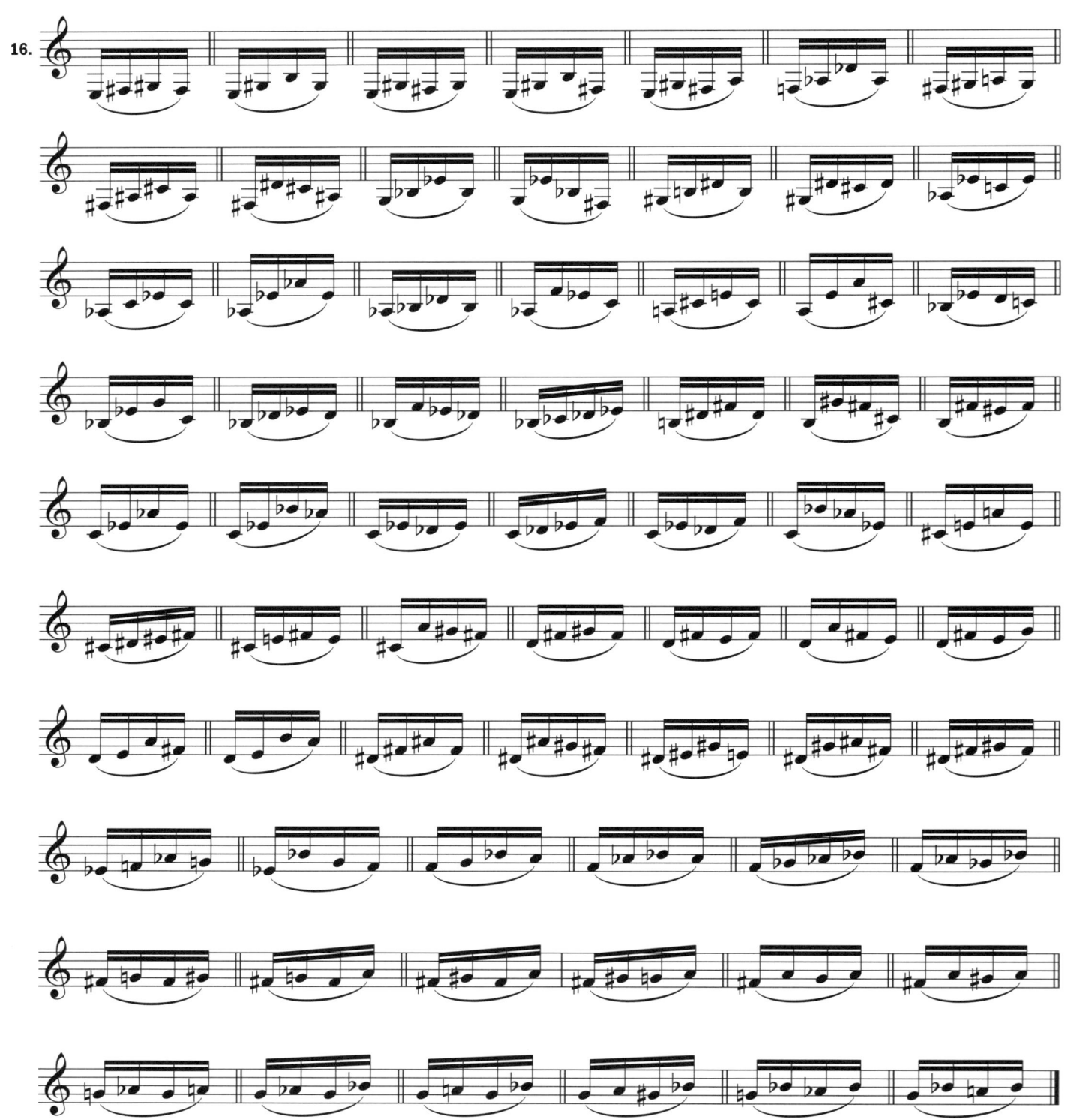

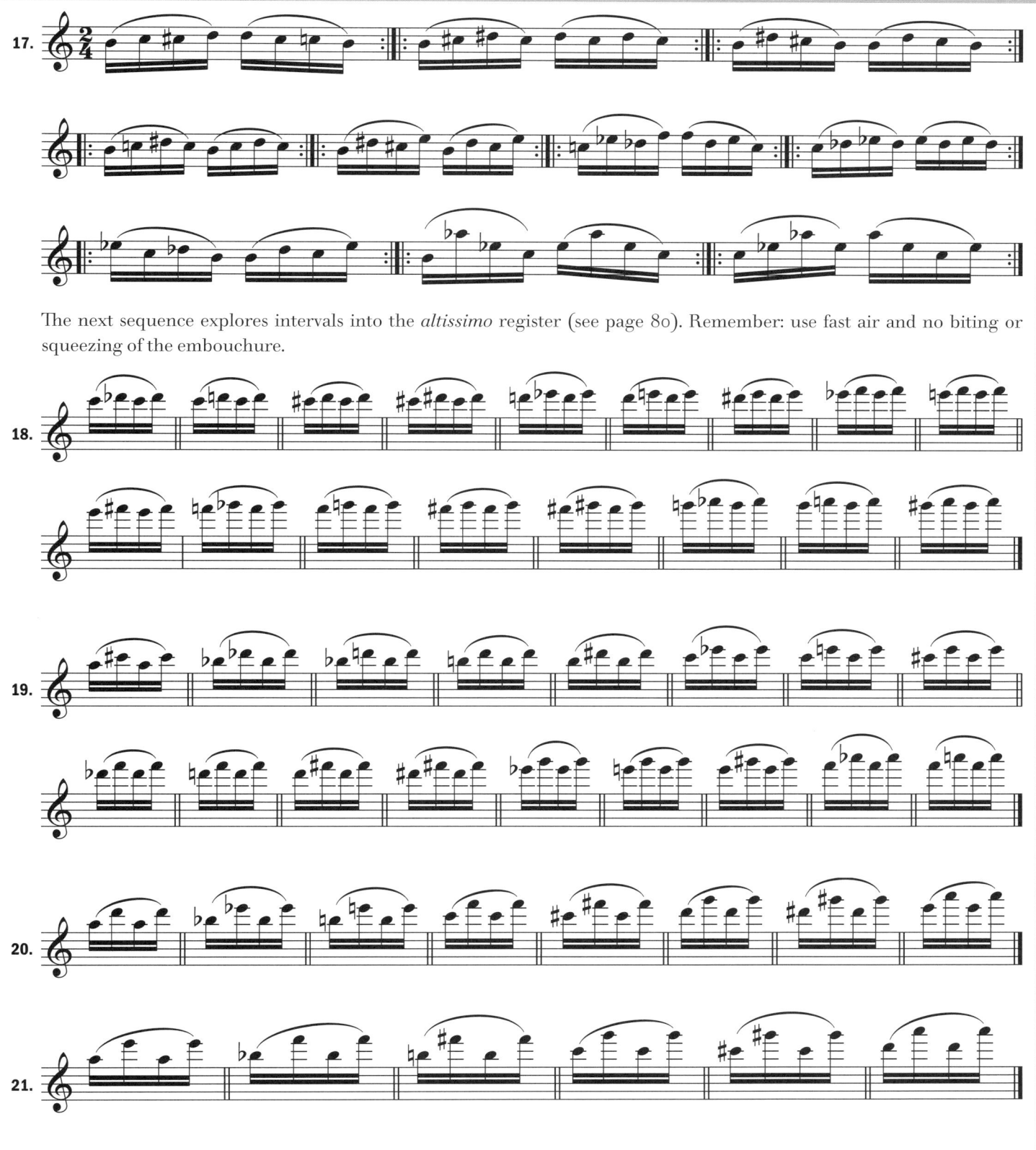

The next sequence explores intervals into the *altissimo* register (see page 80). Remember: use fast air and no biting or squeezing of the embouchure.

EXERCISES

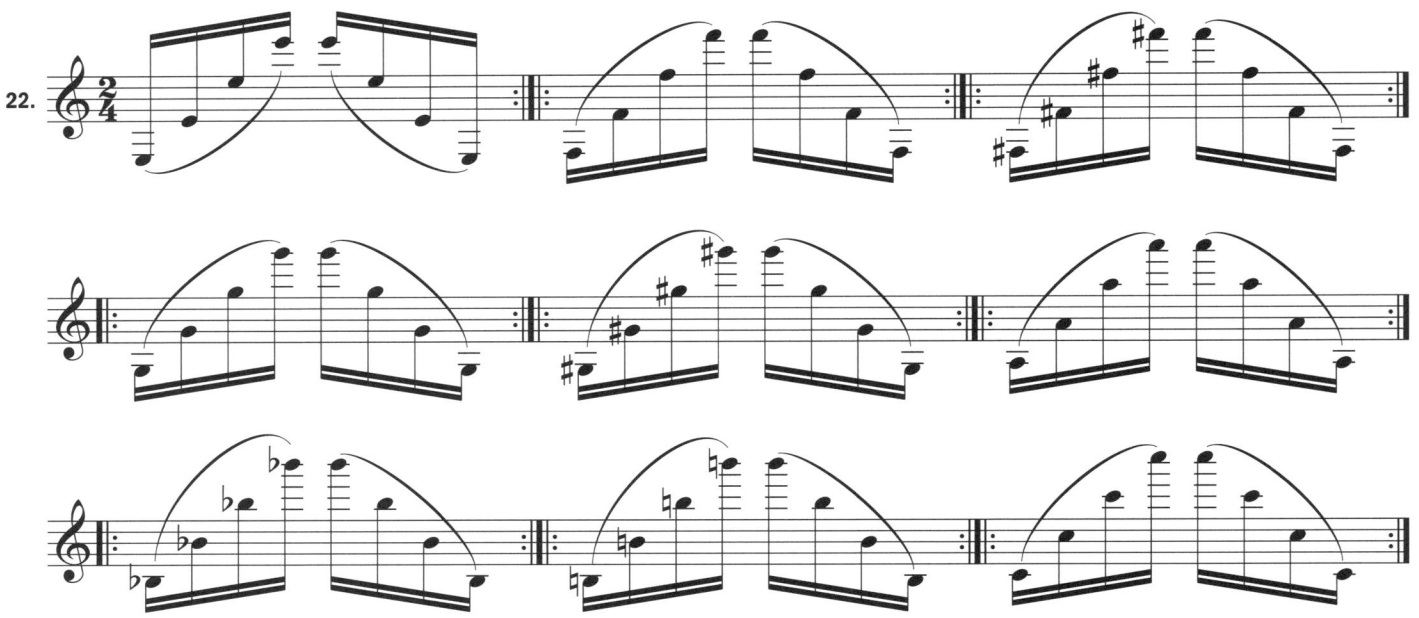

The next sequence mixes intervals of seconds and thirds.

The next sets of sequences explore crossing the breaks. Play the exercises with different articulations: *legato*, *tenuto* (*legato-tonguing*) and *staccato*. Be especially aware of any tension that might creep into the fingers when playing passages that repeatedly cross the break. Sustain an energetic and steady airflow and don't bite or squeeze the embouchure.

FINGER-WORK AND DEXTERITY

SET 1: THE FIRST BREAK

Vary exercises 28–30 using the following patterns:

EXERCISES

SET 2: THE SECOND BREAK

The final sequences are very helpful for warming up the fingers, especially before a concert performance or examination. Choose a particular note in each example and aim, mentally, for that one as you play. It is not to be articulated or played louder – just felt strongly in the mind. This will help the brain to maintain control by splitting the exercise up into manageable units. It will also encourage thinking about phrasing by grouping particular notes together.

This is a technique you can apply to other semiquaver (sixteenth-note) passages (especially long ones); splitting them up will give the brain moments of repose and so facilitate mental relaxation and ease of performance. Choose different notes when you repeat the exercise. Some examples are given below.

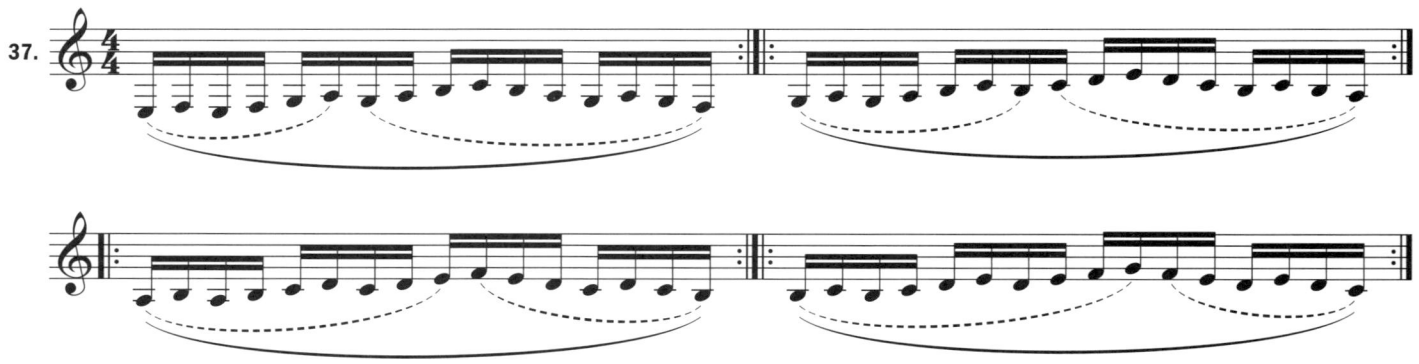

FINGER-WORK AND DEXTERITY

Manuscript: Mendelssohn Clarinet Sonata

Performance

Bringing the music to life

Playing with 'style'

Potential performance issues for clarinettists

Bringing the music to life

Practice and the *power of intention*

As you spend quality time thinking about and practising the techniques and exercises in this book, hopefully you will constantly be developing and improving your playing. More importantly, you will simultaneously be developing an *instinctive and unconscious* control over what you are doing. The keyword here is *thinking* – thinking as you practise. For optimum learning – whether it's a physical skill, a musical thought or concept, or a theoretical understanding – we must continually contemplate and reflect upon that learning. Ideally a practice session should be a constant conversation with yourself.

Maybe you've just been working at some exercises to improve slurring up to the *altissimo* register. As part of the process it's very useful to reflect on what you've been doing.

There are some general reflections to consider, for example:

- What have I just learned? … *to relax my jaw more, and maintain a faster flow of air as I ascend.*
- Why did I learn it? … *in this instance, so that I can better control the opening of Brahms' Clarinet Sonata No. 1.*
- How did I learn it? … *by becoming more aware of what I'm doing with the appropriate muscles.*

There are some more specific questions to ponder also:

- What exactly did I do? … *concentrated on the amount of tension in my jaw muscles and an appropriate control of air until I became fluent in slurring upwards.*
- How exactly did I do it? … *thought about the jaw biting, played some long notes first, and then the exercises slowly.*
- Should I do it again? … *have I achieved my goal of slurring comfortably up to the altissimo register? … maybe not yet. There's still a way to go to reach an instinctive control.*

And maybe the most crucial question of all:

- What effect does this new learning have on what I can already do and what I already know? *It's given me more confidence and I find I can also play other leaps with confidence.*

Learning something new, or extending something we already know or can do, will almost always have a knock-on effect. It may suddenly put other aspects of what we know or can do into a different or clearer context. It might mean that what we can already do now, needs to be reassessed – for example, a new fingering may have an effect on the whole way we approach a particular phrase. It might give us a lot more confidence to try other things. Awareness of that knock-on effect is a great boost to the significance and value of our learning.

Once we are learning efficiently, that learning can become *internalised*, meaning it becomes instinctive and unconscious, but that's not our final destination as learners. Each minuscule component, each tiny detail (be it part of the physical, musical or theoretical journey) will become instinctive and unconscious if we take the trouble to *think* and process what we are doing as we are doing it. The process is cumulative: it gradually builds up.

If this kind of study and learning becomes routine (gradually building our technique), then conscious thought on the process becomes unnecessary. Our minds now have the space and freedom to connect directly with the music and so might spontaneously imagine a new way to shape a phrase, put in a *diminuendo* we hadn't thought of before, or play a note more softly – anything at all in response to the musical moment.

The essence of the matter

This gives us the **power of intention**: *this is what I want to do with this music at this moment and I know instinctively that I can do it – so I do.* It's very important to understand that this process can happen at any level, which is why I call it 'cumulative'. If elementary players know and understand what they are doing, their ability to do it and apply it in other contexts as they progress is heightened.

Of course, there are always some who are able to do all this seemingly without much effort, and they can do it at any level. We often applaud such individuals for their *innate talent*, and maybe label them 'prodigies', but they are generally just processing more quickly and making connections faster. For many, taking a more thoughtful approach to learning the clarinet will ultimately result in the same thing: unlocking and accelerating the speed of learning, and so producing equal progress and achievement. What's more, the investment of time and effort can, in the end, prove as durable and perhaps more practical, as this results in the ability to pass on skills to others in meaningful and effective ways.

Once the appropriate technical skills have been developed, we are liberated to express the music without barriers, hindrance or obstacles. If we decide to do something – for example, play a leap with more *diminuendo*, or a passage with a lighter *staccato* – then that *intention* will almost always just happen. We *will* be able to control it technically. If we *want* it to happen, it will happen. It's a powerful reflex.

Intentional practice

This takes us to the heart of practice. There has been much written about this often perplexing activity. Some enjoy it; many don't. Some seem to make strides forward at great pace; others seem to get stuck and plateau for ages. For most, though, it's probably a mixture of these two extremes.

Here, I'd just like to add one thought about getting the best out of the time we do spend practising. Spend a lot of time practising in *slow motion*. Not literally slow motion, but just taking as much time as you need. Whatever you do, do it with great care. Careless practice can result in mis-programming the brain, which will impede progress. In the process of thorough learning, don't be in a hurry. Ultimately progress will be much more profound and lasting.

Whether it's an exercise, a scale or a piece, set up every note and every technical manoeuvre with extreme care. Never just do it, but do it *thinking about what you're doing*. Choose a slow pulse and use the time between the notes to think exactly what you will do to play the next note as successfully and with as much control as possible, with the maximum of effect and the minimum of tension.

Maybe our mantra should be: **fast thinking … slow playing.**

THE THIRD NOTE

As players (and teachers), we sometimes find it difficult to master a particularly tricky passage, despite much practice. Sometimes the best way to overcome awkward technical manoeuvres is to consider the *third note*. For example, a two-note figure is identified as being the cause of a tricky passage. After some slow-motion practice on the notes in question, add the previous note. The solution is often found in exploring the best way to move to the tricky pair via the note before. *The third note!*

REPETITION

If you're going to repeat something during the process, think *why?* What are you particularly concentrating on? Never do something mindlessly. It just wastes time and risks building the wrong movements into your muscle memory.

Practice is a process of building each phrase, exploring and finding the solution to each technical challenge, one careful step at the time. Aim, ultimately, to find everything you do 'easy'. That's not to say that we are not continually seeking out new musical and technical challenges, but if each step is the right one, progress is smooth and continuous.

Eventually the brain will be so well-programmed that you will simply be able to do whatever it is you want to do, and do it instinctively and unconsciously.

Just a few 'rules' for getting the best out of your practice time:

- Practise regularly, but not for too long at a time. Take lots of short breaks.
- Stay relaxed and work patiently and methodically. Never allow yourself to get frustrated. If you are, you're doing the wrong thing – or maybe you're doing the right thing, but at the wrong time or in the wrong order!
- A mistake is where something goes wrong because you don't really know how to do it or it has been set up without enough preparation. So don't do it! A slip happens on the way to perfection. If you do make a slip, reflect and carefully consider the cause, decide on *what you are going to change when you try it again* and then have another go. Mistakes are frustrating. Slips are opportunities.
- Never play faster than you can, but play slowly often.
- Try to imagine, or even sing, *your* ideal shape for a phrase before you play it, so that technical aspects don't influence your musical decisions.
- Practice is a place – enjoy being there.

Interpretation and Quantum Phrasing

Much of our discussion has been on the technical side of playing. Let's look briefly at interpretation, and in particular at phrasing. Players of different instruments, when considering phrasing, take into account a variety of factors: for example, string players will consider up- and down-bows, pianists will consider textures and multiple lines, singers have words to think about. In phrasing clarinet music, we are just thinking about supporting a single line through our breathing.

Phrasing is a multi-faceted subject and musicians are constantly trying to unlock its secrets.

FROM SPEAKING TO PLAYING

When we speak, we do so in phrases. It makes what we say intelligible and meaningful and gives it the personal perspective we wish to convey.

Aloud, say the line: 'I'm good at scales.'

Now say it as a …
- … simple statement
- … question
- … with pride
- … thoughtfully
- … as if you don't believe you are

Now say the line again, trying to convey a more complex sentiment. For example, you may say it with a degree of incredulity, delighted at having achieved full marks on scales at an exam having thought you'd done poorly.

Now try putting an emphasis on individual words and see what the phrase suggests …

- '*I'm* good at scales.' … *and you're good at …*
- 'I'm *good* at scales.' … *even if you don't think so.*
- 'I'm good *at* scales.' … *and also at aural and sight-reading.*
- 'I'm good at ***scales***.' … *but not so good at aural work and sight-reading.*

The difference in meaning conveyed between these examples varies between slight and really quite significant. It's all down to inflection, timbre, nuance, emphasis, vocal punctuation and, to a certain extent, rhythm. Once you've said those words with the meaning you wish to convey, we might say you've given the phrase *a shape*.

The same is the case in musical phrasing. Let's take the first phrase in Brahms' Sonata No. 2, Op. 120:

There are several ways of phrasing this:

- You may wish to make the G (an *appoggiatura*) your most glowing note (this movement is full of expressive *appoggiaturas*); it's also the highest note in the phrase.

- Maybe you might also wish to direct the phrase to the B♭ or right to the end of the final E. Knowledge of the harmony will also help here.
- Perhaps you might like to put some energy into the secondary upbeat E (the leading note) in the first bar.[75]

Would any of these be inappropriate? Some may argue that one or another may be more effective – but really it's down to personal preference. These decisions ultimately result in developing your own *interpretation* of that phrase.

One of the exciting aspects of phrasing is that it can be as complex, subtle and multi-layered as you like. You might wish to put that little energy on the second note, make the third glow, but still aim for the B♭ and maintain a clear sense of movement right through to end of the final E. Behind all these nuances, additionally there would be delicate *crescendos* and *diminuendos* and maybe a touch of *rubato*. This is what I think of as *Quantum Phrasing*, elaborate and multi-layered phrasing, which gives shape, direction, colour and meaning. Of course, you don't have to think through and analyse every phrase you play. Once into this kind of thinking it will begin to happen instinctively.

Of overriding importance of course, is to think in long, beautiful, unbroken lines. Thinking through the tiny details of each phrase during practice sessions opens the mind to many potential possibilities. Spontaneously in a performance, you might just feel a leaning towards a shape that lends itself, at that instant, to creating an exquisite musical moment. It must be similar to how actors give shape, direction and meaning to their words. For example, in Shakespeare's immortal line: 'To be, or not to be, that is the question', there are so many ways to phrase those words – each of them effective in their different ways.

Where you breathe (during longer phrases) is another issue to consider, which will be dependent on your personal breath control. How many notes or bars can you play before you run out of breath? If you need to breathe within a phrase take care not to 'close' or taper the note before taking the breath (see page 61). By not diminishing the dynamic at the end of the note, the listener is deceived or misdirected into not noticing that breath. Karl Leister sometimes recommends taking the breath somewhat theatrically, not in any way trying to hide it, as part of the drama of the music. There are a number of instances in the Brahms Sonatas where *dramatic breathing* might add to the intensity of the performance. It's up to you.

There is yet another level to *Quantum Phrasing*, but in getting there we need first to look at upbeats and downbeats.

Upbeats and downbeats

In the act of walking, what exactly propels us forward? Scientifically it's quite a complex manoeuvre to do with friction and forces, but if we look at walking more simply, one foot is put downwards on the ground, then the other is picked up, swung forward and put down, then the other is picked up again, swung forward and put down, and so on. We are walking; we are moving forwards. Simplify that further – one foot goes down and then the other up.

Where does the *movement* come in this action? It is the foot that comes up and swings forward that produces the onward movement. The foot that's on the ground is, temporarily, motionless. The analogy with upbeats and downbeats is very revealing. We might say that downbeats are, to some extent, passive or static whilst upbeats are essentially active or dynamic.

---

75. I refer to secondary upbeats as upbeats to notes other than the first beat of the bar.

PERFORMANCE

Often the energy in a phrase or passage is found in the upbeats. So to give music a sense of rhythm, a sense of forward drive, and a sense of shape and direction, we need to study upbeats. But just before we do, let's look at the word 'rhythm'.

> **Rhythm** derives from the Latin *rhythmus* meaning 'movement in time' and the Greek *rhythmos*, meaning 'measured flow or movement'. Movement is the essence. Movement gives a sense of flow, energy, action, and progress. When music is played without these qualities, without movement, it can sound dull, inactive, lifeless and immobile. Interestingly, these qualities sometimes occur as musical character. But there is a difference between musical character (in whatever guise it may be) and the rhythmic drive that causes music to move forward giving phrases shape and direction.

Let's look at the beginning of the Brahms again. There are a number of ways we could interpret the inner rhythmic drive based on the upbeats. The second note is an upbeat, and therefore has some internal energy propelling it towards the expressive appoggiatura G and the next F, its resolution.[76] What happens next is interesting. In the following examples the dotted lines are not there to show slurring but rather how you might *think* the phrase; the articulation always remains Brahms' own.

- The A and D could be felt together as an upbeat to the B♭:

- Or just the D:

In each case there is a slightly different feel to the phrase. Those notes are not really noticeably emphasised (certainly not accented) – but they are thought of as our way to give rhythmical movement and will contribute to the shape of the phrase.

- There is yet another and even more subtle way where the F can be played both as a resolution and as part of the upbeat:

Experiment and see what you might discover.

Now, consider the phrasing of semiquaver (sixteenth-note) passages. There are literally endless passages throughout the entire repertoire to choose from as examples, but here's one from the first movement of the Mozart Concerto:

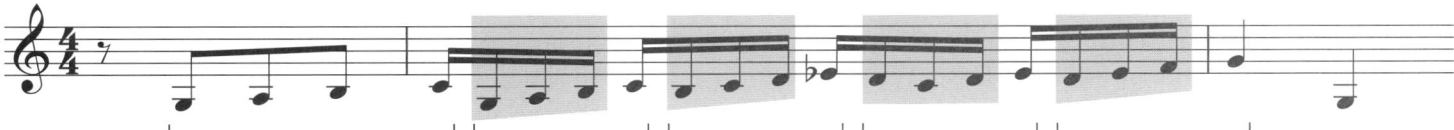

The brackets don't indicate slurring, just the musical grouping of the notes. The three upbeat semiquavers (sixteenth notes) in each beat leading to the next beat (let's call those *secondary downbeats*) will suddenly take on more life and direction if you consider them with this shaping. You may like to give a greater sense of flow, whilst still maintaining the inner rhythmic energy, by feeling it in $\frac{2}{2}$ where it would take on this shape:

This may also influence how you articulate the phrase, and it will certainly change the rhythmic feel in your mind. You will find that just thinking in this way will cause those semiquavers (sixteenth notes) to sparkle with real rhythmic vigour!

Finding the inner rhythmic impulse in a phrase by becoming more aware of upbeats, will add immensely to its shape, and so to its phrasing. It's yet another layer of *Quantum Phrasing*.

---

76. In fact, the concept of tension-resolution should always be a prime consideration behind players' decisions in their phrasing, especially when playing in the Austro-Germanic style, e.g. the resolution of an *appoggiatura*, or any dissonance to a consonance.

Playing with 'style'

Players today do their best to bring some stylistic thinking and interpretation into their performances. Just as there are varied styles of playing the clarinet in different genres such as classical or jazz, an accomplished player should be able to adapt their playing to reflect something of the historical period in which a particular piece was written. Since we have no recordings of musical performances before 1890 to listen to, we must turn to contemporary writings, editions and paintings as our source materials.[77] Since we can't actually hear any recorded clarinet performances from before the 1900s, this means that however authentic we might like to feel our playing to be, ultimately it is to some considerable extent conjecture and guesswork.

If you are able to play a period instrument, set up with the appropriate reed and mouthpiece, you would find that many adjustments would be needed in terms of your technique and tone production. In these circumstances, you would be able to gain at first hand some insights into playing in the style of the period.

For most of us this won't be possible. However, we can still aim to play with musical conviction, coupled with an awareness of the style of the period. This doesn't mean making our performances sound tedious and uninteresting by a misguided attempt to conform to certain received 'conventions' that may be constricting or difficult to interpret. Nevertheless we do need to shape and fashion our interpretations based on some knowledge of the time in which the works were created.

On the other hand you may like to take a much more exploratory or even *provocative* view; art, after all, should challenge, and allow the imagination to run in all sorts of directions. I recall a fascinating performance where Antony Pay mixed movements of the Saint-Saëns Sonata and John Cage's Solo Sonata, at one point playing a movement of the Cage simultaneously with the solo piano passage that makes up the second half of Saint-Saëns' third movement. Would you consider putting a jazz cadenza in the Mozart Concerto? One's initial reaction may be of horror, but think about it!

Baroque

Owing to the clarinet's birthday being around the beginning of the 18th century the repertoire from this period is fairly limited. However, there are significant works by Handel (Overture in D Major, for two clarinets and horn), Molter (Six Concertos), Telemann (Concerto for Two Chalumeaux) and Vivaldi (Three Concerti, for two oboes and two clarinets).[78]

Composers from this period rarely added markings to their music, so dynamics and articulation found in printed editions will have been added by the editor based either on research or their best guess about contemporary performance. This means it is quite acceptable to make alterations for your own ease of playing or if you feel more expressive phrasing would result.

Choosing tempi is also open to experimentation. For example, the term *Andante* derives from the Italian *Andare* meaning 'to go' suggesting that music so marked may be better interpreted as a little faster than the traditional 'at a walking pace' definition might imply. Since ornamentation was an essential element in Baroque performance, it's important to have some knowledge of ornaments and the various ways of interpreting them. Robert Donington's book *The Interpretation of Early Music* (1963) is very helpful, also in its excellent overall discussion of everything pertaining to the Baroque style.[79]

Many original manuscripts are now available online if you wish to study them and discover exactly what the composer did write. Johann Quantz's famous book, *On Playing the Flute* (1752) will also provide much insight into playing Baroque music.[80]

---

77. In fact, the first known acoustic recording was made in 1888 – a performance of Arthur Sullivan's song *The Lost Chord*. The first 'professional' recordings began in 1901 and were made in Russia, featuring personalities from the Imperial Russian Opera including the great bass Feodor Chaliapin. The first clarinet recordings were made very early in the 20th century, but these were mainly arrangements of operatic melodies or variations. Charles Draper recorded the first standard repertoire work, Weber's Concertino, in about 1908 – probably the first significant recording of a professional clarinet player. The first complete recording of the Mozart Concerto was by Haydn Draper in 1929.
78. Graupner, Faber, Rathgeber, Paganelli and Kölbel are other Baroque composers who wrote for the early clarinet.
79. At the time of publication, this book is freely available: https://archive.org/details/interpretationof010975mbp/page/n47/mode/2up.
80. Faber and Faber Ltd., 1996.

Classical

There is a vast repertoire for the clarinet in this period and composers began to add more performance markings: articulation, dynamics and markings of attack (such as accents etc.). This means that markings in modern printed editions are more likely to be the composer's own.[81] In keeping with the Classical style you should be aiming for simplicity of tone, delicacy of line and measured expression. Do look at architecture, interior design, paintings and sculpture of the period for inspiration.

Disappointingly, the majority of the original manuscript of one of the most important works in the repertoire, Mozart's Clarinet Concerto, is lost, so all editions are based on the first printed edition – not on Mozart's autograph.[82] On the plus side, this means that it is quite acceptable to adapt the articulation to fit your particular tonguing capabilities.

The Classical Style[83] by the American pianist and author Charles Rosen is a marvellous read for those wishing to study this period in depth, as is Leopold Mozart's *A Treatise on the Fundamental Principles of Violin Playing* (1756).[84]

It also has to be taken into account that these composers were writing their music with quill and ink. What if the tip of their quill was a bit worn after a long day's composing, or the ink a little less viscous than usual, or the paper a little more porous? It's quite possible that some of their markings may not be quite what they had intended!

Romantic

By this time composers were adding many more performance details to their scores. Instead of expecting players to improvise (cadenzas, occasional decorations etc.), composers wanted to indicate to performers more of what they had in mind. At the same time there was an increasing amount of freedom for the performer in terms of dynamic range, tempi, etc., simply because music of this period was meant to be much more expressive and flexible, particularly in terms of tempo.

The Romantic period also saw the rise of the great virtuosi – solo performers who brought their own very individualistic interpretations to the music.[85] Music from this period is marked by a broader and more dramatic use of dynamic levels and attack, as well as a certain expressive flexibility to the pulse.

In terms of tempo, from 1817 onwards it became common for composers to add metronome markings. Although it's important not to follow these too slavishly, having some idea of what the composer had in mind makes it much easier to choose an appropriate tempo. Additionally, venue, acoustic, mood, the size of the accompanying orchestra (if appropriate) and your own personal capabilities are among other factors to consider.

Interestingly Weber's very important clarinet works, written between 1811 and 1816, bridge both the Classical and Romantic styles. Most of these works were written for Heinrich Baermann, probably the greatest player of the time, and interesting editions of many of these works were produced by Carl Baermann – (Heinrich's son) based on Heinrich's own marked-up solo part. These provide fascinating insights into the way players of the time might have interpreted the music. Weber's manuscripts are fairly sparse, and Carl's editions include a plethora of dynamic makings, articulations, extra notes and little embellishments as well as some more lengthy cadenzas. So, when playing Weber, within the harmonic and melodic conventions of the time, feel free to be creative.

In playing middle- or later-period Romantic music, for example Spohr, Schumann, Brahms and Reger, there is much room for creative phrasing, imaginitive use of tone colour and *rubato*. However, with late Romantic music it would be unstylistic to change or add to the composer's actual text.

---

81. Markings in brackets or broken slurs in a printed edition usually indicate that they were added by the editor.
82. According to most scholars, we have the first 199 bars of the original – the rest is lost.
83. Faber and Faber Ltd., 2005.
84. Oxford University Press, 1948.
85. Heinrich and his son Carl Baermann, Bernhard Crusell, and Johann Hermstedt were among the great clarinet virtuosi of the 19th century.

THE CLARINET

AUTOGRAPHED EXAMPLES FROM THE CLARINET REPERTOIRE

Weber, Clarinet Quintet Op. 34, I

Schumann, *Fantasiestücke* Op. 73, II

Debussy, *Première Rhapsodie*

PERFORMANCE

La belle époque[86] and 20th-century French composers

As the 19th century rolled into the 20th century there was something of a reaction against the highly charged, intense, personal and emotion-packed style of the Romantics. This was seen particularly in France where some very important clarinet repertoire was emerging. It caused a move towards a more 'impressionistic' style, with parallels in painting and the visual arts. Also seen at this time was a resurgence of interest in Classical structures (neo-Classicism). Much of the music of this period is in fact a kind of amalgam of both of these 'movements'.

Interestingly, 'impressionist' composers (Debussy especially) didn't much approve of the label themselves, but their music is certainly more detached, more concerned with mood and atmosphere than with individualistic expression. Aim to evoke a Classical elegance and reserve in interpretation, with a meticulous, neat, and delicate control and fluidity in performance. Think of the difference between oil paintings and watercolours: we're looking more towards watercolour now in the textures of the sound and in the interpretation.

French composers were obsessed with markings. In playing the music of Debussy, Widor, Rabaud, as well as Poulenc and Françaix (amongst others) all markings – dynamics, articulation, performance directions – should be observed strictly.

There needs to be a lightness in the sound – even in *forte* playing. Listen to French players. Consider the sense of rhythmic movement too, particularly in the more flourish-like gestures. For example, Karl Leister suggests the demi-semiquaver flourishes in Debussy's *Première Rhapsodie*, (between bars 46 and 50 as shown on page 198) are played as a 'wash of colour, as if moving the paintbrush swiftly across the canvas'.[87]

In the more neo-Classical styles of Poulenc and Françaix, it is important to avoid playing slow music overly lugubriously or indulgently. Listen, for example, to the available performances of Poulenc playing Poulenc.[88]

Modern

When it comes to music from about 1900 onwards, in the words of Cole Porter's great 1934 musical, 'anything goes'. Stylistically music became very diverse, some composers continuing in the neo-Classical or neo-Romantic styles, some moving towards the avant-garde, some embracing the emergence of jazz, and some incorporating older folk styles such as klezmer. Despite all this diversity, experimentation and apparent freedom, composers are often increasingly prescriptive and detailed in their directions and markings for the player. However, the range of tone, articulation and rhythmic fluidity you can bring to such repertoire can be as broad as your technique might accommodate.

There are fascinating and widely available recordings of performances, where composers and the players for whom the works were written have collaborated. Copland and Arnold, for example, have both recorded their concertos with Benny Goodman (the dedicatee). These are essential listening in developing an understanding of the appropriate style.

Of course there are specific stylistic considerations to be followed if you are playing music particular to jazz or klezmer for example. Some of these techniques (e.g. pitch bending and *glissandi*), are discussed earlier (see *Sounding good*, page 46). If you are interested in developing these techniques further there are always specialists in these particular contemporary styles who can be of help.

> In summary, an awareness of stylistic conventions is vital for the informed player. However, the great joy of music making is in the individual performer's own interpretations. If we are to ensure the future of the wonderfully rich clarinet repertoire we have inherited, players must seek to maintain a freshness each time a work is re-performed, a sense that each new performance is, to some extent, a rediscovery.

---

86. A period in European history between about 1870 and 1914 where there was great optimism and development in all areas of life especially the arts and technology.
87. In a wonderful masterclass that he gave in my house a few years ago.
88. Sadly there is no recording of the Clarinet Sonata accompanied by Poulenc himself, who died before the work was published, but there is a recording of Poulenc accompanying the Flute Sonata and much can be learned about stylistic interpretation from this. There is no hint of sentimentality in the slow movement. Philippe Cuper told me that in his lessons with André Boutard (who was the only clarinettist to have played it with the composer) Poulenc asked that the precise rhythms be truly respected and that no rubato should disturb the 'sentences'.

Potential performance issues for clarinettists

Much has been written on performance and performance anxiety. Rather than duplicating information, here we will consider some specific aspects that clarinet players in particular are sometimes prone to in moments of stress. Of course making your technical and musical preparations for concerts, recitals, exams or auditions as comprehensive and thorough as possible will contribute significantly to reducing stress levels. Here are some potential problem areas connected to such events and some thoughts and possible recommendations on how to deal with them.

Warming up

Choose some of your favourite warming- and limbering-up exercises from the chapter *Be prepared!* to start. Some deep breathing is very helpful. It will slow down the pulse rate and make you feel calmer. Blowing some notes with the reed set around 5mm above the mouthpiece is particularly recommended. It will invigorate the breathing muscles very quickly. Nerves affect breathing – it becomes shallow. This should help alleviate that possibility.

Dry mouth

Singers sometimes apply a little lemon juice, or lemon-scented cream on their hands as the aroma can help to get the saliva glands working. Drinking a small glass of water with a squeeze of lemon or lime will increase saliva production.

Too much saliva

Avoid chocolate and sugary drinks that thicken saliva by releasing enzymes.

Tight throat

Another potential result of nerves is a tight throat. Again, be prepared. Think about the back of your tongue in your warming/limbering up and maybe do the soft palate exercise on page 37. Spend a few moments breathing gently with a slightly open mouth. Singing and playing simultaneously (if you can) will relax the throat.

PERFORMANCE

Embouchure tightness

This is so often a result of nerves. *Be aware* of the embouchure tightening, or even of the *possibility* of it tightening. If it does, silently 'talk' your way through it. '*I must relax those muscles.*' Consciously relax both embouchure and jaw muscles (but be careful not to let this affect breath support). As part of preparation, think through the possible moments in the repertoire where such tightness might occur – before a section involving leaps, or in a sustained passage that uses higher notes, for example, and practise them reminding yourself to remain in control of those muscles. Maybe do some embouchure and posture flexibility exercises (see page 43). Particularly recommended is hissing with fast air and moving your lips around.

Grace-note gambit

If there is a passage you feel you really do need to play, then play it in the GNG manner. Insert a short grace note between the notes (see page 64).

Improvising

Improvise around the pieces you are going to be playing in the appropriate keys, using scales and other related patterns. Maybe improvise around particular technical areas, for example, downward leaps, light *staccato*, or very quiet playing. Avoid actually playing sections from the pieces themselves, unless you have a lot of time where you can play sections very slowly. If things go wrong it can affect your confidence.

Reeds and mouthpieces

Even with really careful preparation there can still be last-minute problems. Maybe the favoured reed doesn't work with the acoustic. The simple solution is always to have a number of reeds on the go. There's always the very unlikely possibility that you might drop your mouthpiece, so having a spare (especially if the event is an important one) is also not a bad idea. As a general rule, harder reeds are more suitable to dryer acoustics and softer reeds to more reverberant acoustics, but ultimately it is the music that is of overriding importance. Don't let mouthpieces and reeds become too distracting.

Problems caused by food and drink

Take care what you eat and drink before a performance. Avoid heavy foods that can impede the movement of the breathing muscles and make you tired (and avoid fatty foods that can increase phlegm production). If you need to eat, choose lighter foods like salad and vegetables, soup, and apples, which digest quickly. Complex carbs like porridge, nuts or a banana will give a quick release of energy. Try not to eat anything substantial within around an hour of a performance. Be careful with caffeine and alcohol – both are dehydrating. Caffeine can also affect the central nervous system and cause minor tremors, especially in the hands. It's a good idea to brush your teeth before a performance, preferably without toothpaste which may affect saliva production.

The clarinet

Reeds – straight out of the box?

The mouthpiece

Taking care of your clarinet

Reeds – straight out of the box?

Many players and teachers subscribe to the practical view that you take a reed out of the box and you do your best. If on the other hand you discard those that don't meet your requirements, probably and uneconomically, this will mean consigning a number to the bin. For some players reeds can become a source of irritation – even exasperation. This needn't be the case.

With just a little knowledge and some basic (and inexpensive) tools, it's possible to begin to manage your reeds, making the good ones better and the not-so-good ones usable.

Managing your reeds

What you'll need:

- Ideally, a piece of glass to which you need to bond a piece of very fine sandpaper. Try to get some holes punched into the sandpaper that will allow it to be *really* flat.
- Some additional very fine sandpaper (grit 400–600)
- An implement for filing reeds (you can use reed rush or a glass reed stick)
- A reed clipper (optional)

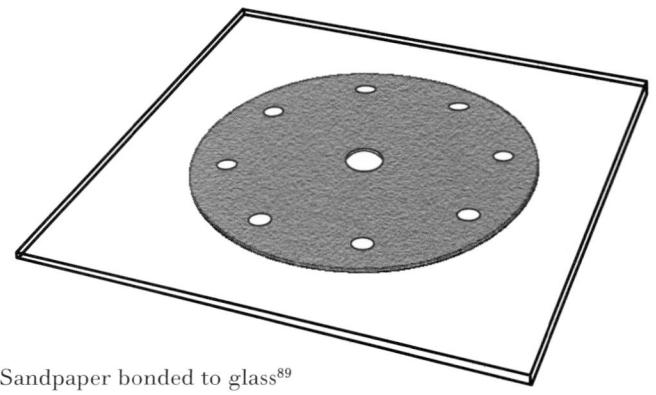

Sandpaper bonded to glass[89]

Reed anatomy

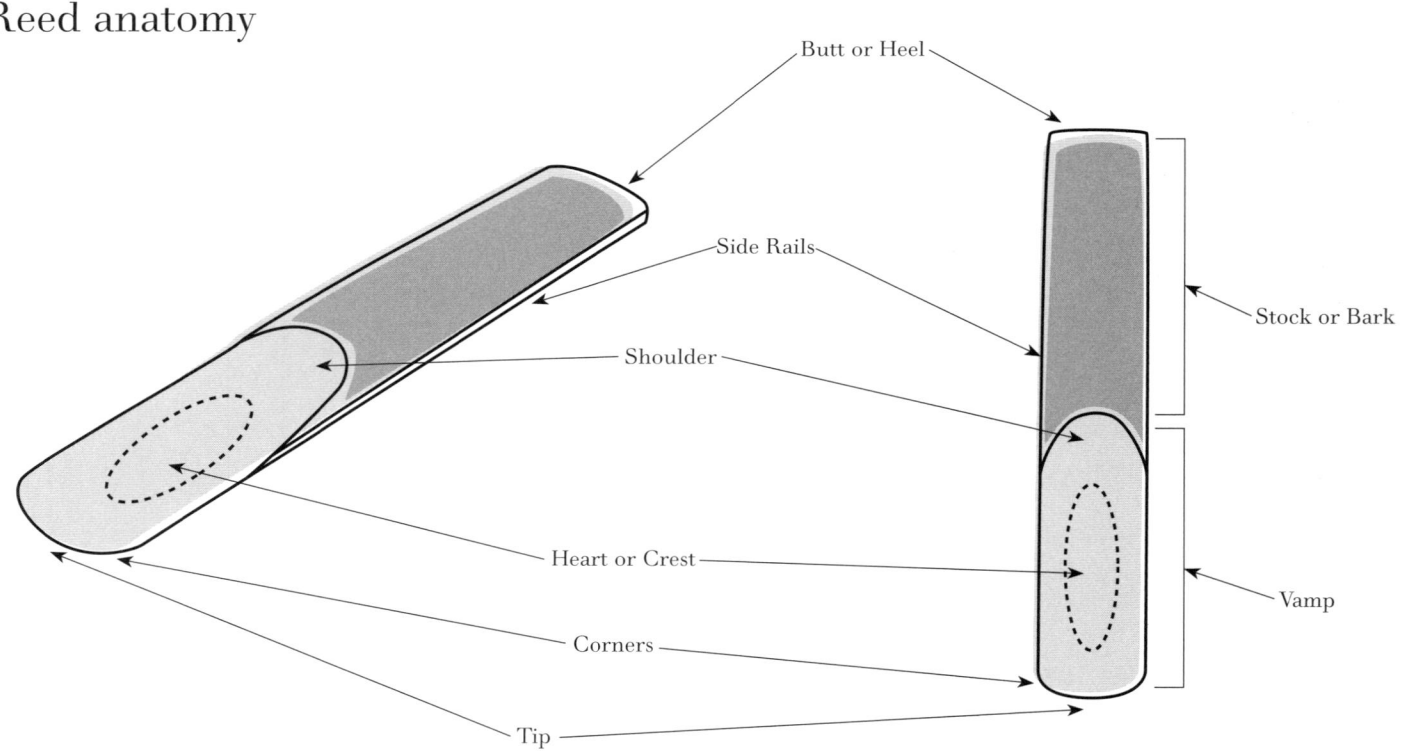

---

89. This particular design has been developed by Gaspare Buonomano and Xiya Cheng.

The characteristics of a good reed

Here are some useful characteristics to look out for:

- Look at the heel: a thicker reed will generally give a better response compared with a thin one. Check that it has a good symmetrical curve.

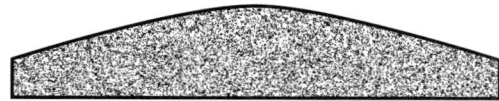

A good shape and thickness

A poor shape and too thin

- The fibres should be reasonably evenly distributed and aligned straight up and down the vamp.
- A consistent light or creamy colour usually indicates a good reed. Some say a few dark spots on the bark are usually a good sign (but this may well be an example of clarinet folklore!).

Filed and unfiled reeds

This affects the part of the reed just behind the vamp. On filed reeds (sometimes called 'French' or 'double cut'), just behind the vamp, you'll find a thin layer of bark sanded in a straight line. This can encourage a more free blowing response, with a slight ease of production in soft articulation. They will usually provide a brighter tone. Moderately resistant mouthpieces generally work well with filed reeds.

Unfiled reeds (sometimes called 'American' or 'single cut') have a U-shape where the vamp joins the bark. These usually provide the player with a darker, more resistant tone. Easy-blowing mouthpieces work well with unfiled reeds.

Some players do have a preference for one over the other, but, practically speaking, for most players the two cuts will feel very similar.

On the table

The underside of a reed is called the *table*. An ideal reed needs a really flat table that will cause it to vibrate evenly and provide you with a good response. Making the table absolutely flat (even by factory standards) is difficult and sometimes the reed warps over time.

Try this test. Using a very soft pencil, draw three parallel lines on the table (as shown below).

Now gently sand in a side-to-side motion the underside of the reed on your glass for a few moments and then have a look at the result. If all three lines have disappeared or are equally faint then the reed is flat. More likely is that they appear slightly uneven, so a little more sanding is necessary until they have all disappeared. The reed is now likely to be much more even, which will give you a better response.

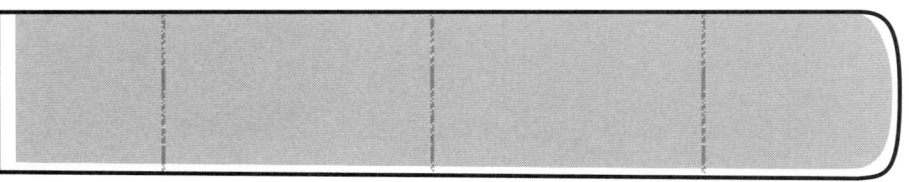

THE CLARINET

The first tests

Having made sure the table of the reed is completely flat, we now turn our attention to the topside, or vamp, of the reed.

Place the reed on the mouthpiece, carefully checking its position. It is very important to have the reed really centred. Check the placement of both the tip (which should be parallel with the tip of the mouthpiece) and the heel. At this point, try to avoid handling the vamp and especially the tip of the reed. Instead hold it on the stock (or bark) to protect the reed tip. Adjust until it is really centred.

Then, holding the reed on the mouthpiece with your left-hand thumb (rather than attaching it with the ligature), very softly – somewhere between ***ppp*** and ***pp*** – play an open G (G^2), with firm breath support and a well-formed embouchure (and absolutely no biting, see page 41). Play for about 10 seconds (or more) and listen closely:

- If the sound has an airy quality then the reed is probably too hard.[90]
- If the note is difficult to keep even and the sound has an unrefined, buzzy and unfocussed quality, then the reed is probably too soft.
- If you hear a beautifully clean, warm, rich and stable sound with ideal resistance, you're very lucky and you probably have an excellent reed.

Further tests

If the result of your test was either of the first two outcomes above then try these further tests:

- Pivot the reed a few millimetres to the left (holding it about halfway down and keeping the heel as centred as possible) and play again at ***pp*** – this will test the right side of the reed.
- Again, listen carefully and feel the response. Decide whether it is too hard and resistant or too soft.
- Now test the left side.

It is not uncommon for each side to have a slightly different response.

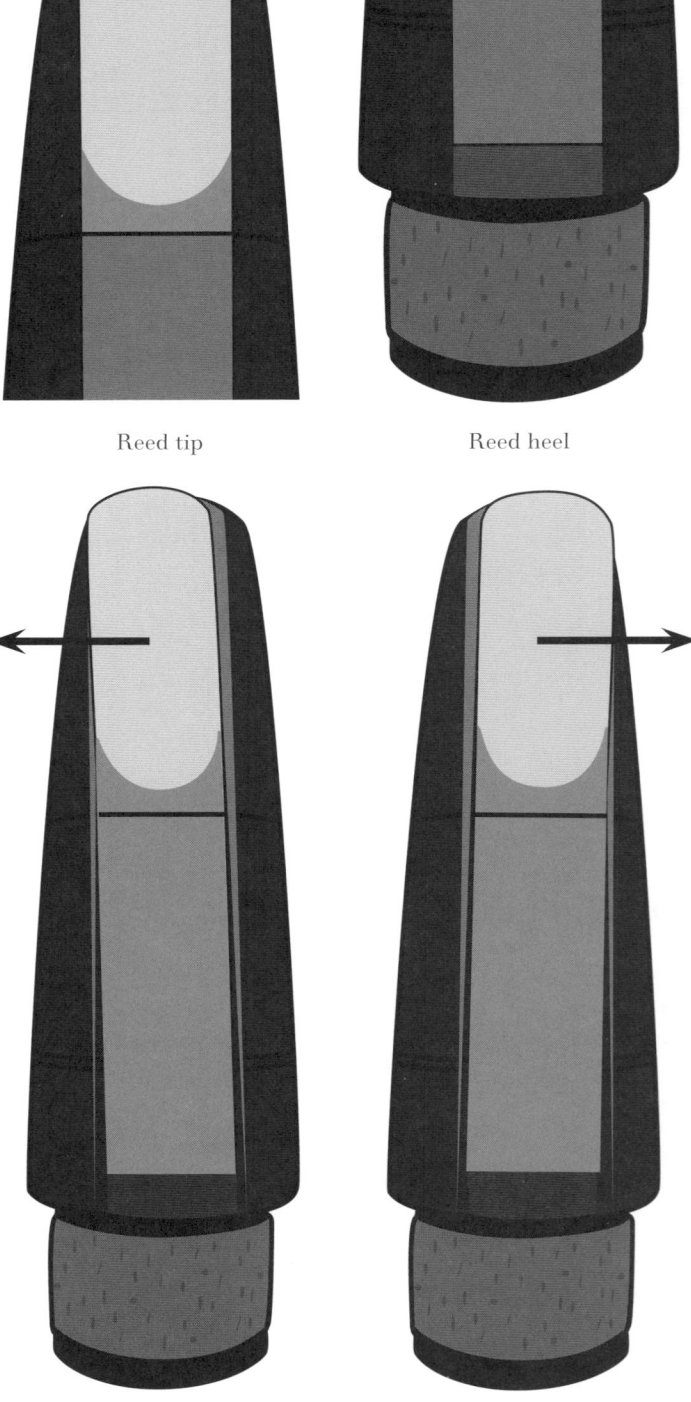

Reed tip

Reed heel

Reed left

Reed right

90. We normally describe reeds as being either hard or soft. It would actually be more accurate to talk of their resistance which varies according to the density of the cane they are made from. A hard (stronger) reed is a more resistant reed and a soft (more flexible) reed, less resistant.

If the side you have tested is too hard, using some Dutch rush,[91] gently sand the appropriate side roughly in the shaded areas, being careful to avoid the heart of the reed (roughly the area inside the oval).

If *both* sides are too soft you can cut the tip with a reed clipper if you have one. Be careful to take off just a tiny amount, test and then take off a little more if necessary. Most reed cutters leave the corners of the reed poorly shaped in relation to most mouthpieces. You might try shaping these with some very fine sandpaper – this is a skill that will probably take some time to master.

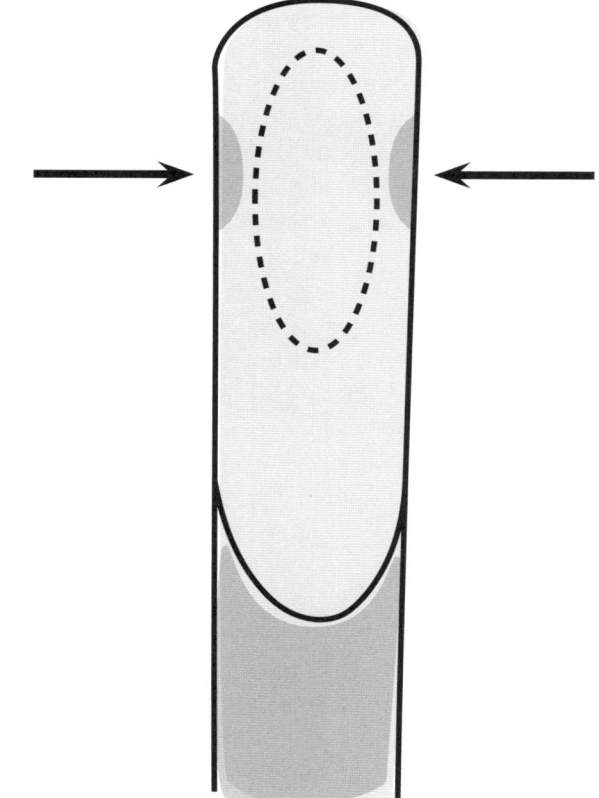

If just one side is too soft then place the reed on its side (with the appropriate side rails on the sandpaper) and sand it very carefully on the glass. Sand only the smallest amount and then test. Repeat the process until you get the desired response when you play.

Take care not to over-sand as this ultimately will render the reed unusable.

With practice you should find that you become quite adept in this kind of basic reed maintenance.

Placing the reed so that the tip protrudes slightly above the mouthpiece tip will cause a harder (more resistant) response and conversely, placing it slightly below the tip, a softer (less resistant) response. Some players suggest that very gently flexing the corners (think of it as gently massaging the corners of the reed) will cause an increase in the warmth of the sound.

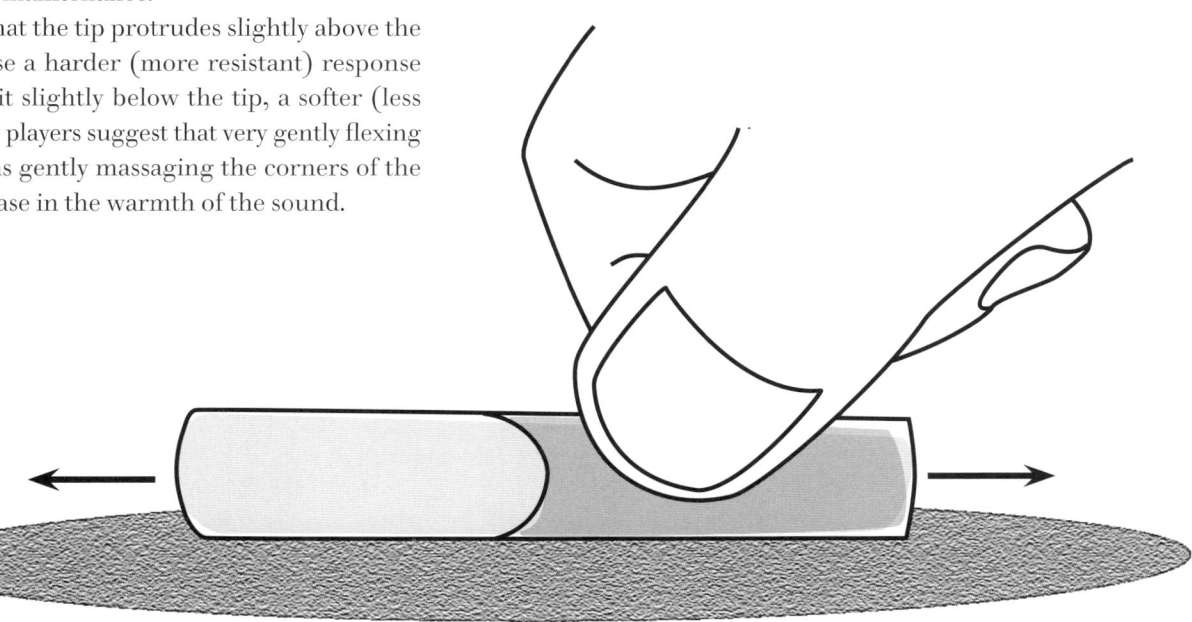

91. Or some sandpaper, or a glass reed stick.

Looking after your reeds

Ideally once you have chosen and made any appropriate adjustments to your new reed, play it in – between about five to ten minutes a day for the first week or so, preferably just using the lower register as upper register notes cause the reed to vibrate too fast.[92] Play at about ***mf***. This will help a reed to develop good moisture retention qualities.

Try to have a number of good reeds on the go and rotate them. The most interesting and clearly sensible advice I've ever heard is always to have seven reeds on the go, one for each day of the week. When one is past its best, replace it. I've known very few to follow this advice! If you enjoy longer practice sessions (more than two hours for example) use more than one reed. As a result, your reeds will last longer and give you better service.

Store reeds in a good quality reed case that holds them flat and keeps the moisture out. After each play you may wish to rinse the reed under a tap, then dry it carefully with a soft cloth or by running it between your thumb and index finger, always moving towards the tip, and then place it in the case. Drying reeds thoroughly after playing will often extend a good reed's life significantly. Reeds can also be placed on a piece of glass after playing. The important point is to keep them flat.

During the interval in concerts keep the mouthpiece cap on to stop the reed from drying out.

Reeds and oral hygiene

Reeds need moistening prior to playing. Usually this is done by placing the reed in the mouth for a few moments. This is conventional practice though some players prefer to moisten the reed in clean water. Try to avoid eating food or drinking acidic beverages immediately before playing as these can damage the reed. If you have had food or drink beforehand, clean your teeth or use a mouthwash before playing.

Take particular care with reeds if you have a cold, flu or any infection as they can harbour germs and bacteria.

The calcium in saliva can also affect reeds, forming a coating on the reed's surface causing it to vibrate less effectively. Some players occasionally soak reeds in a 3% hydrogen peroxide solution. This will dissolve calcium deposits and generally give the reed a good clean and prolong its life. Make sure to rinse *thoroughly* before you play (though this concentration of hydrogen peroxide is usually quite harmless, it is better not to ingest any). It hardly needs saying that clarinet players should look after their teeth!

Synthetic reeds

Plastic reeds have been available for many decades. Today, non-cane reeds are made from quite high-tech synthetic materials and many players are using them. There are a number of different makes on the market; some are fully synthetic and others are fashioned by coating the vamp of a wooden reed with plastic. The response of these reeds varies with different mouthpieces and so some careful experimentation is necessary.

Synthetic reeds are inevitably significantly more expensive than cane reeds, but there are advantages. Once you have a preference for a make and a strength (which often come in quarter sizes), they will all be fairly consistent in response and are unlikely to be affected by temperature and humidity. In addition, they won't need the careful playing-in and maintenance of a cane reed, will generally be more reliable, and will probably last substantially longer.

Reed strengths and myths

I have occasionally heard it suggested that the harder the reed, the better the player. This is a myth! Though, to some extent, the more practice you do, the harder the strength you'll need.

Beginners, generally speaking, will probably use number 2 reeds. Some may prefer half a strength softer. As the embouchure muscles develop, a harder reed will be necessary. Number 3 or 4 reeds (with a suitable mouthpiece) are probably ideal for most players, though if the mouthpiece opening is small you'll probably need a harder reed. It's best to discuss this with a reed expert or with a teacher.

There are many other conditions that may affect a reed's response: the altitude (maybe you're playing up in the Mexican mountains!), the humidity, temperature, acoustic qualities and size of the space in which you are playing.

Choosing the appropriate strength reed is important, since playing on inappropriate reeds can produce unwelcome muscle tension in the embouchure. A good embouchure is all about developing the control and durability of the muscles – not just muscle strength. The right reed will aid enormously in this development.

If you find yourself becoming more interested in reed maintenance there are some good books available to study.[93]

On the other hand, my teacher, John Davies, was of the opinion that you simply do the best with what you've got. In many respects this will develop a more resourceful ability to adapt and reduce worry over having the perfect reed. Maybe somewhere between the two approaches is a prudent place to be.

---

92. The exercises in the *chalumeau* register section (pages 65–69) are ideal for this.
93. See Bibliography, page 232.

The mouthpiece

It is not the intention of this section to go into too much detail about mouthpieces, but a little knowledge can be useful. Certainly, a good quality and well chosen mouthpiece will help a more modest instrument produce surprisingly enhanced results without excessive expense, and having the right mouthpiece might save a lot of money on reeds.

It's important to be aware that mouthpiece behaviour is highly dependent on the subtleties of each individual player's facial physiology, embouchure, technique and personal preferences. Mouthpiece response is not an exact science.

Try to have as good a mouthpiece as possible from as early on as possible. Generally, those that come with instruments are not up to the specifications of those from specialist mouthpiece manufacturers – such a mouthpiece can make a huge difference.

The mouthpiece and reed is where the instrument and the player connect. It's the point where the airflow transforms into beautiful clarinet tone. It affects timbre and tuning, potential dynamic range, flexibility, projection, resistance and response.

Mouthpieces: a very brief history

At the beginning, the mouthpiece was personalised by a relationship between maker and player. By the 1920s there were hundreds of mouthpieces to choose from – probably a greater variation than today. Curiously, the choice then narrowed until the 1960s, but since then it has expanded again and there are now a multitude of mouthpiece models from which to choose. It's salutary to remember though that there have always been great players even when there was little choice. So while having the choice will certainly add another dimension to your playing it's not a decisive factor.

Knowing your mouthpiece

The way in which a mouthpiece plays is determined by a number of intricate factors. Many of these are beyond the scope of this book.[94] The most important feature, however, in determining the interaction between the mouthpiece and the reed is known as the 'facing curve'. The nature of the facing curve affects how the instrument feels when you blow. It might blow very easily, as if you're blowing into a big space (or as if you're playing the recorder), or it might feel more resistant.

So, what do we mean by resistance when associated with a mouthpiece? A mouthpiece that is too free-blowing – where you don't feel *resistance* when playing – may be uncomfortable and not allow you to do all you wish to do.[95] Appropriate resistance will give you a good *response* – in other words, while feeling comfortable, the instrument will respond to your playing with evenness and uniformity throughout its entire range.

The facing curve of your mouthpiece is central to all this. Understanding it will help you to choose a suitable reed for your particular mouthpiece.

The facing curve

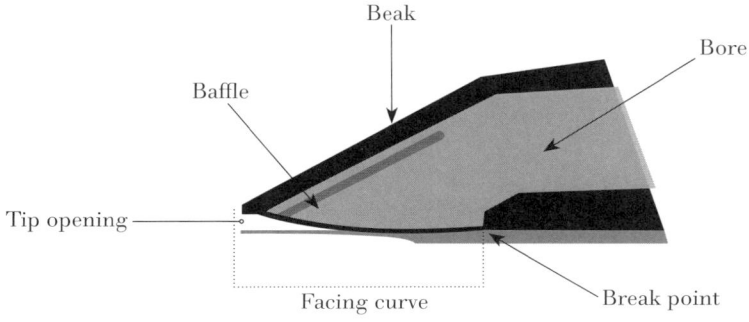

94. For example, the shape of the baffle (the space extending back into the mouthpiece from the tip rail), the internal tone chamber, the angle of the mouthpiece walls and the width of the tip rails and side rails will all have some effect on the response. For those interested in this level of detail it is suggested they contact a mouthpiece maker.
95. The reed also plays an important role in determining how free-blowing a mouthpiece will feel.

THE CLARINET

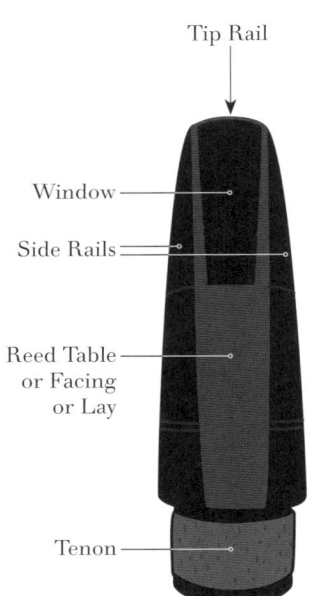
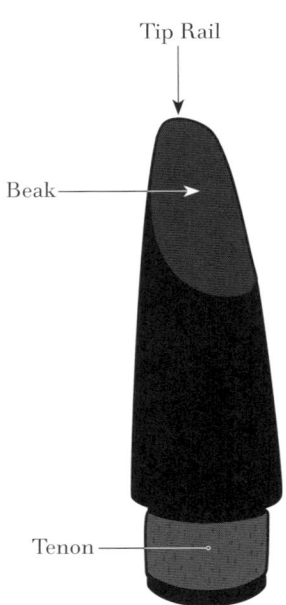
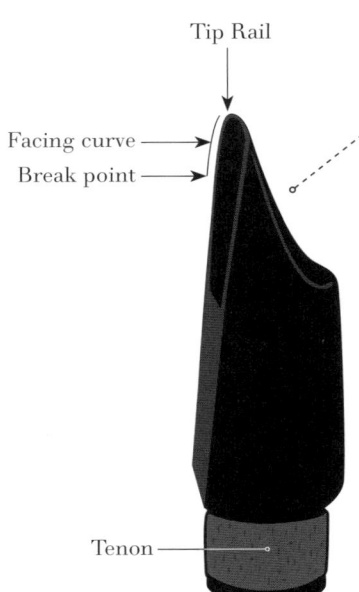

Lowering the beak (as in this mouthpiece design), thus making the beak thickness thinner, can have a significant effect on the resonance of the mouthpiece.

In understanding the facing curve, we need to start at the tip of the mouthpiece. The distance between the reed tip and the tip of the mouthpiece is called the *tip opening* which can be narrow or wide.[96] It is said that in the 19th century, the tip opening was the width of three playing cards (approximately 0.90mm). This trick would have been useful to players at the time, as accurate measuring tools were rare. Great players of the mid-20th century like Jack Thurston and Reginald Kell also played with a similar, though slightly wider opening of about 1.10–1.20mm (Benny Goodman also favoured the 1.20mm opening). All these players used a soft reed – Thurston was known to use number one-and-a-half reeds.

The reed is placed on the table. The portion of the reed that vibrates is specifically the area between its tip and the point where it comes into contact with the table (the *break point*). The break point is where the facing begins to curve. Thus, this area is known as the *facing curve*.

There are two variables with regard to facing curves:

- The *length* of the curve (which can be short or long).[97]
- Its curvature (more curve will result in a wider tip opening, less curve in a narrower tip opening).

This, therefore, gives rise to four main combinations:

a) Short facing curve + small degree of curvature = narrow tip opening:

b) Short facing curve + greater degree of curvature = wide tip opening:

c) Long facing curve + small degree of curvature = narrow tip opening, and greater area of vibration:

d) Long facing curve + greater degree of curvature = wide tip opening and again, greater area of vibration:

So ...

- If you have a mouthpiece with a narrower tip opening (example a or c) you'll need a harder, more resistant reed.
- If you have a mouthpiece with a shorter facing curve (example a or b) you'll need a softer (less resistant) reed.
- If you have a mouthpiece with a wider tip opening (example b or d) you'll need a softer (less resistant) reed.
- If you have a mouthpiece with a longer facing curve (example c or d) you'll need a harder (more resistant) reed.

---

96. To give some figures, a narrow tip opening would typically be 0.95mm–1.12mm; a medium opening would be 1.13mm–1.25mm and a wide opening would be 1.27–1.70mm.

97. Of course, in some mouthpieces the facing curve measurement will be somewhere between short or long, but for the purposes of explanation it is easier to look at the two extremes and the effect they have on playing.

Therefore …

- Mouthpieces with a wide tip opening and short facing curve giving a higher resistance (b) would require a softer reed. This would often be a suitable combination for jazz performers.
- Mouthpieces with a narrow tip opening and long facing curve giving a lower resistance (c) would require a harder reed. This will give a more refined sound that lends itself to solo and orchestral playing. They may also require more mouthpiece in the mouth. The crucial point is not to find yourself dampening the reed which will inhibit the sound.
- Examples a) and d) are more neutral and each have features from both of the above.

Don't worry if all of this sounds a little impenetrable! Mouthpiece manufacturers generally offer clear guides to each of their mouthpieces and will recommend appropriate reed strengths and cuts.[98]

Choosing a mouthpiece

Mouthpieces are typically made from hard rubber (known as ebonite), glass (crystal), plastic or (much less commonly) wood. Most beginner mouthpieces will be made from plastic. These are resilient but limited in tone production and control. Crystal mouthpieces are relatively more resistant in their blowing response, and are unlikely to warp or change in internal dimension with continual cleaning. The tonal properties are slightly different – experiment if you are interested. They have a distinctive appearance but will need very careful looking after, since they can chip fairly easily. Wooden examples are quite rare, have a rather limited dynamic range, lack projection and warp easily. The majority of players use ebonite mouthpieces that will enable a warm, focussed and singing tone quality, combined with good projection.

There are a great many variations in commercial mouthpieces. Seek the advice of a specialist who will direct you to the most appropriate mouthpiece for your needs. All models will indicate tip opening size and facing length.

Make sure you try out a variety of similar models using both a trusted reed and new reeds.[99] A good first test would be to play a chromatic scale over the entire range of the instrument loudly at a reasonable speed thus eliminating the possibility of adjusting your technique to the mouthpiece. Then play the same scale very softly – it's essential to find a mouthpiece that will comfortably play quietly. Don't warm up on the mouthpiece as this will give you cause to get used to it and begin adapting. Then try another one and compare.

Once happy, test for the following across the whole range of the mouthpiece:

- Intonation
- Evenness and uniformity of tone at all dynamic levels (especially *p*)
- *Crescendo* and *diminuendo*
- Response both to *legato* and *staccato* playing, and various other types of articulation
- A comfortable balance between free-blowing as well as resistance
- An appropriate attainability of harmonics
- Bugling

Spend a good deal of your testing time playing slowly! You'll discover more that way.

Mouthpiece patches

Many players like to attach an adhesive patch to the beak of the mouthpiece. These aid comfort and protect the mouthpiece from scratching (especially from sharp teeth). They help to stop the mouthpiece slipping and to avoid biting, and eliminate the potentially distracting vibration through the teeth.

Take care not to place the patch right at the tip of the beak. For best results, fix it about 5mm down from the tip. If the patch is too close to the top of the mouthpiece, it can adversely influence the airflow when playing. Different thicknesses may slightly affect the sound.

Looking after your mouthpiece

Like reeds, mouthpieces require careful maintenance for optimum results. After playing, it is considered better not to clean the mouthpiece with your instrument pull-through, but rather to wash it in cool soapy water. You can buy smaller, dedicated mouthpiece pull-throughs that are less likely to cause any damage to the bore with repeated use.

If well looked after, mouthpieces can last a good number of years though some players like to change fairly often and have a number in their collection.[100] Unless you have a crystal mouthpiece, there is a small possibility of warping in the table area and with a magnifying glass, you may find tiny chips in the tip rail. Both of these will compromise the response.

---

98. Reeds can be bought in a number of different cuts where the particular dimensions differ.
99. Visit a shop or dealer if possible, or order a number to try out at one time.
100. I know a number of players who own many hundreds!

Taking care of your clarinet

Clarinets will often continue to work even when their condition might not be 100%. Under such circumstances response in all departments will be impaired. The result is either frustration or the development of poor habits that might seem temporarily to overcome the problems. Keeping the instrument in best condition is therefore essential.

General daily maintenance

Try to wash your hands before playing. This will both protect and give longer (and more beautiful) life to the keywork.

Wooden instruments should always be allowed to adjust to room or hall temperature. If you begin to play a clarinet when it's still too cold, it may develop cracks.

New clarinets

If your new clarinet is plastic, there is not much to do in addition to all the suggestions given. In the case of a wooden instrument be very careful to limit the amount of playing time in the first few weeks otherwise the wood may crack. Instrument makers differ slightly in their advice, but the average recommendation is not to play for more than about 15–20 minutes a day for the first week, rising to maybe two sessions of 15–20 minutes a day in the second, then rising to 30-minute sessions for the remainder of the first month. Thereafter a normal amount of playing should be safe. Having said that, some players take exceptional care and a crack will still appear, and others very little care at all and no cracks. Luck and the capricious nature of things will always play their part!

When assembling, occasionally apply some cork grease to the tenons so that excessive hand pressure on the keywork is avoided, but be careful not to use too much grease; it will be absorbed into the cork and ultimately can work the cork loose from the tenon. Never use any force in fitting the joints together and take care not to put any pressure on the keywork. It's very easy to bend keys. Depress the rings of the upper joint thus lifting the correspondence mechanism and ensure the link keys on both joints are well-positioned. Play a 'long' $B\flat^3$ (first finger of each hand in the *clarion* register) if you wish to check this.

Stiff joints can mean that the wood has swollen – this is particularly a problem with new clarinets. Ideally it is best to take the instrument to a repairer as soon as possible, however an emery board can be used *very gently* to remove excess wood. The swelling is likely to be either above or below the tenon cork and is often indicated by shiny wood. Many technicians advise not to make any structural changes to an instrument until it's at least two years old as the wood can both swell and contract in that time.

After playing, first remove the ligature and reed, then the mouthpiece. Dry both reed and mouthpiece carefully, then pull through the rest of the instrument slowly, from the bell to the barrel, to avoid the pull-through catching on the speaker tube and any moisture being deposited in the tone holes. Then dry the tenons and the tenon joints. Always disassemble the instrument, otherwise tenon corks will become loose. Check for water in the tone holes.

Some mouthpieces can cause the discolouration of silver-plated keys, so it is recommended to keep them either outside the case or in a protective pouch.

With a duster or similar, wipe the keys and the surface of the instrument gently.

THE CLARINET

- Barrel or Socket
- Joint ring
- Upper joint
- Keys
- Rings
- Tone holes
- Lower joint
- Rod
- Post
- Bell

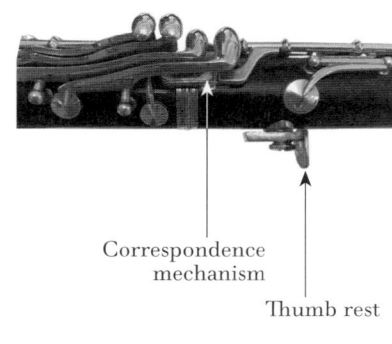

- Correspondence mechanism
- Thumb rest

Main Image © Denis Gliksman for Buffet Crampon.

213

Occasional maintenance

Using a soft brush (a paintbrush or soft toothbrush would work) brush gently around the keywork, rods, posts and springs to remove dust.

From time to time check for loose screws (the A and G♯ throat keys are often prone to working themselves loose). Tighten them carefully, but not too much.

If a screw falls out while the instrument is in use (this does occasionally happen!) locate it immediately and take care not to dislodge any mechanism involved. With a suitable screwdriver reinsert the screw and tighten appropriately. However, if you feel you cannot reinsert the screw yourself, place it and any compromised mechanism into a bag or safe container until you are able to take it to a professional technician.

You may wish very carefully to apply some oil to the junction of rods and posts. Use a good quality and reputable specialist oil.[101] Apply a tiny drop to a needle and then the needle to the point where the rod and post connect. Activate the appropriate key a few times. Ensure none gets onto the wood or the body of the instrument, and dry immediately if it does.

If you wish to clean the wood or body of the instrument more thoroughly, simply use a non-fluffy duster. Never use liquid polish – untold damage may result! Some players like to remove all the keywork – only do this if you *really* know what you're doing!

Annual maintenance

Some players like to oil the inside of the bore occasionally. This is often recommended by reputable instrument makers, and particularly important if you live in a dry climate that might affect the natural moisture of the instrument. If you do, use a specialist bore oil. Prepare the instrument by placing some thin paper (cigarette paper has been traditionally used for this purpose[102]) under each pad and then put just a few drops onto a dedicated swab and pull through a few times. It is essential that no oil reaches the pads.

Professional maintenance

Ideally take the instrument to an experienced technician approximately once a year or if you feel something is not working properly.

PADS

If you suspect a pad is not covering properly owing to a note not speaking immediately, or producing a persistent squeak, you can use a piece of very thin and lightweight paper to test its all-round *sealing*. Cut the paper to a point at one end and place the pointed end under a section of the pad. Use the paper as a 'feeler gauge' by closing the pad over the paper and giving it a couple of light tugs. If you feel resistance there are no problems with that part of the pad. 'Feel' all the way around – you'll notice if the pad is not covering the tone hole equally as this area will give less resistance when the paper is tugged. Replacing pads is best done by an experienced technician. You may also notice small tears that will usually cause a buzz in the tone. Such pads should be replaced as soon as possible.

KEYWORK

Check that each key is working properly. If a key has become particularly noisy, doesn't operate easily or you suspect a loose or lazy spring, take the instrument to an experienced technician. Technicians can also (to varying degrees) regulate the tension of some keys – some players have a preference for a tighter or looser mechanism.

---

101. There are a number of different brands available from specialist woodwind dealers.
102. You could also use Mylar paper.

Potential improvements

Good technicians (independent or specific makers) may be able to help in various ways, including the following:

- Manufacturers normally have reamers made for the bore of their instruments and high-tech measuring equipment to check the dimensions of the bore (which may very slightly change over time).
- Register-key (speaker-key) tubes can be changed to improve response. They come in different sizes and materials.
- The shape of the register-key pad (if made from cork) can be adjusted to improve response.
- The venting of keys can be adjusted. That is, the clearance between the pad and the tone hole – if it is too narrow you will hear a fuzziness in the sound.
- The material that pads are made from can make a difference (most commonly, leather, cork, or synthetic materials). Cork pads can provide more resonance (the upper joint keys can benefit particularly from being cork) but they can be harder to fit with a good seal in the larger keys and on older instruments. Leather pads are softer and seal more universally. Some players have a mixture of both.
- Tone holes can be voiced by undercutting – this can help with the projection of certain notes. Avoid having any such work done until an instrument is at least a couple of years old and has settled.

The clarinet and orange juice (and other sugary drinks)

Do not drink anything sugary or fizzy for at least an hour before you play the clarinet. Such drinks may condense onto the pads that will cause them to stick. Sugary fizzy drinks can also increase the acidity of saliva that could damage the reed, mouthpiece and even the bore of the instrument (as well as your teeth!).

Further Information

Historic timeline
Clarinet dynasties
Repertoire timings
Recommended orchestral *tutti* cuts
Recordings

THE CLARINET

Historic timeline

1700	Johann Christoph Denner makes the first clarinets – an instrument modelled on the earlier *chalumeau* (the development of which he also played an important part). The clarinet is distinguished from the *chalumeau* by an additional finger hole at the upper end of the tube, a narrower reed and the fact the register-key tube and key are moved higher up away from the 'A' key (creating an instrument overblowing at the 12th).
1706	The first known tutor for the *chalumeau* appears, published under the title *The Compleat Book for the Mock Trumpet*. By all descriptions the 'Mock Trumpet' and the *chalumeau* were probably one and the same.
1707	Denner dies. Work on the clarinet is taken over by his son Jacob, who engineered the end of the tube into the more familiar bell-shape that we know today to enhance tonal projection. These instruments had two keys roughly equivalent to the 'register' (B♭) and the 'A' key of the modern instrument.
1710	The first orders for clarinets were made to Jacob Denner.
1712	The earliest known works were written for the clarinet: a set of duets published by Estienne Roger.
1716	The chorus *Plena nectare* from Vivaldi's oratorio *Juditha Triumphans* was the first orchestral work to use the clarinet.
1728	Probably the first example of the clarinet used as a solo instrument with orchestra: two concerti by Johann Valentin Rathgeber for 'clarineto and strings'.
1730s	The use of the word 'clarinet' (literally from the Italian meaning 'little trumpet') became more common.
1740	Antonio Vivaldi composed his two *Concerti Grossi* for two *chalumeau* (clarinets) and two oboes.
1740s	The third key/flap, the 'B/E', was added. There is little evidence to indicate who made this addition.
1743	Johann Melchior Molter began composing his 6 Concerti for Clarinet in D.
1748	Handel composed an overture for two clarinets in D and *corno di caccia*.
1749	The clarinet was introduced to Paris in the opera *Zoroastre* by Jean-Philippe Rameau.
1755	Johann Stamitz is widely considered to have composed the first concerto for B♭ clarinet.
1759	Due to the influence of Stamitz, the clarinet became an official component of the Manheim Court Orchestra.
1750s	The fourth (right-hand A♭/E♭) and fifth (left-hand C♯/F♯) keys were added by Brunswick organ builder, Barthold Fritz.
1764	The first clarinet tutor was written by Valentine Roeser (*Essai d'instruction*), which contains a description of the instrument and some basic technical exercises.
1770	Gregorio Sciroli composed the first clarinet sonata.
1770s	The bass clarinet and basset horn were developed. The bass clarinet was created by wind-maker Gilles Lot in Paris, but the inventor of the basset horn is unknown.
1789	Mozart composed his Clarinet Quintet K. 581.
1791	Mozart composed his Clarinet Concerto K. 622. Jean-Xavier Lefèvre popularised, (but most likely did not invent), the left-hand C♯/G♯ key, the sixth to be added.
1801	Lefèvre wrote his famous *Méthode de clarinette*, which included 12 sonatas.
c.1806	Iwan Müller updated the key pads by replacing the previously-used leather or felt strips with more flexible leather or gut stuffed with wool. He also developed the metal screw ligature and thumb rest.
1811	Weber composed his two Clarinet Concertos and Clarinet Concertino.
1812	Müller produced a clarinet with 13 keys and more precise finger holes. The mechanism (the construction, venting and padding of the keys) is considered the greatest advance since Denner. Louis Spohr had his first clarinet concerto published.
c.1820	German clarinettists began to play with the reed on the underside of the mouthpiece, which was subsequently adopted by players in Paris.
1822	Müller's clarinet tutor *Anweisung zu der neuen Clarinette* is published.
1823	Roller keys are developed by Cesar Janssen, which allowed clarinettists to slide between (little-finger) notes.
1830	Berlioz incorporated the E♭ clarinet into his *Symphonie Fantastique*.
1839	Hyacinthe Klosé and Auguste Buffet adapted the Boehm flute mechanism to the clarinet, producing an instrument with six rings and 17 keys, which was very similar to the modern clarinet.
1844	Berlioz wrote his *Treatise on Instrumentation*, which advised many composers on how to write for the clarinet.
1850s	Mouthpieces began to be made out of hard rubber (in fact, a mixture of rubber and sulphur).
1869	Reeds were first machine-made.
1894	Brahms composed his two Clarinet Sonatas.
1900	The use of African blackwood for clarinet manufacture became more common due to increased exports from Mozambique and Tanzania. Formerly, clarinets were generally made from boxwood.
1908	Charles Draper made possibly the first recording of a consequential clarinet work, Weber's Concertino in E♭ major, Op. 26.
1909	Debussy composed his *Première Rhapsodie*.
1920s	The clarinet begins to play a major role in the development of jazz.

FURTHER INFORMATION

1924	Gershwin wrote *Rhapsody in Blue*, including perhaps for many music lovers the most iconic solo in the clarinet repertoire.
1925	Metal clarinets were introduced in the USA.
1928	Nielsen composed his Clarinet Concerto Op. 57.
1939	Bartók's *Contrasts* is first performed by Benny Goodman – the first of his many commissions.
1948	Copland wrote his Concerto for Clarinet and String Orchestra for Benny Goodman.
1950s	The first plastic clarinets were manufactured, made from a material called *resonite*.
1954	F. Geoffrey Rendall wrote his seminal book on the history and construction of the clarinet.
1962	*Stranger on the Shore* (Acker Bilk) reached No. 1 in the American Billboard Hot 100.
1969	The crew of Apollo 10 took a recording of *Stranger on the Shore* to play on the moon – it was the first piece of music ever to be played on the moon.
2004	The 300th anniversary of the clarinet is celebrated by a major Symposium at the Musikinstrumenten-Museum SIMPK in Berlin.
2008	Mozart's and Brahms' Clarinet Quintets were placed in the top ten of the Best 100 Chamber Works of all time' by a survey conducted by the Australian Broadcasting Company.

THE CLARINET

Clarinet dynasties

Who was your teacher's teacher's teacher? My teacher, John Davies, was taught by George Anderson who was taught by the legendary Henry Lazarus. The fact that I can trace my dynasty back to the greatest British player of the 19th century by only three degrees of separation is because each of these great characters lived to a very great age! I also had a few lessons with Georgina Dobrée whose dynasty can be traced back to Lefèvre and Beer.

Below are some more clarinet family trees. Stanley Drucker, the great American player, can be traced back to the father of German clarinet playing, Franz Tausch. Drucker was a member of the New York Philharmonic for an extraordinary 61 years, 49 of them as principal. Sabine Meyer can be traced back to Jules Yublar but sadly (and unusually) no further. The extensive family tree opposite/below began growing after a conversation with my friend, the French clarinettist Philippe Cuper. It was fascinating to trace Philippe's clarinet dynasty back to the Lefèvre brothers and the very establishment of the Paris Conservatoire towards the end of the 18th century. There are so many interesting interconnections. Virtually everyone who plays the clarinet can probably connect with this tree somehow. Can you find your way into it?

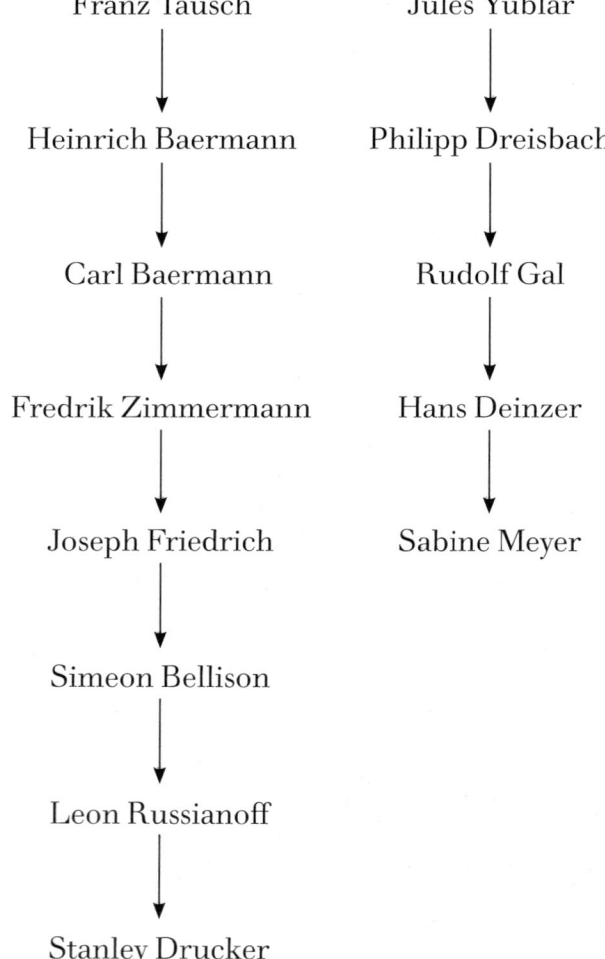

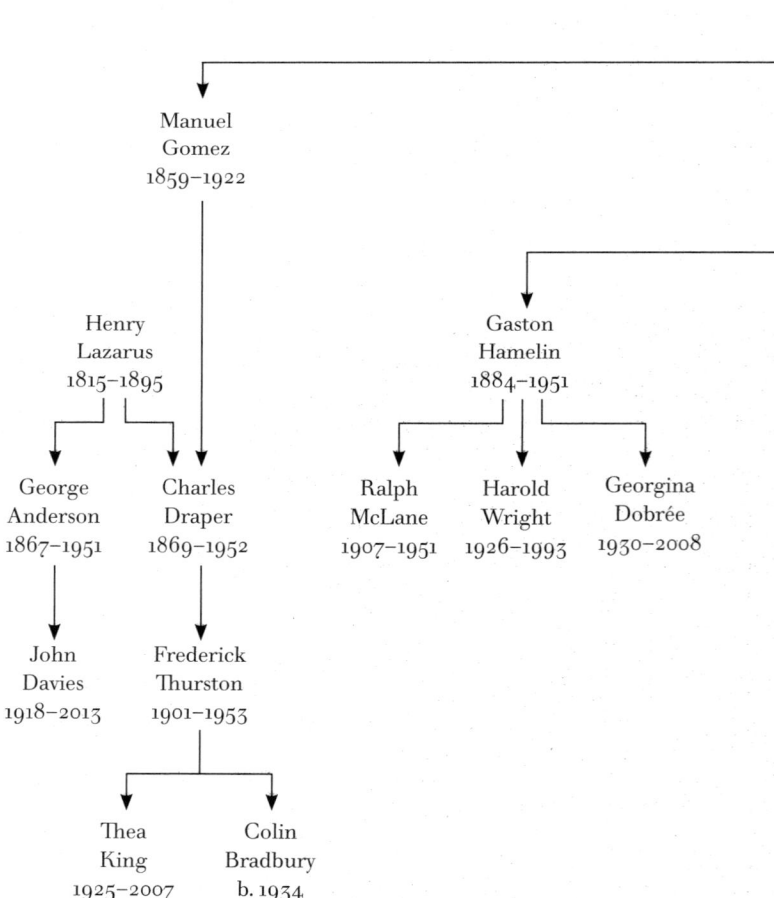

FURTHER INFORMATION

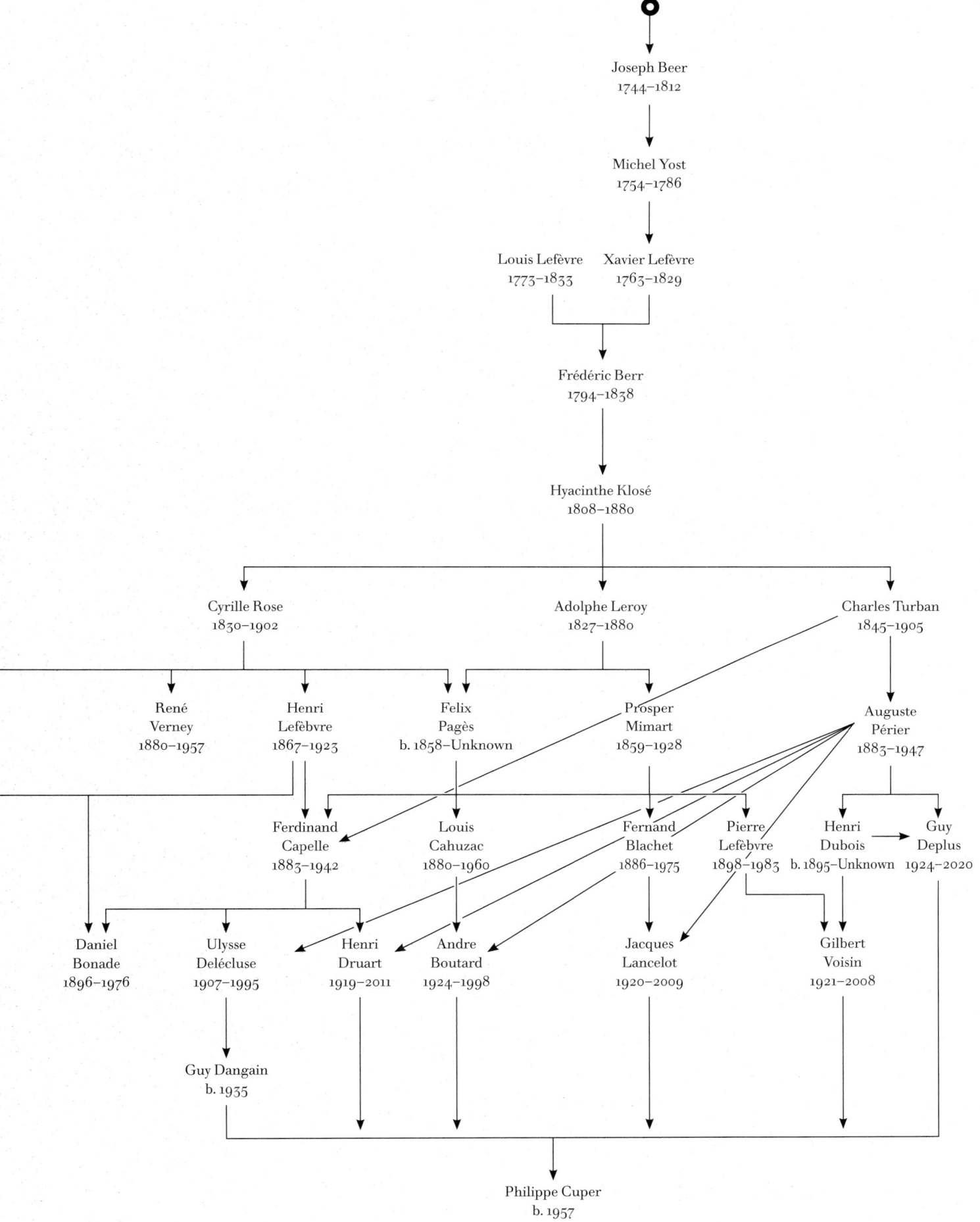

Repertoire timings

In selecting works for recitals, auditions, concerts and exams, timings are always a crucial factor. The list below includes timings for most works likely to be considered (it would have been impossible to list every work written for the clarinet). Of course, specific works have no definitive speeds and so timings will much depend on interpretation. However, the timings given here are based on taking an average from many performances of each work, so it should give a very helpful indication when considering your choice.

Timings of works with orchestra are given inclusive of orchestral *tutti*.

Name	Title	Duration
Alwyn, William	Sonata in E♭	11'10
Arnold, Malcolm	Sonatina Op. 29, I	2'35
Arnold, Malcolm	Sonatina Op. 29, II	2'29
Arnold, Malcolm	Sonatina Op. 29, III	2'07
Arnold, Malcolm	Concerto Op. 20 No. 1, I	7'08
Arnold, Malcolm	Concerto Op. 20 No. 1, II	7'20
Arnold, Malcolm	Concerto Op. 20 No. 1, III	3'25
Arnold, Malcolm	Concerto Op. 115 No. 2, I	5'30
Arnold, Malcolm	Concerto Op. 115 No. 2, II	7'38
Arnold, Malcolm	Concerto Op. 115 No. 2, III	2'27
Baermann, Heinrich	Adagio	4'28
Bax, Arnold	Sonata, I	8'55
Bax, Arnold	Sonata, II	5'27
Benjamin, Arthur	Le Tombeau de Ravel	14'17
Berg, Alban	Four Pieces Op. 5	8'36
Bernstein, Leonard	Sonata, I	3'39
Bernstein, Leonard	Sonata, II	6'44
Bizet, Georges (arr. Sarasate, P., arr. Baldyrou, N.)	Carmen Fantasy	10'00
Bliss, Arthur	Pastoral	4'44
Bowen, York	Sonata Op. 109, I	7'11
Bowen, York	Sonata Op. 109, II	3'01
Bowen, York	Sonata Op. 109, III	5'00
Brahms, Johannes	Sonata Op. 120 No.1, I	7'59
Brahms, Johannes	Sonata Op. 120 No.1, II	5'09
Brahms, Johannes	Sonata Op. 120 No.1, III	4'15
Brahms, Johannes	Sonata Op. 120 No.1, IV	5'12
Brahms, Johannes	Sonata Op. 120 No.2, I	8'19
Brahms, Johannes	Sonata Op. 120 No.2, II	5'14
Brahms, Johannes	Sonata Op. 120 No.2, III	7'27
Burgmüller, Norbert	Duo Op. 15	12'14
Busoni, Ferruccio	Concertino Op. 48	10'51
Busoni, Ferruccio	Elegie in E♭, BV 286	4'50
Castelnuovo-Tedesco, Mario	Sonata Op. 128, I	7'58
Castelnuovo-Tedesco, Mario	Sonata Op. 128, II	3'12
Castelnuovo-Tedesco, Mario	Sonata Op. 128, III	5'36
Castelnuovo-Tedesco, Mario	Sonata Op. 128, IV	4'00
Cimarosa, D. arr Arthur Benjamin	Concerto, I	2'39
Cimarosa, D. arr Arthur Benjamin	Concerto, II	2'32
Cimarosa, D. arr Arthur Benjamin	Concerto, III	2'43
Cimarosa, D. arr Arthur Benjamin	Concerto, IV	2'24
Cooke, Arnold	Sonata in B♭, I	6'35
Cooke, Arnold	Sonata in B♭, II	3'42
Cooke, Arnold	Sonata in B♭, III	6'19
Cooke, Arnold	Sonata in B♭, IV	3'48
Copland, Aaron	Clarinet Concerto	16'37
Crusell, Bernhard	Concerto Op. 1 No. 1, I	10'27
Crusell, Bernhard	Concerto Op. 1 No. 1, II	3'50
Crusell, Bernhard	Concerto Op. 1 No. 1, III	6'24
Crusell, Bernhard	Concerto Op. 5 No. 2, I	11'07
Crusell, Bernhard	Concerto Op. 5 No. 2, II	5'23
Crusell, Bernhard	Concerto Op. 5 No. 2, III	6'18
Crusell, Bernhard	Concerto Op. 11 No. 3, I	10'10
Crusell, Bernhard	Concerto Op. 11 No. 3, II	6'14
Crusell, Bernhard	Concerto Op. 11 No. 3, III	7'15
Debussy, Claude	Petite Piece	1'34
Debussy, Claude	Première Rhapsodie	7'43
Donizetti, Gaetano	Concertino in B♭, I	4'03
Donizetti, Gaetano	Concertino in B♭, II	3'54
Dunhill, Thomas	Phantasy Suite Op. 91, I	1'47
Dunhill, Thomas	Phantasy Suite Op. 91, II	1'28
Dunhill, Thomas	Phantasy Suite Op. 91, III	1'14
Dunhill, Thomas	Phantasy Suite Op. 91, IV	1'57
Dunhill, Thomas	Phantasy Suite Op. 91, V	0'46
Dunhill, Thomas	Phantasy Suite Op. 91, VI	3'18
Finzi, Gerald	Five Bagatelles: Prelude	3'40
Finzi, Gerald	Five Bagatelles: Romance	4'20
Finzi, Gerald	Five Bagatelles: Carol	2'01
Finzi, Gerald	Five Bagatelles: Forlana	2'58
Finzi, Gerald	Five Bagatelles: Fughetta	2'13
Finzi, Gerald	Concerto Op. 31, I	8'01
Finzi, Gerald	Concerto Op. 31, II	11'32
Finzi, Gerald	Concerto Op. 31, III	8'16
Françaix, Jean	Concerto I	8'01

FURTHER INFORMATION

Name	Title	Duration
Françaix, Jean	Concerto II	5'39
Françaix, Jean	Concerto III	4'54
Françaix, Jean	Concerto IV	6'09
Francaix, Jean	Tema con Variazioni	8'34
Gade, Niels	Fantasiestücke Op. 43 No. 1	2'13
Gade, Niels	Fantasiestücke Op. 43 No. 2	2'28
Gade, Niels	Fantasiestücke Op. 43 No. 3	4'39
Gade, Niels	Fantasiestücke Op. 43 No. 4	3'15
Giampieri, Alamiro	Carnival of Venice	7'04
Grovlez, Gabriel	Sarabande et Allegro	5'28
Harris, Paul	Adagio	3'46
Harris, Paul	Sonata da Camera, I	1'01
Harris, Paul	Sonata da Camera, II	2'23
Harris, Paul	Sonata da Camera, III	1'02
Harris, Paul	Sonata da Camera, IV	1'20
Hindemith, Paul	Sonata, I	5'09
Hindemith, Paul	Sonata, II	2'50
Hindemith, Paul	Sonata, III	7'13
Hindemith, Paul	Sonata, IV	2'31
Hindemith, Paul	Concerto, I	8'10
Hindemith, Paul	Concerto ,II	2'07
Hindemith, Paul	Concerto, III	7'10
Hindemith, Paul	Concerto, IV	6'18
Honegger, Arthur	Sonatine H.42, I	3'44
Honegger, Arthur	Sonatine H.42, II	2'23
Honegger, Arthur	Sonatine H.42, III	1'08
Horovitz, Joseph	Sonatina, I	5'02
Horovitz, Joseph	Sonatina, II	4'08
Horovitz, Joseph	Sonatina, III	3'41
Howells, Herbert	Sonata, I	11'08
Howells, Herbert	Sonata, II	10'08
Hurlstone, William	Four Characteristic Pieces: Ballade	5'46
Hurlstone, William	Four Characteristic Pieces: Croon Song	3'05
Hurlstone, William	Four Characteristic Pieces: Intermezzo	2'24
Hurlstone, William	Four Characteristic Pieces: Scherzo	3'45
Ireland, John	Fantasy Sonata	14'39
Krommer, Franz	Concerto in E♭ Op. 36, I	10'28
Krommer, Franz	Concerto in E♭ Op. 36, II	4'58
Krommer, Franz	Concerto in E♭ Op. 36, III	5'26
Lefèvre, J. Xavier	Sonata No. 1, I	2'26
Lefèvre, J. Xavier	Sonata No. 1, II	4'09
Lefèvre, J. Xavier	Sonata No. 1, III	1'08
Lefèvre, J. Xavier	Sonata No. 2, I	3'29
Lefèvre, J. Xavier	Sonata No. 2, II	3'37
Lefèvre, J. Xavier	Sonata No. 2, III	1'58
Lefèvre, J. Xavier	Sonata No. 3, I	3'42
Lefèvre, J. Xavier	Sonata No. 3, II	3'06
Lefèvre, J. Xavier	Sonata No. 3, III	2'02
Lefèvre, J. Xavier	Sonata No. 4, I	4'26
Lefèvre, J. Xavier	Sonata No. 4, II	5'24
Lefèvre, J. Xavier	Sonata No. 4, III	2'23
Lefèvre, J. Xavier	Sonata No. 5, I	4'00
Lefèvre, J. Xavier	Sonata No. 5, II	2'52
Lefèvre, J. Xavier	Sonata No. 5, III	2'28
Lefèvre, J. Xavier	Sonata No. 6, I	3'19
Lefèvre, J. Xavier	Sonata No. 6, II	3'47
Lefèvre, J. Xavier	Sonata No. 6, III	4'20
Lefèvre, J. Xavier	Sonata No. 7, I	5'04
Lefèvre, J. Xavier	Sonata No. 7, II	3'42
Lefèvre, J. Xavier	Sonata No. 7, III	2'41
Lefèvre, J. Xavier	Sonata No. 8, I	4'21
Lefèvre, J. Xavier	Sonata No. 8, II	2'40
Lefèvre, J. Xavier	Sonata No. 8, III	4'10
Lefèvre, J. Xavier	Sonata No. 9, I	5'25
Lefèvre, J. Xavier	Sonata No. 9, II	5'46
Lefèvre, J. Xavier	Sonata No. 9, III	3'37
Lutosławski, Witold	Dance Preludes 1	0'56
Lutosławski, Witold	Dance Preludes 2	2'43
Lutosławski, Witold	Dance Preludes 3	1'11
Lutosławski, Witold	Dance Preludes 4	3'32
Lutosławski, Witold	Dance Preludes 5	1'36
Martinů, Bohuslav	Sonatina H.365, I	5'38
Martinů, Bohuslav	Sonatina H.365, II	2'38
Martinů, Bohuslav	Sonatina H.365, III	2'24
Mendelssohn, Felix	Sonata in E♭, I	11'20
Mendelssohn, Felix	Sonata in E♭, II	4'21
Mendelssohn, Felix	Sonata in E♭, III	6'51
Messager, André	Solo de Concours	5'26
Milhaud, Darius	Sonatine Op. 100, I	3'10
Milhaud, Darius	Sonatine Op. 100, II	4'09
Milhaud, Darius	Sonatine Op. 100, III	2'32
Milhaud, Darius	Duo Concertant	6'49
Molter, J. M.	Concerto No. 1, I	4'10
Molter, J. M.	Concerto No. 1, II	4'44
Molter, J. M.	Concerto No. 1, III	3'19
Molter, J. M.	Concerto No. 2, I	4'53
Molter, J. M.	Concerto No. 2, II	4'59
Molter, J. M.	Concerto No. 2, III	2'16
Molter, J. M.	Concerto No. 3, I	4'46
Molter, J. M.	Concerto No. 3, II	4'59
Molter, J. M.	Concerto No. 3, III	2'23
Molter, J. M.	Concerto No. 4, I	4'55
Molter, J. M.	Concerto No. 4, II	4'26
Molter, J. M.	Concerto No. 4, III	2'53
Mozart, W. A.	Concerto K.622, I	12'08
Mozart, W. A.	Concerto K.622, II	7'22
Mozart, W. A.	Concerto K.622, III	8'40
Muczynski, Robert	Time Pieces Op. 43 No. 1	2'35

THE CLARINET

Name	Title	Duration
Muczynski, Robert	Time Pieces Op. 43 No. 2	6'10
Muczynski, Robert	Time Pieces Op. 43 No. 3	2'15
Muczynski, Robert	Time Pieces Op. 43 No. 4	5'19
Nielsen, Carl	Concerto Op. 57	24'45
Penderecki, Krzysztof	Three Miniatures, No. 1	0'55
Penderecki, Krzysztof	Three Miniatures, No. 2	1'37
Penderecki, Krzysztof	Three Miniatures, No. 3	1'22
Pierné, Gabriel	Canzonetta Op. 19	2'57
Poulenc, Francis	Sonata, I	5'19
Poulenc, Francis	Sonata, II	5'03
Poulenc, Francis	Sonata, III	3'15
Reger, Max	Sonata Op. 49 No. 1, I	7'46
Reger, Max	Sonata Op. 49 No. 1, II	4'09
Reger, Max	Sonata Op. 49 No. 1, III	4'20
Reger, Max	Sonata Op. 49 No. 1, IV	4'34
Reger, Max	Sonata Op. 49 No. 2, I	9'10
Reger, Max	Sonata Op. 49 No. 2, II	2'35
Reger, Max	Sonata Op. 49 No. 2, III	4'43
Reger, Max	Sonata Op. 49 No. 2, IV	5'51
Reger, Max	Sonata Op. 107 No.3, I	12'45
Reger, Max	Sonata Op. 107 No.3, II	5'15
Reger, Max	Sonata Op. 107 No.3, III	5'47
Reger, Max	Sonata Op. 107 No.3, IV	7'41
Richardson, Alan	Roundelay	3'39
Ridout, Alan	Concertino, I	1'36
Ridout, Alan	Concertino, II	2'36
Ridout, Alan	Concertino, III	1'46
Ridout, Alan	Sonatina, I	2'19
Ridout, Alan	Sonatina, II	2'20
Ridout, Alan	Sonatina, III	1'50
Rossini, Gioachino	Introduction, Theme and Variations	12'23
Saint-Saëns, Camille	Sonata in E♭ Op. 167, I	4'16
Saint-Saëns, Camille	Sonata in E♭ Op. 167, II	2'09
Saint-Saëns, Camille	Sonata in E♭ Op. 167, III	3'53
Saint-Saëns, Camille	Sonata in E♭ Op. 167, IV	5'11
Schumann, Robert	Fantasiestücke Op. 73 No. 1	3'31
Schumann, Robert	Fantasiestücke Op. 73 No. 2	3'16
Schumann, Robert	Fantasiestücke Op. 73 No. 3	4'05
Spohr, Louis	Concerto Op. 26 No. 1, I	11'04
Spohr, Louis	Concerto Op. 26 No. 1, II	3'32
Spohr, Louis	Concerto Op. 26 No. 1, III	6'21
Spohr, Louis	Concerto Op. 57 No. 2, I	11'34
Spohr, Louis	Concerto Op. 57 No. 2, II	5'06
Spohr, Louis	Concerto Op. 57 No. 2, III	7'57
Spohr, Louis	Concerto No. 3, I	11'01
Spohr, Louis	Concerto No. 3, II	9'43
Spohr, Louis	Concerto No. 3, III	7'57
Spohr, Louis	Concerto No. 4, I	10'53
Spohr, Louis	Concerto No. 4, II	7'20
Spohr, Louis	Concerto No. 4, III	8'02
Stamitz, Carl	Concerto No. 3 in B♭, I	8'12
Stamitz, Carl	Concerto No. 3 in B♭, II	4'01
Stamitz, Carl	Concerto No. 3 in B♭, III	4'03
Stanford, Charles V.	Concerto in A minor Op. 80, I	5'35
Stanford, Charles V.	Concerto in A minor Op. 80, II	8'02
Stanford, Charles V.	Concerto in A minor Op. 80, III	6'44
Stanford, Charles V.	Three Intermezzi Op. 13 No. 1	3'42
Stanford, Charles V.	Three Intermezzi Op. 13 No. 2	2'28
Stanford, Charles V.	Three Intermezzi Op. 13 No. 3	2'44
Stanford, Charles V.	Sonata Op. 129, I	7'48
Stanford, Charles V.	Sonata Op. 129, II	6'48
Stanford, Charles V.	Sonata Op. 129, III	5'54
Stravinsky, Igor	Ebony Concerto	8'44
Stravinsky, Igor	Three Pieces No.1	1'46
Stravinsky, Igor	Three Pieces No.2	1'09
Stravinsky, Igor	Three Pieces No.3	1'14
Sutermeister, Heinrich	Capriccio	5'57
Szałowski, Antoni	Sonatina, I	2'15
Szałowski, Antoni	Sonatina, II	3'45
Szałowski, Antoni	Sonatina, III	2'23
Tartini, G. arr Gordon Jacob	Concertino, I	2'11
Tartini, G. arr Gordon Jacob	Concertino, II	2'38
Tartini, G. arr Gordon Jacob	Concertino, III	2'41
Tartini, G. arr Gordon Jacob	Concertino, IV	3'44
Templeton, Alec	Pocket Size Sonata No.1, I	2'32
Templeton, Alec	Pocket Size Sonata No.1, II	3'13
Templeton, Alec	Pocket Size Sonata No.1, III	1'43
Templeton, Alec	Pocket Size Sonata No.2, I	2'48
Templeton, Alec	Pocket Size Sonata No.2, II	2'57
Templeton, Alec	Pocket Size Sonata No.2, III	1'24
Vanhal, Johann B.	Sonata No. 3 in B♭, I	6'05
Vanhal, Johann B.	Sonata No. 3 in B♭, II	3'41
Vanhal, Johann B.	Sonata No. 3 in B♭, III	4'34
Vaughan Williams, Ralph	Six Studies in English Folk Song No. 1	1'36
Vaughan Williams, Ralph	Six Studies in English Folk Song No. 2	1'20
Vaughan Williams, Ralph	Six Studies in English Folk Song No. 3	1'36
Vaughan Williams, Ralph	Six Studies in English Folk Song No. 4	1'25
Vaughan Williams, Ralph	Six Studies in English Folk Song No. 5	1'33
Vaughan Williams, Ralph	Six Studies in English Folk Song No. 6	0'54
Weber, C. M.	Grand Duo Concertant Op. 48, I	8'24
Weber, C. M.	Grand Duo Concertant Op. 48, II	5'33
Weber, C. M.	Grand Duo Concertant Op. 48, III	6'03
Weber, C. M.	Concertino for Clarinet Op. 26	9'18
Weber, C. M.	Concerto No. 1 in F minor Op. 73, I	8'18
Weber, C. M.	Concerto No. 1 in F minor Op. 73, II	6'42
Weber, C. M.	Concerto No. 1 in F minor Op. 73, III	6'14
Weber, C. M.	Concerto No. 2 in E♭ Op. 74, I	8'30
Weber, C. M.	Concerto No. 2 in E♭ Op. 74, II	7'10
Weber, C. M.	Concerto No. 2 in E♭ Op. 74, III	6'17
Weiner, Leó	Peregi Verbunk	6'12
Widor, Charles-Marie	Introduction and Rondo Op. 72	6'54

Recommended orchestral *tutti* cuts

In preparing pieces for exams or auditions it may be necessary to make cuts in the orchestral *tutti*. Those given here are merely suggestions but may help in giving guidance.[103] Not all of the cuts suggested have to be employed, only those that are best suited to the performer (in terms of stamina) and the performance (considering, for example, the quality of piano or time available).

MOZART CONCERTO K. 622

Movement 1 – Allegro	• Finish bar 8 on the first quaver (quarter note) of the third beat and begin again at bar 53, with the upbeat semiquaver (sixteenth note). • Play the first beat of bar 154 and begin again with the second beat of bar 168. • Cut from the end of bar 232 to bar 246. • Play the first beat of bar 343 and begin again on the second beat of bar 356.
Movement 2 – Adagio	• Finish on the first quaver (quarter-note) beat of bar 8 and begin again on the second quaver (quarter-note) beat of bar 16. • Play the first quaver (quarter-note) beat of bar 24 and begin again on the second quaver (quarter-note) beat of bar 32. • Finish on the first quaver (quarter-note) beat of 75 and begin again on the second quaver (quarter-note) beat of 83.

WEBER CONCERTO NO. 1

Movement 1 – Allegro	• Begin from bar 38. • Cut from the end of bar 148 to bar 166.
Movement 3 – Rondo Allegretto	• Cut from the end of bar 87 to bar 108. • Cut from the end of bar 184 to bar 194.

WEBER CONCERTO NO. 2

Movement 1 – Allegro	• Cut from the end of bar 17 to bar 39. • Cut from the end of bar 136 to bar 148. • Cut from the end of 192 to bar 203.

KROMMER CONCERTO IN E FLAT

Movement 1 – Allegro	• Cut from the end end of bar 3 to bar 40 or to bar 48. • Cut from the end of bar 133 to bar 161. • Cut from the last beat of bar 244 to bar 251. • Cut from the end of 328 to bar 339.
Movement 2 – Adagio	• Cut from the end of bar 1 to bar 11.

SPOHR CONCERTO NO. 2

Movement 1 – Allegro	• Cut from the end of bar 7 to bar 68. • Cut from the end of bar 168 to bar 179.
Movement 3 – Rondo Alla Polacca	• Cut from the end of bar 38 to bar 60.

---

103. With thanks to Scott Mitchell, Senior Staff Accompanist and lecturer in Piano Accompaniment at the Royal Conservatoire of Scotland, for help with these cuts.

Recordings

This list represents a very small proportion of the available recordings of clarinet music, but will make a good basis for any focussed listening.

The players and their recordings have been divided into national schools and specific genres. Though there are sometimes clear and discernible differences in the sound and in the style of playing from one school to another, sometimes these differences are less marked. Many have tried to describe the various schools – the French, for example, as bright and colourful, the German as centred and dark – but such descriptions are helpful only to a degree being both somewhat subjective and generic. Also, it is worth bearing in mind that it is not the school that creates the style, but the player's personal approach that becomes a model for others to follow. In addition, there is often a divergence of approach within a school and the qualities of playing can be heard to have changed over time.

Nevertheless, the concept of 'clarinet schools' is still an interesting and valid one. In the days before mass communication and travel, national styles of playing, as well as instrument design and manufacture, were certainly much more individual.

There were clear national styles of playing in the 18th century, notably initiated by Franz Tausch (1762–1817) in Germany and Joseph Beer (1744–1812) in France. These particular schools retained individuality in both sound quality and instrument manufacture for a long time, but as time has moved on, their defining characteristics have become less clear.

It is therefore recommended that you listen to the suggested recordings (and others) and form your own opinions, choosing the descriptive words you find best define the different schools of playing.

All these performances are available in one form or another. Specific media (CDs, various online sites, streaming sites etc.) have not been specified and are left to your preference.

THE GERMAN SCHOOL

Karl Leister	Brahms – Clarinet Sonata Op. 120 Nos. 1 and 2 (the Orfeo recordings are recommended)
	Brahms – Clarinet Quintet in B minor Op. 115
	Schumann – Fantasy Pieces for Clarinet and Piano Op. 73
	Spohr – Concerto for Clarinet Nos. 1, 2, 3 and 4
Dieter Klöcker	Mozart – Clarinet Quintet K. 581
	Weber – Clarinet Concerto Nos. 1 and 2
Sabine Meyer	Mozart – Clarinet Concerto K. 622

THE AUSTRIAN SCHOOL

The Ottensamer family	Any recordings
Leopold Wlach	Mendelssohn – Concert Piece No. 1, Op. 113 and No. 2, Op. 114
Alfred Prinz	Weber – Clarinet Quintet in B♭ Major Op. 34

THE FRENCH SCHOOL

Jacques Lancelot	Stamitz – Clarinet Concerto No. 2
	Molter – Clarinet Concerto in A major, MWV 6.41
	Ravel – Introduction and Allegro
	Françaix – Concerto (first recording)
André Boutard	Poulenc – Sonata for Clarinet (first recording, Boutard studied with Poulenc)
Philippe Cuper	Françaix – Concerto
	Cahuzac – Complete Works
	Breval – Concerto
Ulysse Delécluse	Widor – Introduction and Rondo for Clarinet and Piano Op. 72
Guy Deplus	Messiaen – Quatuor pour la fin du temps
Patrick Messina	Debussy – Première Rhapsodie

FURTHER INFORMATION

SOLO DE CONCOURS
Ulysse Delécluse	Messager – Solo de Concours
Pierre Genisson	Chausson – Andante and Allegro for Clarinet and Piano
	Debussy – Première Rhapsodie
Andre Moisan	Rabaud – Solo de Concours Op. 10

THE ITALIAN SCHOOL
Alessandro Carbonare	Bassi – Rigoletto: Fantasia di concerto pour clarinette et piano
Corrado Guifredi	Bassi – Rigoletto: Fantasia di concerto pour clarinette et piano
Alamiro Giampieri	Gagliano – Fantasia Rapsodica

THE ENGLISH SCHOOL
Jack Brymer	Mozart – Clarinet Concerto K. 622
	Mozart – Clarinet Quintet K. 581
Reginald Kell	Brahms – Clarinet Quintet in B minor Op. 115
Gervase de Peyev	Ireland – Fantasy Sonata for Clarinet and Piano
	Brahms – Clarinet Sonata Op. 120 Nos. 1 and 2
	Horowitz – Sonatina for Clarinet and Piano
Fredrick Thurston	Stanford – Sonata for Clarinet and Piano
Thea King	Finzi – Clarinet Concerto Op. 31
	Jacob – Sonata for Clarinet and Piano
Emma Johnson	Michael Berkeley – Clarinet Concerto

THE AMERICAN SCHOOL
Stanley Drucker	Bernstein – Sonata for Clarinet and Piano
	Corigliano – Concerto for Clarinet
Robert Marcellus	Mozart – Clarinet Concerto K. 622
Benny Goodman	Copland – Clarinet Concerto
Larry Combs	Copland – Sonata for clarinet and piano
Jon Manasse	Brahms – Clarinet Sonata Op. 120 Nos. 1 and 2
Harold Wright	Mozart - Clarinet Concerto K. 622
	Bartók – Contrasts

HISTORIC RECORDINGS
These players were all born in the 19th century

Charles Draper	Weber – Concertino in E♭ Op.26
	Henry Bishop – Variations on Home Sweet Home
Simeon Bellison	Gretchaninov – Sonata
Gaston Hamelin	Debussy – Première Rhapsodie
August Perier	George Marty – Premier Fantaisie

PERIOD INSTRUMENTS
Antony Pay	Weber – Clarinet Concerto Nos. 1 and 2
Eric Hoeprich	Mozart – Clarinet Concerto K. 622
Colin Lawson	Lefèvre – Clarinet Concerto No. 4 in G minor

JAZZ
Acker Bilk	Acker Bilk – Stranger on the Shore
Benny Goodman	Any of his jazz recordings
Artie Shaw	Artie Shaw – Concerto for Clarinet
Doreen Kitchens	Any of her jazz recordings

THE CLARINET

| Eddie Daniels | Vivaldi – Four Seasons (in the jazz style!) |

NORDIC
| Kari Kriikku | Magnus Lindberg – Clarinet Concerto |

KLEZMER
Giora Feidman	Traditional – Maya Freilach
	Kostakowsky – Bulgar
Harold Seletsky	Seletsky – Klezmer Fantasy

TODAY'S PLAYERS

Today's players do not really fit a particular national school or generic style. The approach to sound and interpretation has become more international and less disparate.

Julian Bliss	Nielsen – Clarinet Concerto
Shirley Brill	Françaix – Clarinet Concerto
David Campbell	Bliss – Clarinet Quintet
Michael Collins	Spohr – Clarinet Concertos
István Kohán	Weiner – Peregi Verbunk
Ricardo Morales	Poulenc – Sonata for Clarinet
	Bartók – Contrasts
Thorston Johanns	Richard Strauss – Romanze for Clarinet and Orchestra
	Copland – Clarinet Concerto
Pierre Genisson	Mozart – Clarinet Quintet K. 581
Han Kim	Brahms – Sonatas
Martin Fröst	Hilborg – Peacock Tales
	Nielsen – Clarinet Concerto
	Crusell – Clarinet Concerto in F minor Op. 5
Sharon Kam	Françaix – Theme and variations
Giovanni Punzi	Krommer – Concerto in E♭ for Clarinet Op. 36
Annelien van Wauwe	Debussy – Première Rhapsodie
	Pierne – Canzonetta
Victoria Samek	Richard Rodney Bennett – Duo Concertante

Appendices

Glossary of terms
Bibliography

THE CLARINET

Glossary of terms

Accentuation/Accent Emphasises a specific note, usually shown by: >

Agogic accent An accent indicating when a note should be held for its full duration, while simultaneously giving it extra prominence. This is normally referred to as a *tenuto*.

Air column All the energised air in both halves of the clarinet: inside the player and the instrument.

Alexander Technique A technique of reducing tension via adjustments to posture and movement, as well as taking emotional factors into consideration.

Altissimo The register of the clarinet which consists of all notes above C^3.

Amplitude The maximum height of a soundwave.

Aperture The opening between the reed and the mouthpiece tip, usually labelled as the 'tip opening'.

Appoggiatura A grace-note ornament that delays the next note of the melody and is typically one degree higher or lower. It is often referred to as a 'leaning note', coming from the Italian *appoggiare*, 'to lean upon'.

Articulation Starting and ending notes to influence their length and 'attack'.

Atmospheric pressure The pressure of the air around us.

Baffle The inside slope of the clarinet mouthpiece located opposite the mouthpiece window.

Bark The lower section of the reed, distinguished by its smooth texture and darker colour.

Baroque A term denoting the specific style of music composed between c. 1600 and c. 1750; prominent composers include Bach, Handel, Purcell and Vivaldi.

Barrel The section of the clarinet that sits between the mouthpiece and the main body of the instrument, mostly used to adjust intonation.

Beak The flat surface of the clarinet mouthpiece where the player places their top teeth or a mouthpiece patch.

Beats (intonation) The acoustic interference pattern between marginally different frequencies, heard when there is a conflict of intonation between simultaneously sounded notes.

Bell The bottom joint of the clarinet, named after its bell-like appearance.

Bending The technique of deliberately flattening the intonation of a note to bring it down to a lower pitch.

Blade (tongue) The section of the tongue's upper surface located just behind the tip, typically used for anchor-tonguing.

Body The combined length of the upper and lower joints.

Bore The cylindrical cavity inside the clarinet.

Break The point of crossing between two registers, found on the clarinet between $B\flat^2$ and B^2, and C^3 and $C\sharp^3$.

Break point The point on the mouthpiece where the facing begins to curve.

Breath articulation Starting a note using only the breath, not the tongue.

Bugling The process of moving between the harmonics of a particular fingering by altering tongue (oral cavity) shape, so named because of its application to brass playing.

Bulging The unnecessary action of making small *crescendi* on individual notes that can disturb *legato*, and therefore the phrasing.

Bumping Alighting on a note with too much accentuation.

Butt (reed) The short edge located at the opposite end of the reed to its tip, also known as the heel.

Chalumeau The lowest register of the clarinet, between E^1 and $F\sharp^2$.

Clarinet (*clarion*) The register of the clarinet after the first break, ranging between B^2 and C^3; it is sometimes referred to as the *clarion* or the *clarino* register.

Classical A term denoting the specific style of music composed between c. 1750 and c. 1810; prominent composers include Mozart, Haydn and Schubert.

Closed pipe A type of instrument design that includes a tube with one open end and one closed end.

Corners (reed) The upper corners of the of the reed vamp, also referred to as the 'ears'.

Correspondence mechanism The two interlocking keys that join the mechanisms of the upper and lower joints, located under the right-hand trill keys.

Crest (reed) Another name for the heart of the reed.

Cylindrical stopped pipe (See 'Closed pipe').

Decibel A unit of sound intensity.

Dissonant An adjective deriving from the term 'dissonance' denoting a lack of agreement within the harmony of music.

Double-tonguing The alternation of stopping the air with the tongue tip and stopping the air with the back of the tongue to achieve a faster speed of articulation.

Dutch reed rush A natural material used to adjust and improve the response of resistant reeds.

Dynamics The variation in how loud or how soft notes are played.

Ears (reed) (See 'Corners').

Embouchure The action of the facial muscles enclosing the mouthpiece.

Facing The flat surface of the mouthpiece where the reed rests, stretching from the tip rail until the tenon begins. Other names include the 'reed table' or the 'lay'.

Facing curve The curvature of the upper section of the facing.

Flat (intonation) A note that sounds marginally below the desired pitch.

Flutter-tonguing An articulation technique that involves rolling the tongue whilst blowing to create a 'fluttering' sound.

Fundamental The lowest perceived pitch of a note over which harmonics may be heard.

Glissando The technique of sliding cleanly between notes.

Harmonics Notes that can be sounded using the same fingering as the fundamental.

Heart (reed) The central part of the reed vamp, also known as the crest.

Heel (reed) (See 'Butt').

Interval The heard distance between two pitches.

Intonation The accuracy of the pitch of the note played in relation to 'concert pitch'.

Key-pad height The distance between the key-pads and their respective tone holes.

Lay (See 'Facing').

Legato Articulation technique that involves joining notes as smoothly as possible, without any gap.

Ligature The device that holds the reed to the mouthpiece.

Lipping (up/down) Changing the intonation of a note with the embouchure.

APPENDICES

Lower joint The part of the clarinet located between the upper joint and the bell, operated by the right hand.

Mezzo-staccato An articulation technique involving playing notes with the smallest degree of separation, while still detaching them.

Modern A term denoting the specific style of music composed c. 1910 onwards; prominent composers include Sibelius, Arnold, and Stravinsky.

Multiphonics Multiple notes played simultaneously.

No-tongue articulation (See 'Breath articulation').

Open pipe A type of instrument design that includes a tube with both ends open.

Oral cavity The space inside the mouth that is influenced by the shape of the tongue.

Orchestral tutti The sections of concerti where the solo instrument does not play.

Overtones (See 'Harmonics').

Partials (See 'Harmonics').

Phrasing Shaping a sequence of notes to maximise musical expression.

Pitch The frequency (number of Hertz) of a note, denoting to how 'high' or 'low' it sounds.

Portato (See '*Mezzo-staccato*').

Posture The position in which the body and the instrument are held.

Projection Creating a sound that can maintain its intensity and quality after travelling distance.

Pulse The periodic beats, changing with tempo, which are the basis of rhythm.

Reed The small section of cane that vibrates to create sound.

Reed table (See 'Facing').

Register Groups of notes that share tonal characteristics relating to pitch-range, tone and timbre. The clarinet has four: *chalumeau*, throat, clarinet and *altissimo*.

Register key The key depressed by the left thumb to produce notes a 12th higher.

Resonant A high quality of sound that possesses richness, depth and colour.

Ring keys The five round metal keys that the fingers depress to cover the tone holes.

Romantic A term denoting the specific style of music composed between c. 1810 and c. 1910; prominent composers include Brahms, Weber, Spohr and Reger.

Sharp (intonation) A note that sounds marginally above the desired pitch.

Shoulder (reed) The portion of the reed just above the U-shaped cut.

Side rails (mouthpiece) The thin flat edges either side of the mouthpiece window.

Side rails (reed) The side edges of the reed.

Slur A notation that denotes the smooth joining of notes (see '*Legato*').

Speaker key (See 'Register key').

Squeak A high, unintentional overtone.

Staccatissimo An articulation even shorter than a *staccato* note.

Staccato A short, articulated note.

Stock (See 'Bark').

Support The control enacted by the abdominal muscles to create a steady column of air.

Table (mouthpiece) The section of the facing on which the non-vibrating part of the reed lays.

Table (reed) The flat underside of the reed that sits on the mouthpiece.

Tempo The speed of the pulse, measured in beats per minute.

Tenon The corked parts of the joints.

Tension Unnecessary muscular stress that inhibits an action.

Tenuto (See 'Agogic accent').

Throat register The range of notes between G^2 and $B\flat^2$.

Timbre The distinctive quality of sound an instrument produces.

Tip (reed) The very thin end of the reed.

Tip (tongue) The thinnest part of the tongue that sits just behind the top teeth.

Tip opening The distance between the tip of the reed and the mouthpiece.

Tip rail The narrow, flat edge found at the tip of the mouthpiece.

Tone The quality of a musical sound.

Tone holes The holes in the instrument that open and close to produce different pitches.

Travel The feeling of movement within a held note.

Triple-tonguing A fast articulation technique carried out in groups of three articulations, alternating the tip of the tongue and the back of the tongue.

Undertone The unwanted sounding of the fundamental or other lower harmonics when playing higher notes.

Upper joint The section of the clarinet located between the barrel and the lower joint, operated by the left hand.

Vamp The scraped section of the reed that includes the reed heart.

Voicing (See 'oral cavity').

Wavelength The distance over which the shape of a soundwave repeats (e.g. the distance between two peaks).

Waves (sound) Vibrations of molecules of any substance that generate sound.

Window The opening in the mouthpiece table just behind the reed.

Bibliography

It's rather heartening that there are so many books on the clarinet. My list below is by no means exhaustive but represents those I have on my shelves and to which I often refer.

BOOKS

Baines, A., *Woodwind Instruments and their History* (Dover, 1991)
Bartolozzi, B., *New Sounds for Woodwind* (Oxford University Press, 1967)
Brymer, J., *Clarinet* (Kahn & Averill, 1977)
Drapkin, M., *How to Work on Clarinet Reeds* (Carl Fischer, 2019)
Ferron, E., *The Clarinet Revealed* (International Music Diffusion, 1996)
Garbarino, G., *Metodo per Clarinetto* (Boosey and Hawkes, 1979)
Gibson, O. L., *Clarinet Acoustics* (Indiana University Press, 1998)
Guy, L., *Selection, Adjustment, and Care of Single Reeds* (Rivernote Press, 1997)
Harvey, P., *The Clarinettist's Bedside Book* (Fentone, 1980)
Heaton, R., *The Versatile Clarinet* (Routledge, 2006)
Hoeprich, E., *The Clarinet* (Yale University Press, 2008)
Kell, R., *Clarinet Staccato from the Beginning* (Boosey and Hawkes, 1968)
Kroll, O., *The Clarinet* (Batsford, 1968)
Lawson, C., ed., *The Cambridge Companion to the Clarinet* (Cambridge University Press, 1995)
Lawson, C., *The Early Clarinet: A Practical Guide* (Cambridge University Press, 2000)
Mazzeo, R., *The Clarinet, Excellence and Artistry* (Alfred Music, 1981)
Mozart, L., *A Treatise on the Fundamental Principles of Violin Playing* (1756) (Oxford University Press, 1985)
Pino, D., *The Clarinet and Clarinet Playing* (Scribners, 1998)
Porter, M., *The Embouchure* (Boosey & Hawkes, 1970)
Puwalski, T., *The Clarinetist's Guide to Klezmer* (Zephyr, 2001)
Quantz, J., *On Playing the Flute* (1752) (Faber & Faber, 2001)
Albert R., Rice *Notes for Clarinetists: A Guide to the Repertoire* (Oxford University Press, 2017)
Rehfeldt, P., *New Directions for Clarinet* (Scarecrow Press, 1994)
Rendall, F., G., *The Clarinet* (Williams & Norgate, 1954)
Ridenour, T., *Clarinet Fingerings* (Ridenour Clarinet Products, 2002)
Ridenour, W. T., *The Educator's Guide to the Clarinet* (Ridenour, 2nd ed: 2002)
Russianoff, L., *Clarinet Method, Book 1 & Book 2* (Schirmer, 1983)
Saska, R., *A Guide to Repairing Woodwinds* (Northeastern Music Pub Inc, 1987)
Sigel, A., *The Twentieth Century Clarinetist* (Franco Colombo, 1966)
Sim, A., *303 Clarinet Fingerings and 276 Trills* (Queen's Temple Publications, 2008)
Stein, K., *The Art of Clarinet Playing* (Alfred, 1994)
Thurston, F., *Clarinet Technique* (Oxford University Press, 3rd ed: 1977)
Weston, P., *Clarinet Virtuosi of the Past* (Robert Hale, 1971)
Weston, P., *More Clarinet Virtuosi of the Past* (Emerson Edition, 2nd ed: 2003)
Weston, P., *Yesterday's Clarinetists: A Sequel* (Emerson Edition, 2002)
Weston, P., *Clarinet Virtuosi of Today* (Egon Publishers, 1989)
Weston, P., *Heroes and Heroines of Clarinettistry* (Trafford, 2008)

PAPERS

Chen, J.M., Smith, J. and Wolfe, J., *How players use their vocal tracts in advanced clarinet and saxophone performance* (School of Physics, The University of New South Wales, Australia, 2010)
Susumu, M., MD, *Laryngeal Control While Playing Wind Instruments* (Journal of the Oto-Rhino-Laryngological Society of Japan, 1989)
Fitz, C. and Wolfe, J., *How do clarinet players adjust the resonances of their vocal tracts for different playing effects?* (University of New South Wales, 2005)
Fitz, C. and Wolfe, J., *Playing frequency shift due to the interaction between the vocal tract of the musician and the clarinet* (Stockholm Music Acoustics Conference, 2003)
Freire, R. D., *Psychoacoustic effects of overtones and undertones on clarinet voicing: developing the tone through collaborative practice with two clarinets* (Universidade de Brasília, 2010)
Lulich, S. M. and Charles S., *The relation between tongue shape and pitch in clarinet playing using ultrasound measurements* (Indiana University, 2017)